LANGUAGE AND LINGUISTICS Monograph Series No.A2-2
《語言暨語言學》專刊甲種二之二
2002-1-002-002-000010-1

Pazih Texts and Songs

巴宰族傳說歌謠集

by Paul Jen-kuei Li and Shigeru Tsuchida

李壬癸・土田滋 著

Institute of Linguistics (Preparatory Office)
Academia Sinica
Taipei
November 2002

中央研究院
語言學研究所籌備處

Pazih Texts and Songs 巴宰族傳説歌謡集

Contents

Introduction

Pazih is a plain tribe language formerly spoken in the central-western part of Taiwan, around Fongyuan areas and along the Dajia River. Some Pazih people started to migrate to Puli, Nantou, in the central part of Taiwan in 1825. There were still nine Pazih villages and the language was still actively spoken during the Japanese period (1895-1945). Although the language has become extinct in the original settlement in the western plain, a few old speakers for both dialects, Pazih and Kaxabu, can still be found in Puli areas. It is partially remembered by only a few old people today. The Pazih language will become entirely extinct before long.[1]

Given in this monograph are all the Pazih texts and songs that have been recorded mostly by the authors, but a few by the previous investigators, including Asai, Ino, and Ferguson for texts, and Nomura for three ritual songs. The monograph contains two main parts: Part One gives the texts and Part Two the songs. Given in the appendices are: (1) three ritual songs of *ayan* recorded perhaps by Nomura during the Japanese period (1895-1945), (2) the Lord's prayer in Sekhoan by Rev. Ferguson in 1896, (3) Pazih sentences by Steere in 1873, and (4) sample of previous scholars's field notes for the Pazih language.

The first field investigation of the Pazih language was done by Steere (1874), and then followed by Ino (1897), Ogawa (1922), Asai (1936-37), Ferrell (1970), Tsuchida (1969), Li (1976, 1998, 2000), Lin (1988, 2000), Blust (1999), and Li and Tsuchida (2001). Most of the earlier studies are mainly short wordlists. Only Ino (1 text), Asai (3), Tsuchida (4), and Li (9) have collected texts over a period of a hundred years, 1897-1997. All these texts are now arranged in accordance with the investigators, Paul Li, Shigeru Tsuchida, Erin Asai, Kanori Ino, and in that order. They have been analysed, with word-by-word and free translations in both English and Chinese.[2] Those texts collected by Ino and Asai were all checked, edited, and corrected, with the help of our Pazih informant, Pan Jin-yu, before they were incorporated in this volume. Among the 17 texts, only two (A Text 6 and C Text 1) have appeared in Li and Tsuchida (2001:369-384), and they are reprinted with minor corrections in this volume. Two

---

[1] This study was supported in part with grants for Paul Li from the Academia Sinica, National Science Council (NSC89-2411-H-001-048, NSC90-2411-H-001-027), and Chiang Ching-kuo Foundation for International Scholarly Exchange (RG-002-D-'00). Shigeru Tsuchida was supported in part with Grant-in-Aid for Scientific Research on Priority Areas (A) The Japan Ministry of Education, Science, Sports and Culture Endangered Languages of the Pacific Rim (Grant No.12039103). We'd like to thank the anonymous reviewers for their valuable suggestions to improve an earlier version of our manuscripts, and Wen Chyou-chu for providing us with the musical notes for the Pazih songs.

[2] The English translation gives morpheme-by-morpheme glosses while the Chinese gives only word glosses. The Chinese translation is for common readers, while the English translation is for those majoring in linguistics.

texts, A Texts 6 and 7, though deal with more or less the same story, they were narrated by different speakers with different expressions and sentence structures, and so are A Texts 1, 2 and 3.

Pazih songs were first recorded by someone (see Appendix 1 and Sato 1934) at an uncertain date, followed by various musicians, such as Hsu Chang-hui and Lu Bing-chuan (1982), and then by Li and Lin (1990), Wu (1998), and Wen (1998). Most of the songs in this volume have been recorded and transcribed by Li in the past fourteen years. Both the words and music notes (transcribed by Chyou-chu Wen and Ching-tsai Lin) for all the songs are presented in this volume. Some of the the songs have appeared in various publications, Li and Lin (1990), Wu (1998), and Wen (1998).

The Pazih reference grammar appeared as the Introduction to *Pazih Dictionary* compiled by Li and Tsuchida (2001:1-56), so interested readers are referred to it. A shorter Chinese version appeared in a conference paper by Li (1998). It is, therefore, decided not to repeat them here but excerpts. Nevertheless, CDs for the recordings of some Pazih texts and all songs have been prepared to go with this publication. Note that the written texts and tape recordings are not necessarily identical.

In these texts and songs, phonetic symbols, such as *ŋ, ʔ,* and *ə* are used, while in *Pazih Dictionary* the romanized letters, *ng, ',* and *e* are used respectively.

Although the meanings of most grammatical particles are clear and defined in the texts and songs, a few of them are not clear in some context, such as *aa, aʔ, ha, hai, hii, i, iu, la,* and *na,* especially in C Texts 1-4, as recorded by Tsuchida, who tried to transcribe everything as he heard in the original tape. Most of them seem to be simply nonsignificant hesitating elements to fill up the time before the next word or sentence appears, but in future studies they may turn out to be important clues for discourse analysis of spontaneous speech.

To faciliate reading and understanding the Pazih texts and songs in this volume, a brief sketch of Pazih grammar is given as the following:

1. Phonology

There are four voiceless unaspirate stops /p, t, k, ʔ/, three voiced stops /b, d, g/, three voiceless fricatives /s, x, h/, one voiced fricative /z/, three nasals /m, n, ŋ/, two liquids /l, r/, two semivowels /w, y/, and four vowels /i, u, ə, a/. The stops are unreleased in the word-final position. Among these consonants, /k/ is a free variant between velar [k] and uvular [q], especially for speakers of the older generation such as Itih and Chen A-jin (Kaxabu), /x/ is a velar or uvular fricative depending on the individual speakers, /h/ is a pharyngeal fricative, /l/ is a voiced lateral, /r/ is a flap or retroflex (only in word-final position). The glottal stop is phonemically significant in the Kaxabu dialect, in which /r/ is lost and there is a contrast

2

between zero and the glottal stop in the word-initial and final position, e.g., *azəm* 'new year'; *ʔazəm* 'stupid'.

The high vowels /i, u/ have their phonetic variants [e, o] respectively when adjacent to /h/ or /r/, e.g., /pazih/ [pazeh] 'self-appelation', /buhut/ [bohot] 'squirrel', /rutuh/ [rotoh] 'monkey', /rarung/ [rarong] 'hole'.

Geminate vowels are phonemic, e.g., *rəzaw* 'leisure' vs. *rəəzaw* 'only'.

Table 1. Pazih Consonants and Vowels

Consonants:				Vowels:	
p	t	k	ʔ	i	u
b	d	g			
	s	x	h	ə	
	z				
m	n	ŋ		a	
	l				
	r				
w	y				

Stress always falls on the final syllable.

2. Morphology

2.1 Affixation

Many roots are bound, e.g., *adu-*, *idəm-*, *əbət-*, *ulah-*, *bisit-*, etc. Each of these bound roots must take one of the affixes to occur as a free form. There are a good number of prefixes, but only two infixes (<*a*> and <*in*>) and five suffixes (-*an*, -*aw*, -*ay*, -*ən* and -*i*) in Pazih.

Among these affixes, many have invariant forms, including both infixes, <*a*> 'progressive' and <*in*> 'perfective', and all suffixes -*an* 'Locative-focus', -*ay* 'Future', -*aw* 'Anticipating', -*i* 'Patient-focus, imperative', -*i* 'vocative', except the Patient-focus suffix -*ən* ~ -*un*, which is phonologically conditioned by the preceding vowel. The Agent-focus prefix has several allomorphs: *m-* ~ *ma-* ~ *mə-* ~ *mi-* ~ *mu-*, which are mostly lexically conditioned, and only *mə-* is phonologically conditioned by the following vowel, e.g., *mə-kən* 'to eat'.

2.2 Reduplication

In addition to the special type of reduplicated syllable, there are four other major types of reduplication in Pazih: (1) reduplication of a complete stem except the coda, e.g., *zaxi-zaxi* 'rough', *rimu-rimu* 'will-o'-lantern', *maa-təbə-təbər* 'to fight each other with fists', *kari-karit* 'swidden field', *ma-zəpə-zəpət* 'crowded'; (2) reduplication of the first CV of the stem, e.g.,

3

su-suzuk 'is hiding'; (3) reduplication of the first CV of the stem with the vowel replaced by /a/, e.g., *da-dius* 'spoon' < *dius* 'to scoop'; (4) reduplication of the first CV of the stem with vowel lengthening, e.g. *dəə-dəpəx* 'is reading'.

Different types of reduplication may indicate different syntactic functions and/or phonological constraints. Briefly speaking,

a. reduplication of a noun stem indicates plurality, e.g. *saw-saw* 'people' or *sa-sa-saw* 'many people' < *saw* 'person', *apu-ʔapu* 'ancestors' < *apu* 'grandma', *aba-ʔabas-an* 'middle-aged people' < *abasan* 'siblings', *sa-sa-səmər* or *səmə-səmər* 'much grass' < *səmər* 'grass';

b. reduplication of a stative verb stem indicates intensity, e.g., *mu-ziza-zizay* 'very old' < *zizay* 'old', *ma-kari-karit* 'very dry' < *ma-karit* 'dry', *ta-ŋiti-ŋiti* 'very angry' < *ta-ŋiti* 'angry', *m<in>a-baza-baza* 'very knowledgeable' < *ma-baza* 'to know', *t<in>ə-rəhə-rəhən* 'very black' < *tərəhən* 'black';

c. reduplication of the first CV of a verb stem indicates the progressive aspect or a repetitive action, e.g., *di-dius* 'is scooping', *ki-kizu* 'is making a mark', *ri-ririx* 'is checking traps', *su-suzuk* 'is hiding';

d. reduplication of the first CV of a numeral indicates an ordinal, e.g., *du-dusa* 'the second' < *dusa* 'two';

e. reduplication of the first CV of the stem with the vowel replaced by /a/ indicates an instrument (Blust 1998), e.g., *da-dius* 'spoon' < *dius-* 'to scoop up', *sa-sipər* 'fishnet' < *sipər-* 'to cast a fishnet to fish', *sa-sapuh* 'broom' < *sapuh-* 'to sweep', *a-aləp* 'door' < *aləp-* 'to close', *a-ixu* 'oar' < *ixu-* 'to row';

f. reduplication of a disyllabic active verb stem indicates a continuous or repetitive action, e.g., *zəzə-zəzəb-i* 'Keep sucking!' < *zəzəp-* 'to suck', *maa-bakə-bakət* 'to hit each other' < *bakət-* 'to hit', *maa-sapa-sapal* 'to join or pile together' < *sapal-* 'to join', *maa-təzə-təzək* 'to kick each other' < *təzək-* 'to kick'.

3. Syntax

3.1 Case Markers

Pazih has the following four case markers:

ki	nominative	*ni*	genitive
di	locative	*u*	oblique

Most of these case markers are optional. In addition to the four case markers listed above, there is a topic marker *ka* and a ligature *a* in Pazih.

3.2 Personal Pronouns

There are four sets of personal pronouns in Pazih:

Table 2. Personal Pronouns

		Neutral	Nominative	Genitive	Locative
1sg		yaku	aku ~ -ku	naki	yakuan, yakunan
2sg		isiw	siw	nisiw	isiwan
3sg	close	imini	mini	nimini	iminiyan
	dist	imisiw	misiw	nimisiw	imisiwan
	invis	isia	sia	nisia	isiaan
1inc		ita	ta	nita ~ ta-	itaan
1exc		yami, yamin	ami	niam	yamian, yaminan
2pl		imu	mu	nimu	imuan, imunan
3pl	close	yamini			
	dist	yamisiw	amisiw	namisiw	yamisiwan
	invis	yasia	asia	nasia	

Most of the pronominal forms in Pazih are derived from Proto-Austronesian; there is only a minor change in the second person singular form: *Su > siw.[3] All the pronominal forms are free. There is only one set of short forms, the nominative, which occurs freely in various positions in a sentence.

3.3 Mood, Focus and Aspect

Table 3. Mood, Focus and Aspect (bakəd- ~ -bakət 'to hit')

		Agent	Patient	Locative	Referential
Realis	Neu	mu-bakət	bakəd-ən	bakəd-an	saa-bakət
	Prf	m\<in>u-bakət	b\<in>akət	b\<in>akəd-an	s\<in>u-bakət[4]
	Prg	baa-bakət	ba-bakəd-ən	ba-bakəd-an	saa-ba-bakət
Irrealis	Fut	baa-bakəd-ay	ba-bakəd-ən	baa-bakəd-ay	
	Ant	mu-bakəd-ay	bakəd-aw		
	Imp	bakət	bakəd-i		

---

[3] The form *imisiw* 'he, she' shows up as *imisu* in formal ritual songs of Pazih. Although we do not think *imisiw* is related to *isiw* '2sg', yet the change in the form of the third person (*imisu > imisiw*) is so suggestive that we may infer that the change in the form of the second person *su > siw* took place fairly recently.

[4] Note that the prefix is *su-* instead of *saa-* or *si-*.

3.4 The Focus System in Pazih

Focus is the agreement between the verb derivation (or inflection) and a noun phrase in a sentence. If the Agentive (actor) case is chosen as the subject, it is called Agent-focus (AF); if the Patient is chosen as the subject, it is called Patient-focus (PF); if the Locative is chosen as the subject, it is called Locative-focus (LF); if the Instrument is chosen as the subject, it is called Instrumental-focus (IF). Like many other Formosan languages and western Austronesian languages, Pazih has four types of focus indicated by verb affixes: (1) Agent-focus by *mu-*, *mə-*, *mi-*, *m-*, *ma* or zero; (2) Patient-focus by *-ən* or *-un*, (3) Locative-focus by *-an*, and (4) Instrumental-focus by *sa-*, *saa-* or *si-* (see Li and Tsuchida 2001 for details).

(1) mu-bakət   rakihan   ki   aba.
    AF-beat   child   Nom   Dad
    'The father beat/is beating a child'

(2) mi-kita akim   ba-bakət rakihan ki   abuk.
    AF-see   Prg-beat child   Nom
    'Abuk saw Akim beating a child'

(3) naki   a   rakihan   rapun-un   ni   hakəzəŋ a   saw.
    I/Gen Lig child   take care-PF Gen   old   Lig person
    'My child is/was taken care of by an old person'

(4) bakəd-ən   ni   sabuŋ rakihan   ka, ma-raxiw   lia.
    beat-PF   Gen   child   Top AF-escape Asp
    'The child beaten by Sabung has escaped'

(5) pu-batuʔ-an   lia   ki   babaw daran.
    pave-stone-LF Asp   Nom   above road
    'The surface of the road has been paved with stones'

(6) k<in>əxəd-an ni   abua naki   a   rima.
    Prf-cut-LF   Gen   my   Gen hand
    'My hand was cut by Abua' (lit., my hand was the place where it was cut by Abua, and the cut is still visible)

(7) saa-xəʔət   nuaŋ ki   saris.
    IF-tie   cow   Nom   string
    'The string was used to tie a cow'

(8) saa-talək   alaw   ki   bulayan.
    IF-cook   fish   Nom   pan
    'The pan was used to cook fish'

(9) si-təʔəŋ   wazu ni   rakihan   ki   batu.
    IF-throw   dog Gen child   Nom   stone
    'The stone was used to throw at a dog by the child'

前言一附：巴宰語法綱要[*]

巴宰族 (Pazih) 是台灣原住民族之一。現存的兩種方言都在埔里鎮採集：一稱 Pazih，主要在愛蘭，另一稱 Kaxabu，在牛眠山、守城份、大湳、蜈蚣崙四庄。這種語言現在已經瀕臨完全絕滅的邊緣。巴宰族的原始社群中心在現在的豐原附近，以大甲溪左右為中心，地理分布頗廣，在日據時代尚有九社。

今日絕大多數的巴宰族人都說台灣閩南語，卻略帶他們自己母語的一些特徵。僅有極少數住埔里附近 80 歲左右的老人對於他們自己的母語仍有一些記憶。據作者所知，目前只有住在愛蘭現年 88 歲的潘金玉老太太稱的上還有不錯的母語能力，可惜她的健康情況似乎欠佳。

本書收錄了所有記錄過的巴宰語文本 (texts) 和歌謠，絕大部分都是作者親自在埔里採集的，只有少數文本和歌謠是前人所採集的，包括淺井惠倫 (1936) 的三篇，伊能嘉矩 (1897) 的一篇，Ferguson (1896) 傳教士的一篇禱告詞，野村氏所藏的三首祭祖歌謠。此外，還有 Steere 最早 (1873) 在烏牛欄所記錄的二十多個句子。這部書主要分為兩部分：前半部是文本，後半部是歌謠。附錄含有四種資料：(一) 野村氏所藏的三首祭歌 aiyan，(二) Ferguson 所翻譯的禱告詞，(三) 美國博物學教授 Steere 所記錄的二十多個句子，(四) 前人所記錄巴宰語田野筆記的手稿影本。把前人的記錄收進本書之前，作者都先跟發音人仔細核對並修訂過的。本書附有部分文本和全部歌謠的 CD，但文本的錄音跟書面記錄有不少出入。

前人對於巴宰語的研究報告相當少。近三十年來所發表的包括費羅禮 (Ferrell 1970)，李壬癸 (Li 1977:380, 389-90; 1978:570-71, 573-82, 1998, 2000, 2002)，林英津 (1988, 2000)，Blust (1999)，Li and Tsuchida (2001)。

關於巴宰族的歌謠，日據時代伊能嘉矩 (1908:47)、不知名人士先後記錄過巴宰族的祭祖歌詞 ayan。小川研究室所藏的三種歌：(一) 開基之歌，(二) 大水氾濫之歌，(三) 氾濫後人民分居之歌。後來由佐藤 (1934) 整理了原文、註解及

---

[*] 本研究李壬癸曾獲以下的研究經費補助：中央研究院主題計畫「平埔族與台灣歷史研究」，行政院國家科學委員會 (編號：NSC89-2411-H-001-048, NSC90-2411-001-027)，蔣經國國際學術交流基金會 (RG-002-D-'00)，土田滋曾獲日本文部科學省特定領域研究 (A)，環太平洋の「消滅に瀕した言語」にかんする緊急調查研究 (編號：12039103)。感謝兩位匿名審查人提供寶貴的修訂和改進意見，溫秋菊副教授和林清財先生分別為巴宰歌謠採譜並提供各首歌謠的五線譜，許淑鈴小姐輸入全部書稿。

大意,在《南方土俗》發表。以上各文獻可惜都沒有附歌譜。李、林 (1990) 合著的就有四庄的歌詞和歌譜。本書收錄了愛蘭和四庄的歌謠並且也都儘量附上歌譜。

　　李壬癸於 1970 年夏天跟土田滋到埔里的愛蘭拜訪巴宰族後裔潘啟明先生。1976 年 7 月起才正式做巴宰語言的調查研究,主要發音人是愛蘭王伊底 (Iteh) 女士 (81 歲),蒐集近千個辭彙和四個文本。後來也蒐集另一個方言 Kaxabu 的資料,先在蜈蚣崙訪問過陳阿金女士(也叫潘天里,78 歲)若干次 (1978-1982),後來 (1988) 才到守城份訪問潘郡乃先生 (83 歲)。以上這幾位發音人都已先後過世了,會說母語的人也愈來愈難找了。為了寫句法,從 1995 年 11 月起再到愛蘭訪問潘榮章先生 (81 歲) 和潘金玉女士 (81 歲),在一年多內訪問了若干次。除了從潘金玉女士錄到二個本文以外,也核對了土田在 1969 年從潘詹梅 (Taruat, 78 歲) 女士和潘萬吉老先生所記錄的相當豐富的詞彙資料以及四篇文本。

　　為了方便讀者閱讀本書中的各篇文本和歌謠,以下分三節簡略說明巴宰語的音韻、構詞、句法以及若干例句。

第一節　音韻
一、音韻系統:
輔音:

		唇音	舌尖	舌根	小舌	咽頭	喉音
塞音	清	p	t	k [k~q]			ʔ
	濁	b	d	g			
擦音	清		s		χ [x]	ħ [h]	
	濁		z				
鼻音		m	n	ŋ			
邊音			l				
閃音			ɾ [r]				
半元音		w	y				

元音:

	前	央	後
高	i		u
中		ə	
低		a	

　　在《巴宰語詞典》中使用羅馬拼音字母 ng, ', e 等,但在本書中卻使用國際音標的語音符號 ŋ, ʔ, ə 等。

二、發音與語音符號說明：

(1) 四個清塞音 /p, t, k, ʔ/ 都不送氣，在字尾也都不解阻 (unreleased)，其中 /k/ 代表舌根塞音 [k] 和小舌塞音 [q] 的自由變體。

(2) 三個清擦音 /s, x, h/，其中 /x/ 是小舌擦音 [χ]，/h/ 是咽頭擦音 [ħ]，/z/ 是和 /s/ 對當的濁擦音。

(3) 詞尾的 -b 清化為 -p，詞尾的 -d 和 -z 都清化為 -t。

(4) /r/ 是閃音或捲舌擦音（捲舌音只在語詞尾出現）。

(5) 高元音 /i, u/ 在 /h/ 或 /r/ 緊鄰時分別成為中元音 [e, o]。

(6) 重音都落在最後音節。

(7) 四庄的方言有進一步的演變：

    (a) 詞尾的邊音都已變成同部位的鼻音：-l > -n。

    (b) /r/ 音大都已丟失，並有抵補音長作用。

    (c) /d/ 音都已變成 [z] 或齒間濁擦音。

第二節　構詞

一、詞綴

巴宰語許多語根都非自由式，例如 adu-, idəm-, əbət-, ulah-, bisit- 等等。這些語根都必須要有個詞綴（前綴、中綴、後綴）才能成為自由式。前綴有數十種之多，中綴只有兩種（<a>, <in>，並以< >符號表示中綴），後綴也只有六種（-an, -aw, -ay, -ən, -i）。

絕大多數的詞綴形式固定不變，包括兩種中綴：<a> '進行式'，<in> '完成式'，五種後綴：-an '處所焦點'，-ay '未來式'，-aw '期待'，-i '命令式（受事焦點）'，-i '呼格'，只有一種後綴 -ən ~ -un '受事焦點' 有兩種形式（前面的元音為 u 時，後綴就是 -un）。表示 '主事焦點' 的前綴形式變化最多：m- ~ ma- ~ mə- ~ mi- ~ mu-，大都視個別語詞而定，只有 mə- 是受限於後頭的元音，如 mə-kən '吃'。表示 '靜態動詞' 的前綴 ha- ~ ma- 也是視個別語詞而定，如 ha-lupas '長'，ma-taru '大'。表示 '使役動詞' 的前綴 pa- ~ paka-，前者用在動態動詞，而後者用在靜態動詞，如 pa-baza '教'，paka-dahu '增加'。

二、重疊

巴宰語的重疊有四種主要類型：(一) 除了語詞輔音尾以外，語根的全部重疊，如 zaxi-zaxi '粗糙'，kari-karit '旱田'，(二) 語根第一音節的重疊，如 su-suzuk '正在隱藏'，(三) 語根第一音節的重疊，但元音以 a 取代，如 da-dius '湯匙' < dius '舀'，(四) 語根第一音節的重疊，元音加長，如 dəə-dəpəx '正在閱讀'。

9

不同類型的重疊可能顯示不同的語法功能或語音限制：

(一) 名詞語根的重疊表示複數，如 saw-saw '許多人' < saw '人'，səmə-səmər '許多草' < səmər '草'；

(二) 靜態動詞語根的重疊表示 '很'，如 mu-ziza-zizay '很舊' < mu-zizay '舊'；

(三) 動態動詞語根第一音節的重疊表示動作在進行中或一再重複的動作，如 di-dius '正在舀'；

(四) 數詞語根第一音節的重疊表示序數，如 du-dusa '第二' < dusa '二'；

(五) 語根第一音節的重疊並且元音以 a 取代，表示工具，如 da-dius '湯匙' < dius '舀'，sa-sipər '漁網'，a-ixu '船槳' < ixu- '划'；

(六) 動態動詞語根的雙音節的重疊表示持續或一再重複的動作，如 bakə-bakət '一直打'。

第三節　句法[5]

一、焦點系統

　　巴宰語的動詞焦點變化有這幾種類型：(一) 主事焦點 mu-, mə, mi-, m-, ma- 或零，(二) 受事焦點 -ən 或 -un，(三) 處所焦點 -an，(四) 指事焦點 saa- 或 si-。由此看來，巴宰語的焦點系統和一般西部南島語以及一些台灣南島語大致相同。

(一) 主事焦點（以主事者當主語）

　　帶主事焦點的動詞表示已發生或正在進行的動作或事件。例如：

1. mu-bakət　rakihan　ki　aba.
   AF[6]-打　孩　主　父
   父親打小孩。

2. yaku　ka　ma-baza　imisiw　ukuazixa　mu-puzah
   我　題　AF-知　他　昨天　AF-來
   我知道他昨天來了。

---

[5] 李壬癸 (1998)〈巴則海語的格位標記系統〉有較詳細的句法解說和例句。更詳盡和更新的分析，請參見英文版，Li and Tsuchida (2001:1-58)。

[6] 本文所使用的縮寫符號如下：AF，主事焦點；BF，受惠焦點；屬，屬格；命，命令式；IF，工具焦點；IR，非現實式；連，連結詞；LF，處所焦點；處，處格；主，主格；題，主題；PF，受事焦點；單，單數；複，複數；Q，疑問；Red，重疊。

(二) 受事焦點（以受事者當主語）

受事焦點以 -ən（或 -un）標示，通常表示已經發生的事，但不是像有的語言（如泰雅、賽德克）表未來。例如：

3. naki a rakihan rapun-ən ni hakəzəŋ.
   我的 連 孩 照顧-PF 屬 老
   我的小孩受老人的照顧。

-un 只是 -ən 的變異，只出現在前面元音是 u，如 huruhur-un "拖"，如：

4. huruhur-un dua dini lai ki adadumud- a luxud- a isia.
   拖-PF 那裡 這裡 了 主 一隻 連 鹿 連 那
   那一隻鹿被拖來拖去。

(三) 處所焦點（以處所當主語）

處所焦點以 -an 標示，都指已發生的事件。例如：

5. pubatuʔ-an lia ki babaw daran.
   鋪石-LF 了 主 上面 道路
   道路上面鋪了石子了。

(四) 指事焦點（以工具或受惠者當主語）

台灣南島語言的指事焦點多用 si-，只有布農用 ʔis-，噶瑪蘭用 ti，巴宰語用 saa-，偶而也用 si-。試比較下列各句所顯示的不同焦點：

6a. mu-xəʔət nuaŋ ki yaku.
    AF-綁 牛 主 我
    我綁牛。

 b. xəʔət-ən naki lia ki nuaŋ.
    綁-PF 我/屬 了 主 牛
    牛被我綁了。

 c. saa-xəʔət nuaŋ ki kahuy.
    IF-綁 牛 主 樹
    樹被用來綁牛。

目前所蒐集到的語料，以 saa- 表示工具或受惠者的主動詞並不多。

7. saa-talək alaw ki bulayan.
   IF-煮 魚 主 鍋
   鍋用來煮魚。

以 si- 表示工具焦點的僅有一例：

8. si-təʔəŋ wazu ni rakihan ki batu.
　 IF-擲　　狗　屬　孩　　主　石
　 小孩用石頭丟擲狗。

　　至於 sas- 和 si- 的區分條件，目前並不清楚。發音人潘金玉（女，83 歲）認為例句 8 中仍以用 saa-təʔəŋ 為宜，si-təʔəŋ 較少用，也有 si-təʔəŋ-ən 的形式，表示"已擲過"。

二、焦點與動貌

　　綜合焦點系統和動貌系統，以語根 bakət-"打"為例，下表顯示動詞的各種變化形式：

表二、巴宰語動詞變化表

	主　事	受　事	處　所	指　事
現實式				
中立式	mu-bakət	bakəd-ən	bakəd-an	saa-bakət
完成式	m\<in>u-bakət	b\<in>akət	b\<in>akəd-an	s\<in>u-bakət
持續式	ba-bakət	ba-bakəd-ən	ba-bakəd-an	saa-ba-bakət
非現實式				
未　來	ba-bakəd-ay	ba-bakəd-ən	baa-bakəd-ay	
期　待	mu-bakəd-ay	bakəd-aw		
命　令	bakət	bakəd-i		

三、格位標記

　　名詞的格位標記有兩種：一種是人稱代名詞，另一種是非人稱代詞，包括普通名詞、人名、疑問詞等。

　　巴宰語有以下四個格位標記：

di　處格　　　*u*　斜格
ki　主格　　　*ni*　屬格

　　此外，還有主題標記 ka 以及連結詞 a。以上這些標記大都可以省略。例句如下：

9. aba ka kasibat rakihan mu-dəpəx babizu.
　 父　題　教　　孩　　AF-讀　　書
　 父親教孩子讀書。

10. aba   a   paray ka   baya?-ən di   rakihan lia.
　　 父   連   錢   題   給-PF   處   孩   了
　　父親的錢給了小孩了。

11. mu-puzah ki   awi, yaku (ka)   kaa-kən sumay.
　　 AF-來   主 人名 我   正在吃   飯
　　阿維來時，我正在吃飯。

12. ma-baza   mu-laŋuy ki   rakihan
　　 AF-會   AF-游   主   孩
　　小孩會游泳。

13. ma-xibariw kahuy ki   yaku.
　　 AF-賣   柴   主   我
　　我賣木柴。

14. ni   saw ki   umamah.
　　 屬   人   主   水田
　　水田是人家的。

15. padaux inusat ni   kalagu ki   atun.
　　 使喝   酒   屬   人名   主   人名
　　佳拉古使阿敦喝酒。

16. isiw taa-tahay u   baruzak?
　　 你   在-殺   斜   豬
　　你正在殺豬嗎？

　　如一般語言，主題都出現在句子的開頭，也就是主動詞或謂語之前。主題標記 ka 出現在它所標記的主題名詞之後，有時也可以省略，但在子題之後都會略為停頓。主格標記 ki 可以標記普通名詞、人名、人稱代詞。屬格標記 ni 可以標記普通名詞或人名。換句話說，巴宰語並不分普通名詞和人名。ni 除了標示所有之外，它的主要功能是標示非主事焦點的主事者。

　　處格 di 標示處所，甚至標示目標。斜格是 u，表示主格、屬格和處格以外的語法關係。至於 a，只是連結兩個名詞之間的從屬關係。它是連接詞 (ligature)，不是真正的格位標記。

主格標記 ki 表示有定 (definite)，而 a 只是連接詞。試比較兩者的不同：

17a. ni　taruat　ki　babizu.
　　　屬　人名　　主　書
　　（這本）書是 Taruat 的。

　　b. ni　taruad-　a　babizu.
　　　屬　人名　　連　書
　　Taruat 的書

四、人稱代名詞

　　人稱代名詞巴宰語有以下這四套：

表一、巴宰語人稱代詞

			I	II	IV		V	
			中立式	主格 (短式)	屬	格	處	格
一	單		yaku	aku ~ -ku	naki		yakuan/yakunan	
二	單		isiw	siw	nisiw		isiwan	
三	單		imisiw	misiw	nimisiw		imisiwan	
		近指	imini	mini	nimini		iminiyan	
三	單	遠指	imisiw	misiw	nimisiw		imisiwan	
		視界外	isia	sia	nisia		isiaan	
包括式			ita	ta	nita ~ ta-		itaan	
排除式			yami	ami	niam/niami		yamian/yaminan	
二	複		imu	mu	nimu		imuan/imunan	
		近指	yamini					
三	複	遠指	yamisiw	amisiw	namisiw		yamisiwan	
		視界外	yasia	asia	nasia			

　　由上表可見大部分的人稱代詞都還保留古南島語的同源詞，只有第二人稱單數的元音發生一點變化：*Su > siw。人稱代詞大都是自由式或長式，只有一套短式的主語。短式的主語大都出現在句子的第二個位置，緊接在謂語之後，這種現象和其他台灣南島語相同，可是也可以出現在句子的不同位置，因此並非真正的後綴 (suffix)，而是依附詞 (clitic)。此外只有一個出現在動詞前的 ta- "咱們"，用在祈求式，例如：ta-kan-i "咱們吃吧！" ta-daux-i "咱們喝吧！" ta-kitaʔ-aw "咱們看吧！" 第三人稱其實是指示代詞，區分近指和遠指，而遠指又區分視界內和視界外。

五、 動貌

如同其他南島語言，巴宰語的"完成式"以中綴 -in-（插在第一個輔音之後）表示。例如：

18. m<in>ə-kən siw　　sumay lia?
　　AF-已-吃　你/主　飯　　了
　　你吃過飯了嗎？

19. awi　ka　p<in>a-kan durun　ni　tata.
　　人名 題 使-已-吃　米糠　屬　繼母
　　繼母給阿維吃米糠。

20. mamah　ka　uzay nisiw　p<in>arisan aku.
　　兄　　題 不是 你的　　已生　　我/主
　　哥哥說我不是你生的。

21. x<in>arəb-an　ki　xuma.
　　已-燒-LF　　主　房
　　房子已經燒了。

表示完成的-in-可以用在主事焦點，也可以用在受事焦點，處所焦點。在受事焦點中，-in-並不和-ən 聯用，也就是通常不使用受事焦點標記-ən。這種現象正和一般台灣與西部南島語言相同。-in-常和處所焦點標記聯用：

22. d<in>idis-an naki　a maxiasu lia　ki　laladan.
　　已-擦-LF 我的　　媳婦　了 主　桌
　　桌子已被我媳婦擦過了。

雖然主事焦點也可以表示已經發生的事件，但是帶-in-才能確定確實已經發生。有時 -in- 的有無，甚至表示相反的意思。例如：

23a. aba ka　paxarihan mu-puzah dini.
　　　父　題 忘記　　　AF-來　　這裡
　　　父親忘了到這裡來。（他沒來）

　 b. aba ka　paxarihan m<in>u-puzah dini.
　　　父　題 忘記　　　AF-已-來　　這裡
　　　父親忘了他已來過這裡了。

出現在動詞組後面的lia有如華語普通話的"了"，表示動作已經開始或完成，例如上面例句22，又如：

24. maŋit   lia   ki   rakihan.
    哭   了   主   小孩
    小孩哭了。

25. yaku   mukukusa   muruput   lia.
    我   工作   完成   了
    我工作完成了。

26. mausay   lia   aku.
    要走   了   我
    我要走了。

正在進行以重疊動詞語根的第一個音節來表示，而且元音都以a取代並且是長元音。例如：

27. yaku   kaa-kən   dukul.
    我   在吃   芋頭
    我正在吃芋頭。

28. yaku   daa-daux   dalum.
    我   在喝   水
    我正在喝水。

29. ina   ka   baa-bazu   siatu.
    母   題   在洗   衣服
    母親正在洗衣服。

正在進行也可以中綴-a-（插在第一個輔音之後）表示。例如：

30. m<a>idəm   lia   ki   rakihan.
    在睡   了   主   小孩
    小孩在睡覺了。

31. abuk   t<a>umala   abua   m<a>aturay.
    人名   在聽   人名   在唱歌
    阿木正在聽 Abua 在唱歌。

未來以後綴 -ay 或 -aw表示。例如：

32. mapaʔ-ay rakihan ki kayu.
　　揹　　將　小孩　　主人名
　　Kayu 將要揹小孩。

33. palazəm a isiw, ta-kitaʔ-aw.
　　過年　　你　咱看將
　　你過年，咱們將要看。

六、否定詞

　　巴宰語有以下這些否定詞：ini '不'，uzay '不是'，kuaŋ～kuah '沒有'，mayaw '還沒'，nah '不要'，ana '別'。其中以ini最常用，它否定動態動詞 (如34) 和靜態動詞 (如35)。uzay出現在名詞之前，它否定整個子句 (如36)，也出現在分裂句或準分裂句 (如37)。kuaŋ是nahada '有' 的反義詞 (如38)。ana出現在主事者焦點動詞之前，也就是帶 -m- 的動詞，這一點巴宰語跟其他台灣南島語（如泰雅語）不同，在其他語言是不帶 -m- 的動詞原形。例如，

34. ini mukusa aku.
　　不　去　　我
　　我沒去。

35. ini bagət aku.
　　不　胖　我
　　我不胖。

36. yaku ka uzay pazih.
　　我　題　不是　巴宰
　　我不是巴宰人。

37. uzay yaku ka hapət məkən dadas.
　　不是　我　題　喜歡　吃　地瓜
　　不是我喜歡吃地瓜。

38. yaku ka kuaŋ a paray.
　　我　題　沒　連　錢
　　我沒有錢。

39. ana m-idəm di dini!
　　別　AF-睡　處　這裡
　　別在這裡睡覺！

REFERENCES 引用書目

Asai, Erin (淺井惠倫). 1936. 埔里烏牛欄、房里 [Auran, Puli]。田野筆記 [field notes]。

Blust, Robert. 1999. Notes on Pazeh phonology and morphology. *Oceanic Linguistics* 38.2:321-364.

Campbell, Rev.William. 1896. *The Articles of Christian Instruction in Favorlang Formosan, Dutch and English from Vertrecht's Manuscripts of 1650.* London: Kegan Paul, Trench, Trübner and Co.

Ferrell, Raleigh. 1970. The Pazeh-Kahabu language. *Bulletin of the Department of Archaeology and Anthropology* 31/32:73-96.

Inô, Kanori (伊能嘉矩). 1897. 蕃語集 [Pazih language]。田野筆記 [field notes]。

----------. 1908. 〈台灣ピイボオ番の一支族パゼツへの舊俗及び思想及一斑〉。《東京人類學雜誌》24 卷 272、273 號。

Li, Paul (李壬癸). 1976. *Pazeh wordlist.* Unpublished MS.

----------. 1977. Morphophonemic alternations in Formosan languages. *Bulletin of the Institute of History and Philology, Academia Sinica* 48.3:375-413.

----------. 1978. The case-marking systems of the four less known Formosan languages. *Pacific Linguistics* C-61:569-615.

----------. 1998. 〈巴則海語的格位標記系統〉 [The case-marking system of the Pazeh language]，《台灣語言及其教學國際研討會論文集》[Papers from the International Symposium on the Languages and Language Teaching in Taiwan] 1:57-81。新竹師院[Hsinchu Normal College]。

----------. 2000. Some aspects of Pazeh syntax. In Videa De Guzman and Byron Bender, eds., *Grammatical Analysis: Morphology, Syntax, and Semantics: Studies in Honor of Stanley Starosta*, 89-108. Honolulu: Oceanic Linguistics Special Publication No.29.

----------. 2002. Nominalization in Pazih. *Language and Linguistics* 3.2:227-239.

Li, Paul (李壬癸) and Lin, Ching-tsai (林清財). 1990. 〈巴則海族的祭祖歌曲及其他歌謠〉 [The Pazeh ritual songs for ancestors and other types of songs]. *Field Materials, Institute of Ethnology, Academia Sinica Occasional Series* 3:1-16.

Li, Paul (李壬癸) and Tsuchida Shigeru (土田滋). 2001. *Pazih Dictionary* 《巴宰語詞典》。Institute of Linguistics (Preparatory Office), Academia Sinica Monograph Series No.A2.

Lin, Ying-chin (林英津). 1988. 〈巴則海語—埔里愛蘭調查報告〉 [Investigation of the Pazeh dialect in Puli]，《臺灣風物》 [The Taiwan Folkways] 39.1:176-200。

----------. 2000. 《巴則海語》[The Pazeh language]。台北 [Taipei]：遠流出版公司 [Yuanliu

Publishing Co.]。

Lu, Bin-chuan (呂炳川). 1982. 《台灣土著族音樂》 [Aboriginal music of Taiwan]。中華民俗藝術叢書 3。台北 [Taipei]：百科文化。

Ogawa, Naoyoshi (小川尚義). 1922. Pazeh 語彙 [Pazih wordlist] (a few hundred items)。田野筆記 [field notes]。

----------. 1939. パゼッヘ語法材料 [Pazih grammatical data]。田野筆記 [field notes]。

Satô, Bun'ichi (佐藤文一). 1934. 〈大社庄の蕃歌〉，《南方土俗》3.1:114-126。葉婉奇譯，〈岸裡大社的歌謠〉，《重塑台灣平埔族圖像》，112-127。台北：原民文化事業有限公司。

Steere, Joseph Beal. 1874. [The aborigines of] Formosa. *Journal of the American Geographical Society of New York* 6:302-334. New York.

Tsuchida, Shigeru (土田滋). 1969. *Pazeh vocabulary.* Unpublished manuscripts, 143pp.

----------. 1969. *Pazeh texts.* Tape-recorded and partly transcribed.

----------. 1982. *A comparative vocabulary of Austronesian languages of Sinicized ethnic groups in Taiwan.* Part I: West Taiwan. Memoirs of the Faculty of Letters, University of Tokyo No.7.

----------. 1993. 〈パゼッヘ語〉 [Pazeh language]，《言語學大辭典》 [Linguistics Encyclopedia] 5:302-310。東京 [Tokyo]：三省堂 [Sanseido]。

----------. 1997. Pazeh-English Vocabulary (Draft). Unpublished manuscripts, pp.126+59.

Wen, Chyou-chu (溫秋菊). 1998. 〈巴則海族祭祖歌 "ai-yen" 初探〉 [A preliminary study on Pazeh's 'ai-yan: The songs for the rite in honor of ancestors]，《藝術評論》 [Arts Review] 9:45-84。

----------. 1999. 〈試探 Pazeh 音樂文化的綜攝—以一首台語聖詩為例〉 [A case study on a Taiwanese psalm to explore Pazeh's syncretism in musical culture]，《藝術評論》 [Arts Review] 10:25-60.

Wu, Rung-shun (吳榮順). 《巴宰族 Ayan 之歌》 [Ayan, Songs of Pazeh]. 平埔族音樂紀實系列 (6)。台北 [Taipei]：風潮有聲出版有限公司 [Wind Records]。

Abbreviations 縮寫

AF, Agent-focus 主事焦點

Ant, anticipating 期待

Asp, aspect 情貌

BF, Beneficiary-focus 受惠焦點

Caus, causative 使役

Conj, conjunction 連接

dist, distant 遠

exc, exclusive 排除式

f, female 女性

Fut, future 未來式

Gen, genitive 屬格

Imp, imperative 命令

Icp, inceptive 起始

IF, Instrumental-focus 工具焦點

inc, inclusive 包括式

invis, invisible 視界外

Ir, irrealis 非現實式

LF, Locative-focus 處所焦點

Lig, ligature 連結

lit, literally 直譯

Loc, locative 處所

m, male 男性

Neu, neutral 中性

Nmz, nominalize 名物化

Nom, nominative 主格

Obl, oblique 斜格

PAn, Proto-Austronesian 古南島語

PF, Patient-focus 受事焦點

per, person 人

poss, possessive 所有格

pl, plural 複數

Prf, perfective 完成式

Prg, progressive 進行式

Q, question particle 疑問助詞

Rec, reciprocal 相互

Red, reduplication 重疊

RF, Referential-focus 指事焦點

sg, singular 單數

Sta, stative 靜態

Syn, synonym 同義詞

Top, topic 主題

Part One: Pazih Texts 巴宰傳說集

A. Pazih Texts Recorded by Paul Li

Text 1. awi ki paasukuan 阿維的故事 *A Story of Awi*

Pazih song written by Pan Chi-min (male, 64) on March 2, 1969
Interpreted by Itih (female, 80) on July 22, 1976.
Recorded in Puli by Paul Li
這個文本是潘啟明（男，64 歲）根據巴宰傳說故事改編的歌詞 (1969.3.2)
王伊底 (Itih，女，80 歲) 口述解說 (1976.7.22)
李壬癸記錄　　地點：埔里

1. awi　　　　　ka　p\<in\>a-kan　durun　　ni　　tata.
   personal name　Top　Caus-Prf-eat　rice-bran　Gen　step-mother
   人名　　　　　題　使吃　　　　米糠　　　屬　　繼母
   Awi 被後母叫他吃米糠。
   Awi was-fed with rice-bran by the step-mother.

2. nahada　batan,　　adadumud-　a　　wazu.
   esixt　　company　only one　　Lig　dog
   有　　　伴　　　　只有一隻　　連　　狗
   他有一個伴，那就是只有一隻狗。
   (He) had only a friend, which was a dog.

3. aba　　ka　maxa-ruaru.
   father　Top　MAXA-sad
   父　　　　　傷心
   父親為他而傷心。
   Father was sad.

4. "mausay[1]　yaku　mi-kita　u　　daxə."
   will go　　I　　　AF-see　Obl　land
   去　　　　我　　看　　　斜　　地方
   「我要去看個地方。」
   "I shall go looking for a place," (Awi said.)

---

[1] The verb form *mausay* is derived from *mausaʔay*, which can be analyzed as *m-a-usa ʔ-ay* 'AF-Prg-go-Fut'.

5. kitakita siaa   na, nahada u rətən.
   AF-see everywhere   exist Obl village
   看 到處   有   村
   看來看去，（看到）有村莊。
   (He) kept looking around, (and) there were villages.

6. mausay lai sia, mata di dapi-dapi.
   will go Asp he from   Red-cliff
   要去 了 他 從   懸崖,山路
   他要去了，走過懸崖峭壁。
   He was leaving, and he (had to) pass through the steep rocky road.

7. kita-kita siaa   na, nahada u dalum.
   Red-look everywhere   exist Obl water
   看 到處   有   水
   看來看去，（看到）有水。
   (He) kept looking around, (and) there was water.

8. m<a>atu-xumak-ay dini.
   build-Prg-house-Fut   here
   要蓋房子   這裡
   （他）要在這裡蓋房子。
   (He) was to built a house here.

9. sasay ki uhuni?
   what Nom now
   什麼 主 現在
   現在要怎麼辦？
   What will he do now?

10. mu-puzah ki aba, ma-hata-hatan.
   AF-come   father AF-Red-laugh
   來   父 高興
   父親來了（看見他有房子而）高興。
   Father came (and) was happy.

11. "naki a lama p<a>uzah di babaw
   my   destiny Prg-come Loc above
   我的   命 來   自 上(上天)
   「我的命是天註定的
   "My fortune is determined by God.

12. yaku uhuni ka kuah a ta-u-xumak."
    I   now   none   Agt-house
    我   現在   沒   妻
    我現在沒有妻子。」
    I do not have a wife now."

13. di rətəl nahada maaxi-zapay
    village exist   unmarried maid
    村   有   閨女
    村裡有待嫁的閨女。
    There was an unmarried maid in the village.

14. apu   ka mu-kawas, "ara-i   dini a mamais."
    old woman Top AF-talk   take-Imp here   lady
    阿婆   講(告訴他)   娶   此地   女
    老太婆告訴他,「娶這裏的女郎吧!」
    An old woman said (to him), "Marry a girl here!"

Text 2. ni awi a paasukuan 阿維的故事 *A Story of Awi*

Narrated by Pan Chi-min (male, 71) on Oct. 24, 1976
Recorded in Auran, Puli by Paul Li
潘啟明（男，71 歲）口述、解說 (1976.10.24)
李壬癸記錄　　地點：愛蘭 (Auran)

1. uhuza   ka   nahada   mamais   ka   lalu,   mamaləŋ   ka   abuk
   ancient   exist lady   personal name man   personal name
   古時   有   女   人名   男   人名

   dusa a saw.
   two   person
   二   人

   古時候有一女名叫 Lalu，一男名叫 Abuk，共兩人。
   Once upon a time, there were two people, a woman named Lalu and a man named Abuk.

2. maa-ʔisakəp   lia   ki   dusa   saw.
   Rec-get together   Asp   two person
   結合   了   二   人

   兩人結合了。
   The two people got married.

3. adaŋ   a   kawas   ma-ŋazəp,   parisan   adaŋ   a   rakihan a   mamaləŋ,   laŋat   ka
   one   year Sta-more   was born   one   baby   boy   name
   一   年   超過   生   一   孩   男   名叫

   awi   sən.
   personal name   is said
   人名   據說

   一年多以後，生了一個男孩，名叫 Awi。
   It is said that in a little more than a year, (they) had a baby boy named Awi.

4. isia   lia   ki   ina   ka   mi-kudər   lia   ki   buxu.
   then   Asp Nom mother   Top AF-sick   Asp Nom body
   那時   母   病   了   身體

   那時他母親病了。
   Then the mother was ill.

5. dusa   ilas   lia   ka   purihat   lia   ki   ina.
   two   month Asp Top die   Asp   mother
   二   月   了   死   了   母

   兩個月之後他母親死了。
   Two months later, the mother died.

6. isia   lia   ki   aba,   "sasai-n   lia   ki   yaku   a   uhuni   nahada   rabəx   a
   then   Asp   father   what to do-PF   Asp   I   now   exist   little
   那時   了   父   怎麼辦   了   我   現在   有   幼小

   rakihan?"
   baby
   孩

   那時父親想，「有一個幼小的孩子，我怎麼辦？」
   Then the father (asked himself), "What shall I do now that (I) have a little baby?"

7. adaŋ   a   dali,   tau-barəd-   a   apu   mu-puzah   lia.
   one   day   neighbor   old woman   AF-come   Asp
   一   天   鄰居   婆   來   了

   有一天，鄰居阿婆來了
   On a certain day, a neighbor (and) old woman came (to him).

8. "abuk,   ara-i   adaŋ   a   ta-u-xumak   aunu   sarap-ən   u   rakihan."
   name   take-Imp   one   Agt-house   for   take care-PF   Obl   baby
   人名   娶   一   妻   可以   照顧   孩

   「Abuk，娶一妻來照顧小孩。」
   "Abuk, take another wife, so that she can take care of the baby."

9. "haw   lia,"   ki   abuk.
   fine   Asp   name
   好   了   人名

   Abuk 說，「好的。」
   "All right," said Abuk.

10. liaka   m-ara   ta-u-xumak.
    then   AF-take   Agt-house
    然後   娶   妻

    然後（他）就娶了太太了。
    Then (he) got married.

11. dusa   kawas   liaka   parisan   u   rakihan   a   mamaləŋ   lia,   laŋat   ka
    two   year   then   was born   baby   boy   Asp   name
    二   年   然後   生   孩   男   了   名

    adaway   sən.
    personal name   said
    人名   據說

    過了兩年，她就生了一個男孩，名叫 Adaway。
    It is said that two years later (she) had a baby boy named Adaway.

12. adaŋ a ilas, adaŋ a ilas, adaŋ a kawas, adaŋ a kawas, ma-taru a
one Lig month one month one year one year Sta-big
一 月 一 月 一 年 一 年 大

rakihan.
child
孩

一個月又一個月，一年又一年，孩子長大了。
Month after month, year after year, the child was growing.

13. ma-baza mə-kən u sumay lia.
AF-know AF-eat Obl rice Asp
知,能 吃 飯 了

他會吃飯了。
(He) knew (how) to eat rice.

14. isia liaka ini mi-kita lia ka awi.
then then not AF-see Asp personal name
那時 然後 不 看 了 人名

那時她瞧不起 Awi 了。
Then (she) looked down upon Awi.

15. tata p<in>arisan ka mə-kən r<iŋ>xaw sumay, awi ka pa-kan-ən
step-mother Prf-born AF-eat Prf-congee rice name Caus-eat-PF
繼母 生的 吃 稀飯 飯 人名 餵

durun.
rice bran
米糠

繼母自己生的吃稀飯，而給 Awi 吃米糠。
The step mother's own child ate rice gruel, whereas Awi was fed with rice bran.

16. isia lia ki awi maxa-kə-kəla[1], ma-kawas aba lia, "mausay ma-rukat
then Asp Nom MAXA-Red-think AF-tell father Asp will go AF-go out
那時 了 想 告訴 父 了 要去 出去

---

[1] The prefix *maxa-* + N 'to produce, to bring forth'; see Li and Tsuchida (2001:13-14).

maanu a daxə."
far   land
遠   地方
那時 Awi 想了想，告訴父親說，「（我）要去很遠地方。」
Then Awi thought it over (and) said to his father, "(I) want to go to a distant place."

17. isia lia ki aba sadiah a hinis.
     then   Asp   father sad   heart
     那時   了   父   難過   心
     那時父親心裡難過。
     Then the father was sad.

18. "haw la, ki nisiw a hinis ka haw i."
     fine   your   heart   good
     好   你的   心   好
     「你的想法也好。」
     "All right, your idea is good."

19. isia lia ki awi ka pikadun lia.
     then   Asp   personal name   set out   Asp
     那時   了   人名   出發   了
     那時 Awi 出發了
     Then Awi set out.

20. mu-kusa mu-ria-riax ka daxə lia.
     AF-go   AF-Red-find   land   Asp
     去   找   地方   了
     去找地方。
     (He) went looking for a place (to live).

21. awi ka pasakən di dida lia.
            arrive   that place   Asp
            到達   那地方   了
     Awi 到了那個地方了。
     Awi arrived at a certain place.

22. mi-kita daya rahut ka, nahada subud- a dalum.
     AF-see east   west   exist   spring   Lig   water
     看   東   西   有   泉   水
     東看西看（看到）有泉水。
     (He) looked to the east (and) to the west, and there was spring water.

23. liaka "riak   ka   dini."
    then   good Top here
    然後   好   這裡
    然後（他）說這地方好。
    Then he said, "It is good here."

24. "m<a>atu-xumak-ay   di   dini,"   lia   ki   awi.
    build-Prg-house-Fut   Loc here   Asp   personal name
    蓋房   處   這裡   了   人名
    Awi 說，「（我）要在此地蓋房子。」
    "(I'm) going to build a house here," Awi said.

25. isia   lia   ki   aba   ka   mu-puzah   mu-riax   awi   lia.
    then   father AF-come   AF-find   Asp
    那時   父   來   找   了
    那時父親來找 Awi
    Then father came to look for Awi.

26. aba   ka   mi-kita   awi.   ma-hata-hatan   awi   maxa-ruaru   lia.
    father AF-see   AF-Red-laugh   produce-tears Asp
    父   看   高興   流淚   了
    父親看見 Awi。Awi 高興得流淚。
    Father saw Awi. Awi was so happy that he shed tears.

27. di   dida   rətən   nahada   ka   apu.
    Loc that   village have   old woman
    處   那   村   有   阿婆
    那村有一個老太婆。
    That village had an old woman.

28. mi-kita   mamaləŋ,   pa-dudu   lia   ki   apu,   "mamaləŋ,   nahada   ta-u-xumak
    AF-see   young man   PA-ask   Asp   old woman   young man   have   Agt-house
    看見   少年   問   了   阿婆   少年人   有   成家

    siw?"
    you
    你
    看見少年人，老太婆就問，「年輕人，你娶了沒有？」
    Seeing the young man, the old woman asked, "Young man, are you married?"

29. "kuah."
    none
    沒有
    「還沒。」
    "Not yet."

30. "ara-i   di   dini   a   maaxi-zapay!"
    take-Imp   Loc   here   unmarried maid
    娶   處   此地   姑娘
    「娶此地的姑娘吧！」
    "Marry a girl here!"

31. "apu,   yaku ka   kuah a   adaŋ a   saysay."
    old woman   I   none   one   anything
    阿婆   我   沒   一個   東西
    「阿婆，我什麼都沒有。」
    "Madam, I haven't got anything."

32. "riak.   ta-si-karum-i   mamais   a   xumak."
    fine   let's-go-inside-Imp   lady   house
    好   咱入贅   女   家
    「好，給女家入贅吧！」
    "Fine, then marry yourself into the girl's family."

33. awi   isia   liaka   ma-sika-sikat.
    personal name   then   then   Sta-Red-shy
    人名   那時   然後   害羞
    Awi 那時害羞。
    Awi was then shy.

34. "haw," lia ki   awi.
    alright Asp Nom personal name
    好   了   主   人名
    Awi 說，「好！」
    "All right," Awi said.

35. liaka   maa-ʔisakəp   isia   lia.
    then   Rec-get together   then   Asp
    然後   結合   那時   了
    然後他就跟那個女子結婚了。
    Then they got married.

36. isia   liaka   maa-ʔisakəp   adaŋ a   kawas   parisan   rakihan   a   mamaləŋ.
    then   then   Rec-get together   one   year   was born   baby   boy
    那時   然後   結婚   一   年   生   孩   男的
    結婚後一年生了一個男孩。
    Then a year after the marriage, (they) had a baby boy.

37. isia   lia   ki   aba   u   tata   mi-kita   ali   lia,   ma-hata-hatan lia.
    then   Asp   Nom father and step-mother   AF-see   grandson   Asp   AF-Red-laugh   Asp
    那時   了   主   父   和   繼母   看   孫   了   高興   了
    那時他父親和繼母看見孫子都很高興了。
    Then (Awi's) father and step mother saw the grandson, (and they were both) happy.

Text 3. ni awi a paasukuan 阿維的故事 A Story of Awi

Written by Pan Tsai-sih
Interpreted by Pan Chi-min (male, 83) on Feb.10, 1988
Recorded in Auran, Puli by Paul Li
根據潘再賜手寫稿，潘啟明口述、改編 (1988.2.10)
李壬癸記錄　　　地點：埔里愛蘭 (Auran)

1. yaku   ka   ta-duduʔ-i   paasukuan.
   I   let's-tell-Imp   story
   我   講   故事
   我要講故事。
   Let's tell a story.

2. uhuza   ka   nahada   mamais   u   mamaləŋ.
   before   exist   lady   and   man
   從前   有   女   與   男
   從前有一女和一男。
   Once upon a time there were a woman and a man.

3. mamaləŋ   ka   abuk   sən   ki   laŋat.
   man   personal name   said   name
   男   人名   據說   名
   男的名叫 Abuk。
   The man was named Abuk.

4. mamais   ka   kalayu   sən.
   lady   female name   said
   女   女子名   據說
   女的叫做 Kalayu。
   The woman was named Kalayu.

5. maa-rəzərət   adaŋ   a   kawas   lia.
   Rec-together   one   year   Asp
   在一起   一   年   了
   他們結婚有一年了。
   They got married for a year.

6. liaka   parisan   rakihan   a   mamaləŋ.
   then   was born   baby   boy
   於是   生   子   男
   於是他們生了一個男孩。
   Then they had a baby boy.

7. awi   sən   ki laŋat. (= laŋat   ka   awi   sən)
   personal name   said   name   name   personal name   is said
   人名   據說   名   名   人名   據說
   據說他的名字叫做阿維。
   It is said that his name was Awi.

8. adaŋ a dali, mi-kudur lia   ki kalayu.
   One   day   AF-sick   Asp   name
   一   天   生病   了   女子名
   有一天 Kalayu 生病了。
   Kalayu got sick on a certain day.

9. adaŋ a dali, adaŋ a dali, ini   riak   ki buxu.
   one   day   one   day   not   good   body
   一   天   一   天   不   好   身體
   一天又過一天，她身體始終不好。
   Day after day, she did not get well.

10. ini   riak   ki kalayu a lama.
   not   good   name   destiny
   不   好   女子名   命
   Kalayu 命不好。
   Kalayu had a bad luck.

11. liaka   purihat lia   ki kalayu.
   then   die   Asp   name
   於是   死   了   女子名
   於是 Kalayu 死了。
   Then Kalayu died.

12. isia   lia   ki abuk ka   maxa-kə-kəla   kalayu lia.
   then   name   MAXA-Red-think   name   Asp
   那時   人名   想念   女名   了
   於是 Abuk 他想念太太 Kalayu。
   Abuk missed Kalayu.

13. "sasai-n   pai ki awi   a   imini tatih-an   a   rakihan?"
   what to do-PF   Q   name Lig   this   little-Nmz   child
   怎麼辦   Q   人名   這個   小的   孩
   「如何處理阿維這個小的孩子？」（Abuk 問自己。）
   "What shall I do with Awi this little child?" Abuk thought.

14. maxa-ru-aruaru lia ki abuk.
    become-Red-sad Asp   name
    傷心   了   人名
    Abuk 很傷心。
    Abuk was very sad.

15. tau-barəd- a rətən ka nahada lia ki apu.
    neighbor   village   exist   Asp   old woman
    隔壁   村   有   了   阿婆
    鄰村有一個老太婆。
    In a neighboring village there was an old woman.

16. mu-kawas ki apu,   "tatih a rakihan. ara-i   adaŋ a ta-u-xumak,
    AF-talk   old woman   little   child   take-Imp   one   Agt-house
    說   阿婆   小   孩   娶   一   妻

    aunu saa-rapun awi"
    for   IF-take care name
    為了 照顧   人名
    阿婆說，「孩子還小，娶個繼室（來）好照顧阿維。」
    The old woman said, "The child is too young. Take another girl to wife, so that she can take care of Awi."

17. "haw   lia." ki   abuk.
    alright Asp Nom   name
    好   人名
    「好吧，」Abuk 說。
    "All right," Abuk said.

18. m-ara   aubil   a ta-u-xumak lia.
    AF-take second   Agt-house   Asp
    娶   後   妻   了
    他娶了繼室。
    Then he married a second wife.

19. aubin   a mamais ka adunu   sən.
    second   lady   female name is said
    後   女   女子名   據說
    據說他繼室名叫 Adunu。
    It is said that the second wife's name was Adunu.

20. aubin a dali adaŋ a kawas maŋazəp parisan rakihan a mamaləŋ.
    later day one year more than was born baby boy
    後 天 一 年 多 生 子 男
    過一年多之後的一天，她生了一個男孩。
    More than a year later she had a baby boy.

21. damuri sən ki laŋat.
    personal name said name
    人名 據說 名
    據說他名字叫做 Damuri。
    It is said that his named was Damuri.

22. ma-taru lia ki awi, suadi ma-baza mu-zakay.
    Sta-big Asp name younger brother AF-able AF-walk
    大 了 人名弟 會 走
    阿維長大了，他弟弟也會走路了。
    Awi was growing up, and his younger brother learned how to walk.

23. ini riak a hinis lia ki aubin a tata.
    not good heart Asp later aunt
    不 好 心 了 後 姨
    後母心不好。
    The step-mother did not have a kind heart.

24. tatalima rakihan ka pa-kan-ən r<iŋ>xaw, awi ya imini ka
    own child Caus-eat-PF Prf-congee name this
    自己 子 使吃 稀飯 人名 這個

    pa-kan-ən durun.
    Caus-eat-PF bran
    使吃 米糠
    自己生的孩子給他吃稀飯，而 Awi 這個孩子只給他吃米糠。
    She fed her own son with rice gruel, yet she fed Awi with bran.

25. tata imini ka sadih a hinis.
    aunt this bad heart
    姨 這個 壞 心
    這個繼母心壞。
    This stepmother was hard-hearted.

26. isia   lia ki awi ka   maxa-kə-kəla   parisan   a ina.
    then   Asp   name   MAXA-Red-think   was born   mother
    那時   了   人名   想念   生   母

於是阿維他想念生母。

Thus Awi missed his own mother.

27. "ini purihat ki naki a ina   ka, ini ma-luhusu   mi-kita yaku," lia ki
    not die   my   mother   not Sta-in that way AF-see   I   Asp
    不   死   我的   母   題 不   那樣   看   我

awi.
name
人名

「我母親要不死，就不會那樣看待我。」阿維想。

"If my own mother had not died, she would not have treated me in that manner," he thought.

28. maamaaləŋ lia ki awi a imini.
    young man   Asp   name   this
    少年   了   人名   此

這個 Awi 長成少年了。

This Awi grew up as a young man.

29. "aba, m<a>a-rukad-ay   lia ki yaku. naki a suadi   ma-taru   lia.
    father AF-Prg-go out-Fut Asp   I   my   younger brother Sta-big   Asp
    爸   要出去   了   我   我的   弟   大   了

yaku ka m<a>-usaʔ-ay mu-riax   riak   a daxə."
I   AF-go-Fut   AF-find   good   land
我   要去   找   好   地方

「爸爸，我要出去了，我弟弟長大了，我要去找個好地方。」

"Daddy, I'm leaving. My younger brother is growing up. I'm going to look for a better place."

30. tumala lia ki aba ka, maxa-ru-aruaru   lia ki aba.
    listen Asp   father   become-Red-sad   Asp   father
    聽   了   父   很傷心   了   父

父親聽了很傷心。

When the father heard this, he was very sad.

31. tata ka ini riak a dais.
    aunt   not good   face
    姨   不   好   臉

後母臉色不好。

The step mother frowned.

32. pikadun   liaka   awi.
    set out   then   name
    起程   然後   人名
    然後阿維起程了。
    Then Awi set out.

33. mu-zakay   ma-dadi   ata?atas,   mu-dakis   ma-dadi   dapi-dapi-an,   ma-rizaux
    AF-walk   Sta-toward cliffs   AF-ascend   Sta-toward Red-steep-Nmz   AF-go down
    走   向   懸崖   爬上坡   向   石壁   下坡

    ma-dadi   rubuŋ   lia.
    Sta-toward lake   Asp
    向   湖   了
    他走向叢林,上峭壁,又下坡到一個湖。
    He walked to the jungle, up the cliffs, down the mountains and got to a lake.

34. kita?-an   di   dakal   ka   nahada   riak   a   subud-   a   dalum.
    look-PF   at   front   exist   good   spring   water
    看   在   前面   有   好   泉   水
    他看見在前面有好的泉水。
    He found nice spring water in front of him.

35. mə-səkət   di   dida   lia   ki   awi.
    AF-rest   at   there   Asp   personal name
    休息   在   那處   了   人名
    阿維在那個地方休息了。
    Awi rested there.

36. maxa-kə-kəla   lia   ki   awi.   "mu-zakay   maanu   a   daran.   dini   ka   riak   a
    MAXA-Red-think Asp   name AF-go   far   road   here   good
    想   了   人名 走   遠   路   此地   好

    daxə."
    land
    地
    阿維想道:「走了很遠的路了,此地是個好地方。」
    Awi thought, "I have walked a long way. This is a good place here."

37. m<a>atu-xumak-ay   di   dini   lia   ki   awi.
    build-Prg-house-Fut   here   Asp   name
    要蓋房   此地   了   人名
    阿維要在此地蓋房子。
    Awi was going to build a house here.

38. taa-tamak-ay kahuy lia ki awi.
    Red-cut-Fut tree Asp name
    要砍 木 了 人名
    阿維砍樹。
    Awi was going to cut trees.

39. raa-razaw lia ki maaxi-zapay a mamais.
    Red-pass by Asp maid lady
    經過 了 未婚 女
    有個未婚姑娘打從那兒經過。
    An umarried girl was passing by.

40. awi ka mi-kita dakan a apu.
    name AF-see front old woman
    人名 看 前面 阿婆
    阿維看見前面來了一個老太婆。
    Awi saw an old woman in front of him.

41. "saysay pai siw?"
    what Q you
    做什麼 Q 你
    「你在做什麼？」
    "What are you doing?"

42. awi ka, "taa-tamak-ay kahuy m<a>atu-xumak-ay di dini ki yaku."
    name Red-cut-Fut tree build-Prg-house-Fut here I
    人名 要砍 樹 蓋房 此地 我
    阿維說，「我要砍樹，要在此地蓋房子。」
    Awi said, "I'm cutting trees to build a house here."

43. "nahada ta-u-xumak siw?"
    exist Agt-house you
    有 太太 你
    「你成家了沒有？」
    "Are you married?"

44. "kuah aku."
    none I
    沒 我
    「我沒有。」
    "Not yet."

37

45. "ta-ara?-ay   di   dini   a   mamais,   haw?"
      Let's-take-Fut   Loc   here   lady   fine
      娶   處   此地   女   好
      「在這兒娶太太，好吧？」
      "How about getting married here?"

46. "mayaw   matuxumak   lia   ki   yaku."
      not yet   build house   Asp   I
      還沒   蓋房子   了   我
      「我還沒蓋好房子呢！」
      "I have not finished building a house yet."

47. "anu   riak   a   barət   mu-kukusa."
      for   good   companion   AF-work
      為了   好   伴   工作
      「（娶一個）好做伴和工作呀！」
      "(A wife) will be your good companion and coworker."

48. m-ara   imini   a   mamais   ka   riak   a   mamais.
      AF-take   here   Lig   lady   good   lady
      娶   此   連   女   好   女
      他在此地娶的女子是好女子。
      The girl he married here was a good one.

49. awi   a   mamais   ka   taruat   sən   ki   laŋat.
      name   lady   personal name   said   name
      人名   女   人名   據說   名
      據說阿維的太太名叫 Taruat。
      It is said that Awi's wife was named Taruat.

50. dusa   lia   ka   mu-tukut   dələm,   piaxun,   tawtaw,   dadas,   dukun;   nahada
      two   Asp   AF-sow   corn   millet   peanut   sweet potatoe   taro   exist
      二   了   撒種   玉米   小米   花生   番薯   芋   有
      lia   ki   t<in>ukut.
      Asp   Prf-sow
      了   種
      二人播種了玉米、小米、花生、甘薯、芋頭，都播種了。
      The couple planted corn, millet, peanuts, sweet potatoes and taroes.

51. aubin a dali, taruad- a imini ka parisan adaŋ a rakihan a mamaləŋ.
　　later　　day　　name　　　this　　was born　one　　baby　　boy
　　後　　　日　　女人名　　這個　　生　　　　一　　孩　　　男
　　後來有一天，這位 Taruat 生了一個男孩。
　　Later on a certain day, Taruat had a baby boy.

52. awi ka ma-hata-hatan nahada rakihan a mamaləŋ.
　　name　　AF-Red-laugh　　exist　baby　　boy
　　人名　　高興　　　　　有　　孩　　　男
　　阿維高興有了一個男孩。
　　Awi was very happy to have a son.

53. dusa ka riak a mu-razaw dali.
　　two　　good　AF-pass　　day
　　二人　　好　　過　　　　日
　　二人過好日子。
　　The two (people) had an easy life = The couple enjoyed their life.

54. dini a daxə ka auran sən.
　　here　land　　place name　is said
　　此　　地　　愛蘭　　　據說
　　據說此地就叫做愛蘭（現地名，古名烏牛欄）。
　　It is said that this place is called Auran.

Text 4. itih[1] a paku paasukuan 《鷹鳥名》的故事
The Story of Transforming into an Eagle

Narrated by Itih (female, 80) on Sept.30, 1976
Recorded in Puli by Paul Li
王伊底口述、解說 (1976.9.30)
李壬癸記錄
地點：埔里

1. ina   ka   puri(a)hat   lia.
   mother   Top   die   Asp
   母   死   了
   她母親死了。
   (Her own) mother died.

2. aba   ka   m-ara   aubil   a   tata ka,   ini   saisim-an   imisiw.
   father   AF-take   second   aunt Conj   not   love-LF   her
   父   娶,拿   後續   姨   不   疼   她
   父親娶了繼母，（可是）並不疼她。
   Although father married a second wife, (she) did not love her.

3. adaŋ a dali,   adaŋ a dali m-aŋit   lia.
   one   day   one   day AF-cry   Asp
   一   天   一   天   哭   了
   她每天都哭。
   (She) cried everyday.

4. ma-kuas ina   ka,   hapət   mu-kusa maki   namisiw a ina.
   AF-tell   mother   Conj   want   AF-go   with   her   mother
   說,告訴   母   愛,要   去   跟   她的   母
   （夢中）她告訴她生母說，她要跟她母親去。
   (She) told (her own) mother (in a dream that she) wanted to go with her mother.

5. namisiw ina   ka,   "hapət   mu-ʔasay   pai siw?"
   her   mother   Top   want   AF-what   Q   you
   她的   母   要   什麼   你
   她的母親問，「妳要做什麼？」
   Her mother (asked), "What do you want?"

---

[1]   A Pazih legend says that Itih is the name of a bird, which cries *kaw* or *kuak* at noon.

6. "hapət maxa-ʔayam; hapət ma-ha-bahar maxa-ʔayam."
   want become-bird want AF-HA-fly become-bird
   要 做鳥 要 飛 做鳥
   「我要做鳥；我要當鳥飛」
   "(I) want to become a bird; (I) want to fly like a bird."

7. namisiw ina, "ara-i a dapas! kəxəd-i a dapas! xəʔəd-i di
   her mother take-Imp dustpan cut-Imp dustpan tie-Imp
   她的 母 拿 糞箕 劈成兩半 糞箕 綁

   abaxa ki dapas!"
   shoulder dustpan
   肩 糞箕
   她的母親說，「拿糞箕！把它劈成兩半！綁在肩上！」
   Her mother (said), "Take a dustpan and cut it into two! (And then) tie them unto the shoulders!"

8. ma-ha-bahar lia.
   AF-HA-fly Asp
   飛 了
   她飛了。
   (She) flew.

9. ma-ha-bahar kāw² babaw tilap.
   AF-HA-fly to above roof
   飛 到(借閩語) 上 屋頂
   飛到屋頂。
   (She) flew to above the roof.

10. ma-ha-bahar kāw babaw kahuy.
    AF-HA-fly to above tree
    飛 到 上 樹
    飛到樹上。
    (She) flew above the trees.

11. ma-ha-bahar kāw babaw kawas.
    AF-HA-fly to above sky
    飛 到 上 天空
    飛到天上。
    (She) flew up in the sky.

---

² The word *kāw* 'to' is a loan from Taiwanese *kau* 'to'.

12. dalian ka mi-kiliw, "kaw, kaw."
    noon   AF-cry
    午   叫
    午時她就叫 "kaw, kaw" （那便是煮午飯之時了）。
    At noon (she) cried, "kaw, kaw."

Text 5. paŋapaŋ 缺了一條腿的美女 *A Pretty Girl Missing a Leg*

Narrated by Itih (female, 80) on Oct.26, 1976
Recorded in Puli by Paul Li
王伊底口述、解說 (1976.10.26)
李壬癸記錄
地點：埔里

1.
nu	uhuza	taubur,	anu	maaka-hapəd-	a	saw	ka	mu-kusa	di
Gen	ancient	gathering place	for	Rec-love		person		AF-go	to
	從前	集會場	為了	相愛		人		去	向

taubur.
gathering place
集會場

從前的會場是相愛的人才去。
As for the ancient gathering place, people who were in love would go there.

2.
mu-puzah	ma-turay	ka	maaxizapay.
AF-come	AF-sing		unmarried girl
來	唱		未婚姑娘

未婚姑娘來唱歌。
Unmarried girls came to sing.

3.
m-itul,	mamaləŋ	ka	mu-kusa	m-apa	anu	mamais.
AF-get up	man		AF-go	AF-carry	for	lady
站起來	男		去	揹	為了	女

（她）站起來，男人就去揹女的。
(As a girl) stood up, a young man (who loved her) would go over to carry the girl on his back.

4.
nahada	adaŋ	a	rubaŋ	mamais,	apaʔ-ən	namisiw	a	ina	mu-kusa	di
have	one		young	lady	carry-PF	her		mother	AF-go	
有	一		年輕	女	被揹	她		母	去	

taubur	a	mi-tuku.
gathering place		AF-sit
集合場		坐

有一個女孩，由她的媽揹著去會場坐。
There was a young lady, carried on the back by her mother to go to the gathering place (and) sit (there).

5. hinaw   riak   a rubaŋ mamais   ka, ini apaʔ-ən ni saw.
   very   good   young lady   not carry-PF   person
   很   好(美)   年輕   女   沒   揹   人
   （她是）很漂亮的女子，但卻沒人揹。
   The young lady was very pretty, yet (she) was not carried by anybody.

6. nahada   rubaŋ   mamaləŋ   maxu-taxa imisiw a kizəx.
   have   young   man   MAXU-wait her   stand up
   有   年輕   男   等   她   站起來
   有個男孩（在）等她站起來。
   There was a young man waiting for her to stand up.

7. namisiw a ina   mu-pudah mi-kita namisiw a rakihan ini asuʔ-un ni
   her   mother AF-come   AF-see   her   child   not carry-PF
   她   母   來   看   她的   孩   沒   被帶
   saw.
   person
   人
   她的母親來看見她的孩子，沒人帶她走。
   Her mother came back to find that her girl was not carried away by anybody.

8. maapaʔay[1] namisiw a rakihan, mu-xalit namisiw a rima.
   shall carry her   child   AF-lead   her   hand
   要揹   她的   孩   拉,牽   她的   手
   （她）要揹她的孩子時，拉她的手。
   Before carrying her child, she took her hands.

9. rubaŋ   mamais m-itul   lia.
   young   lady   AF-get up   Asp
   年輕   女   站   了
   女孩站起來了。
   The young lady stood up.

---

[1] The underlying verb form of *maapaʔay* would have three vowel *a*'s in sequence *maa-apaʔ-ay* 'Rec-carry-Fut', yet the restriction of not permitting more than two identical vowels in sequence deletes one *a*.

10. kuah a adaŋ a karaw.
none one leg
沒 一 腿
（她）少了一條腿。
One leg was missing.

11. rubaŋ mamais ka ma-sikat.
Young lady Sta-embarassed
年輕 女 害羞
女孩很難為情。
The young lady was embrassed.

12. mu-kusa maxa-ʔayam a.
AF-go become-bird
去 做鳥
要去做鳥。
(She) went to become a bird.

13. nah pa-kita saw lia.
not Caus-see people Asp
不要 使看 人 了
不叫別人看見（她）。
(She) did not want people to see her.

14. mausay di maanu a binayu lia.
will go Loc far mountain Asp
要去 處 遠 山 了
她到深山去。
She went to a mountain far away.

15. "na hapət mi-kita yaku a saw ka, alu binayu a ma-laləŋ ka
if want AF-see I Lig people come mountain AF-live
倘 要 看 我 的 人 來 山 住
kita yaku.
see I
看 我
「倘若要看我的人，來山上住就看得到我。
"If people want to see me, they should come to live in the mountain to see me.

16. ahuan aidi binayu a mi-kiliw, 'paŋ, paŋ' ka yaku."
    night at mountain AF-cry I
    夜 在那 山 叫 我
    晚上在山上叫'"paŋ，paŋ"的就是我。」
    At night time (when a bird) cries 'paŋ, paŋ' in the mountain, that is me."

17. namisiw a laŋat ka paŋapaŋ.
    her name personal name
    她的 名 人名
    她的名字是 Paŋapaŋ。
    Her name is Paŋapaŋ.

Text 6. rakihan ka kiusun u rahuay 孩子被老鷹挾走了
The Child Was Seized by an Eagle

Narrated by Itih (female, 80) on Oct.27, 1976
Recorded in Puli by Paul Li

In Japan there is such a story: While a man and his wife were working in the field, their baby sleeping in a cradle was seized away by an eagle. The baby grew up in the eagle's nest. He was left on a pine tree in the yard of a temple by the eagle. Then he was saved and became a disciple of the temple. It took his mother 30 years to find him. Later on he became a famous Buddhist monk. See Hirako Ikeda (1971). *A Type and Motif Index of Japanese Folk-Literature*, pp.182-183.

王伊底（女，80 歲，Taruat 的妹妹）口述、解說 (1976.10.27)

李壬癸記錄　　地點：埔里愛蘭

說明：日本傳說故事有一則，大意如下：父母兩人在田園中工作時，睡在搖籃中的嬰兒被老鷹挾走了。嬰兒就在老鷹的巢中長大。他被老鷹留在廟庭中的松樹上，嬰兒後來獲救了，成為廟裡的學徒。他的生母花了 30 年的時間才找到他。他後來成為有名的佛教高僧。參見 Hirako Ikeda (1971). *A Type and Motif Index of Japanese Folk-Literature*, p.182-183. Helsinki: Suomalainen Tiedeakatemia, Academia Scientiarum Fennica. 感謝 Dr. Warren Brewer 告知我及其相關的參考資料。

1. yaku m<a>a-ka-kawas-ay uhuza paasukuan.
I AF-Prg-Red-tell-Fut ancient story
我　將講　　　　　　古代　故事
我要講古代的故事。
I shall tell an old story.

2. mamais mamaləŋ paxu-karit[1].
woman man work in a field
女　　男　　　做園子
夫妻在做園子。
A woman and a man were working in a field.

3. tumala rakihan a m<a>aŋit.
hear baby Lig AF-Prg-cry
聽　孩　　　一直哭
聽見小孩子一直哭
(They) heard a baby crying.

---

[1] The function of the verbal prefix *paxu-* or *maxu-* is not clear and has limited usage; see Li and Tsuchida (2001:14, 192, 231).

4. m-itul   m-ukusa   mi-kita   lia.
   AF-get up AF-go   AF-look Asp
   站   去   看   了
   站起來去看（個究竟）。
   (They) stood up (and) went to look at it.

5. ara,   pa-sabar[2] di   duhuling   a   axərət.
   Oh!   get-caught Loc interwoven   vine
   呀   掛住   在   成網狀   肉藤
   哎呀！（小孩）掛在爬藤中
   Oh goodness! (The baby) got caught in the interwoven vine.

6. dusa saw   m<a>aki-nua-nualək[3] ma-usaʔ-ay   mu-kalapu rakihan.
   two   people Prg-MAKI-Red-hurry   AF-go-Fut   AF-hold   baby
   二   人   趕緊   去   抱   孩
   兩人趕快去抱孩子。
   The two people rushed there to take down the baby.

7. mu-xalit   axərət   paka-da-daxə.
   AF-pull   vine   Caus-Red-low
   扯   肉藤   使降低
   他們把爬藤扯低。
   (They) pulled down the vine.

8. kalapuʔ-un   ki   rakihan.
   hold-PF   Nom baby
   抱   孩
   孩子抱起來。
   The baby was held up.

9. kita sən   ka   rakihan mamaləŋ.
   look said Top baby   boy
   看   據說 孩   男
   一看是個男孩。
   (They) looked (at it and it was) a baby boy.

---

2 The prefix *pa-* may indicate 'causative' or 'verbalizer;' see Li and Tsuchida (2001:15, 263).

3 The prefix *maki-* has limited usage; see Li and Tsuchida (2001:180).

10. yamisiw   ma[4]   nahada   mamaləŋ   a   rakihan.
    they   also   have   boy   Lig   child
    他們   也   有   男   孩
    他們自己也有男孩。
    They also had a boy.

11. m-iba   rakihan   ka   m-ukusa   di   xumak   lia.
    AF-hold baby   AF-go   home   Asp
    抱   孩   去   家   了
    抱著小孩回家。
    They held the baby in their arms and went home with it.

12. "kaidan,   nahada   suadi   lia."
    name   have   younger brother   Asp
    人名   有   弟   了
    「Kaidan，你有弟弟了。」
    "Kaidan, you have got a little brother."

13. imini   ka   bauki   sən   a   laŋat.
    this   Top   name   said   Lig   name
    這   人名   據說   名
    這個名字是 Bauki。
    This one's name is Bauki.

14. adaŋ   a   dali,   adaŋ   a   dali,   maidəh   kutab-   a   daurik   a   isiz-   a
    one   Lig   day   one   Lig   day   soon   twinkling   eyes   Lig   ten   Lig
    一   天   一   天   很快   眨眼   眼   十

    xasəb-   a   turu[5]   a   kawas.
    five   Lig   three   year
    五   三   年
    一天過一天，一眨眼就是十八年了。
    Day after day, it was soon eighteen (years) at the twinkling of eyes.

---

[4] The form *ma* is a loan from Taiwanese *ma* 'also'.

[5] There are two different ways of saying numerals from eleven to nineteen in Pazih, as recorded in Li and Tsuchida (2001:132). Here is an example of still another way of saying these numerals. Cf. *isit xasəbisupat* 'nineteen' in Sentence 67 in Text 7 below. These differences may have to do with variations of different speakers.

15. abasan   suadi   maxu-papah.
     elder brother   younger brother MAXU-quarrel
     兄   弟   吵架
     兄弟吵架。
     The elder and younger brothers quarreled with each other.

16. "pa-raxiw! uzay   ina   p<in>arisan siw.   t<in>ingi   rahuay siw."
     PA-get out   not   mother Prf-born   you   Prf-snatch eagle   you/Nom
     走開   不是 母   生的   你   挾   老鷹   你
     「走開，你不是媽媽生的，你是老鷹挾來的。」
     "Get out! You were not born by Mother. You were snatched away by an eagle"

17. mu-pudah lia ki   ina   ka   mi-kixi   ina   lia,   "mamah   ka
     AF-return   Asp Nom mother Top AF-complain mother Asp   elder brother Top
     回來   母   訴苦   母   兄

     uzay   ni   siw p<in>arisan aku."
     not   Gen you Prf-born   I/Nom
     非   你   生   我
     媽媽回來時就向她告狀，「哥哥說，我不是你生的。」
     When Mother returned home, (Bauki) complained to her, "My brother said that I was not born by you."

18. "kalaxi. isiw ma naki   a   p<in>arisan."
     untrue   you also my   Lig   Prf-born
     不對   你   也   我的   生
     「不對，你也是我生的。」
     "That's not true. You were also born by me."

19. "uzay nisiw a   p<in>arisan. ma-taaru   lia   aku. m-usay mu-riax   naki
     not   your   Lig   Prf-born   Sta-grow up Asp   I   AF-go   AF-find my
     不是   你的   生   大   了   我   去   找   我的
     a   ina."
     Lig   mother
            母
     「不是你生的，我長大了，我要去找我的生母。」
     "(I) was not born by you. I have grown up. (I) shall go looking for my mother."

20. "usa riax-i! na[6] riax-ən ka, alu pa-kawas-i yaku. na kuah ka,
    go   look-Imp if find-PF Top come tell-Imp   me   if not have
    去   找   若   找   來   告訴   我   若   沒有

    wailu alu xumak."
    early   return home
    快   回來 家
    「去找吧！找到時來告訴我。如果沒有，趕快回家來。」
    "Go looking for (her)! If (she) is found, come to let me know. If there is none, come home early."

21. saasaunan p<a>ikadul mu-pupu sumay pazay anu di daran
    morning   Prg-set out AF-make ball rice glutinous rice for Loc road
    早上   動身   揉(飯糰)   飯   糯米   為 處 路

    a ka-kan-ən.
      Red-eat-PF
      吃
    他早上要動身時，（家裡）做糯米糰到路上吃。
    As (he) was setting out in the morning, (they) made balls of sticky rice to eat on the way.

22. ma-xatukul di binayu, liaka mi-kita u rətəl lia.
    AF-climb   Loc mountain then AF-see Obl village Asp
    爬(山)   處 山   然後 看   村   了
    他爬山，然後看見村子。
    (He) climbed mountains and then saw a village.

23. ma-rizaux m-ukusa di rətəl mu-riax namisiw ina.
    AF-go down AF-go   village AF-find his/Gen mother
    下山   去   村 找   他的   母
    下山去村子找他母親。
    (He) went down to go to a village to look for his mother.

24. pasakən di rətəl ka, səm lia.
    arrive   village Conj late, dark Asp
    到達   村   晚,天黑 了
    到村子時天已黑了。
    Upon arrival at the village, it got dark.

---

[6] Loan word from Taiwanese *na* 'if'.

25. xumak   a   k\<in\>ixid-an   ka, nahada   puŋu kahuy.
    house   Prf-nearby-Loc   Top have   trunk   tree
    房子   旁邊   有   樹幹   樹
    房子旁有一棵樹。
    Nearby a house there was a tree.

26. ma-xatukul   di babaw kahuy.
    AF-climb   up   tree
    爬   上   樹
    （他）爬到樹上。
    (He) climbed the tree.

27. m-ara   namisiw a xuriuk   ka, p\<a\>uhuni xuriuk.
    AF-take his/Gen   flute   Prg-play   flute
    拿   他的   笛   在吹   笛
    拿起他的笛來吹。
    (He) took out his flute to play it.

28. ma-tanga xumak. mi-kiliw, "ima pai siw? saasay ahuan a dali aidi
    AF-open   house   AF-cry   who Q   you   do   night   day there
    開（門） 房   叫   誰   你 做什麼   晚上   天 在那兒
    siw? alu,   alu   yamian."
    you   come come   we-Loc
    你   來   來   我們這兒
    （她）開門叫，「你是誰？這麼晚了在那兒幹嗎？來，來我們這兒！」
    (A woman) called, "Who are you? Why are you there at night time? Come, come over to our place!"

29. p\<a\>udah di asay pai siw?"
    Prg-come   where Q   you
    來   何處   你
    「你從何處來？」
    "Where do you come from?" (the woman then asked).

30. yaku ka p\<a\>udah di   maanu. ri-riax   naki a   ina."
    I   Top Prg-come   Loc far away Red-seek my   Lig mother
    我   來   處 遠   在找   我   母
    「我從遠處來，正在找我媽。」
    "I come from a place far away. (I) am looking for my mother."

31. "saasay ki ri-riax ina?"
    why   Red-seek mother
    為何   在找   母
    「為什麼在找你母親？」
    "Why are (you) looking for (your) mother?"

32. "nimu   a dini ka nahada rakikan kius-un   u   rahuay?"
    you/Gen   here Top have   child   seized-PF   Obl eagle
    你們   這兒   有   孩   挾   老鷹
    「你們這兒有孩子被老鷹挾走嗎？」
    "Did you here have a child snatched away by an eagle?"

33. "uhuda ka naki a rakihan ka kius-un   u   rahuay, ma-sədəm lia."
    former Top my   Lig child   Top seized-PF Obl eagle   Sta-long Asp
    從前   Top 我的   孩   Top 挾   老鷹   久   了
    「從前我的孩子被老鷹挾走，很久了。」
    "Years ago my child was snatched away by an eagle. It has been a long time ever since."

34. "nukuasayan   lia?"
    when   Asp
    何時   了
    「什麼時候？」
    "When was it?"

35. "isiz- a xasəb- a turu a kawas."
    ten   Lig five   Lig three Lig year
    十   五   三   年
    「十八年了。」
    "Eighteen years (ago)."

36. "yaku ka nisiw a rakihan."
    I   Top your Lig child
    我   你的   孩
    「我就是你的孩子。」
    "I am your child."

37. "yaku ki k<in>us-un   rahuay."
    I   Nom Prf-was snatched-PF eagle
    我   被挾   老鷹
    「我被老鷹挾走了。」
    "I was snatched away by an eagle."

38. "liaka   dəkəl-ən   ni   saw   kaxu   uhuni."
    then   pick up-PF   Gen   people   until   now
    然後   揀   人   到   現在
    「被人揀到一直到現在。」
    "Then (I) was picked up by people until now."

39. "ma-taru   lia   -ku   ka,   pudah   mu-riax."
    Sta-big   Asp   I   Conj   come   AF-find
    大   了   我   來   找
    「我長大了才來找。」
    "I have grown up (so I have) come to look for (my mother)."

40. "saasay   pa-yaku   kius-un   a   rahuay?"
    why   Caus-me   seized-PF   eagle
    為何   使我   挾   老鷹
    「我怎麼被老鷹挾走了呢？」
    "Why was I snatched away by an eagle?" (the boy asked).

41. "isiw   ka   ta-aŋit."
    you   Top   baby-cry
    你   哭
    「你很愛哭。」
    "You were a baby-cry."

42. yaku   ka   baa-bazu   siatu.
    I   Red-wash   clothes
    我   正在洗   衣
    我正在洗衣服。
    I was washing clothes.

43. isiw   ka   apaʔ-ən   naki.
    you   Top   carry-PF   by me/Gen
    你   揹   我
    你由我揹著。
    You were being carried on my back.

44. m-aŋit   mə-təzə-təzək.
    AF-cry   AF-Red-kick
    哭   亂踢,掙扎
    （你）卻哭著一直亂踢。
    (You) cried, kicking and struggling.

54

45. liaka m-ukusa di   bayu;   pa-kizih   isiw pa-nunuh.
    then   AF-go   Loc   by water   Caus-low   you   Caus-nurse
    然後   去   水邊   解下   你   餵奶
    我到水旁去，解下你餵你奶。
    Then (I) went by the water to unfasten you (and) nurse (you).

46. liaka pa-idem-en   di   bayu.
    then   Caus-sleep-PF   Loc   by water
    然後   使睡   水邊
    然後讓你睡在水旁。
    Then (I) made (you) sleep by the water.

47. nahada rahuay p<a>udah   di   babaw,   mu-kius isiw lia.
    have   eagle   Prg-arrive Loc   above   AF-seize you   Asp
    有   老鷹   從..來   高處   挾   你   了
    有老鷹從高處下來，挾走了你了。
    There came an eagle from above to snatch you away.

48. mu-taŋar   lia   -ku ka,   kius-un   lia.
    AF-raise head Asp   I   Conj   snatched-PF   Asp
    抬頭看   了   我   被挾走   了
    我抬頭一看（你）已被挾走了。
    (As) I raised my head, (you) had been carried off.

49. m-itul   m-ara   ailuan (yaku) m-usa   mu-siŋar.
    AF-get up   AF-take   pole   I   AF-go   AF-chase
    站起   拿   扁擔   我   去   追
    （我）站起來拿扁擔去追。
    Rising to take up a pole, I went chasing (the eagle).

50. liaka m-aŋit   lia   ku.
    then   AF-cry   Asp   I
    然後   哭   了   我
    我哭了。
    Then I cried.

51. mu-rupud- a mu-bazu,   liaka mu-kusa xumak a m-aŋit.
    AF-finish   AF-wash clothes   then   AF-go   home   AF-cry
    完成   洗衣   然後   去   家   哭
    洗完了衣服，然後我就回家去哭。
    Having finished washing clothes, then I went home to cry.

52. kuah   dini   lai   siw   ka,   ini   ma-taŋa   aaləp.
    without   here   Asp   you   Conj   not   AF-open   door
    無   此地   了   你   沒   開   門
    這兒沒了你，我也就不開門。
    Without you here, (I would) not open the door.

53. nah   mi-kita   ni   saw   a   rakihan.
    not want AF-see   Gen   other Lig   child
    不要   看   人   孩
    （我）不要看人家的孩子。
    (I) did not want to see other people's children.

54. mi-kita   ka   m-aŋid-ay.   uhuni   ma   maxa-kə-kəla."
    AF-see   AF-cry-Fut   now   also   MAXA-Red-think
    看見了   要哭   現在   也   想念
    看了就要哭。現在也會想念。」
    Seeing (them) would (make me) cry."

55. "m<in>u-dəkəl   yaku   a   ina   ka,   saisim-an.
    AF-Prf-pick up   I   mother   love-LF
    揀   我   母   疼
    「揀到我的母親也疼（我）。
    "The mother who picked me up loves me."

56. mausay   m<a>a-kawas   m-iruma   lia   aku   naki   a   p<in>arisan   a
    will Fut   AF-Prg-tell   AF-find   Asp   I   my/Gen   Prf-born
    要去   告訴   找到   了   我   我的   生
    ina   lia   aku."
    mother   Asp   I
    母   了   我
    要去告訴（她）我找到我的生母了。」
    I shall go and tell (her) that I have found my own mother."

57. "nahada   k<in>udis   aidi   namisiw   a   bukun."
    have   Prf-scratch   stay   his/Gen   back
    有   爪痕   在   他的   背上
    「他的背上有爪痕（所以那是一個顯明的標記，也很容易辨認）。」
    "There were scars (left by the eagle's scratching) on his back."

58. "m-iruma naki a p<in>arisan a ina lia."
    AF-find   my/Gen   Prf-born   mother Asp
    找到   我的   生   的 母   了
    「我找到我的生母了。」（他告訴揀到他的父母親）
    "(I) have found my own mother," (he returned home and told the parents who had raised him).

59. "usa ara-i nisiw a ina alu dini a ma-laləŋ!
    go   take-Imp your   mother come here   AF-live
    去   取   你的   母   來 此地   住
    「去帶你的母親來這兒住！
    "Go to bring your mother here to live (with us)!

60. dini ka ma-riax a ribu.
    here Top Sta-broad   field
    此地   寬   園子
    此地有'寬大'（很多之意）的田園
    Here are plenty of fields.

61. alu paxuruma aiŋaiŋar.
    come plant   various vegetables and fruits
    來   種   各種蔬果
    來種各種蔬菜水果。」
    Come to plant various vegetables and fruits.

62. asuʔ-i ki mamah anu maa-parara ma-iliw kapua, siatu,
    take-Imp Nom brother for   Rec-help AF-carry on a pole coverlet clothing
    帶去   兄   幫忙   挑   棉被 衣

    rukus, aidisaysay."
    trousers various objects
    褲   各種物件
    帶去你哥哥去幫著挑被子，衣、褲和各種物件。」
    "Take (your) brother along to help carry coverlet, clothing, trousers, (and) various objects on poles."

63. maku namisiw a mamah mu-kusa dinamisiw a ina lia.
    with his   elder brother AF-go his   mother
    與,跟 他的   哥   去   他的   母
    他跟哥哥到他母親處去。
    (The boy) went to his mother's (place) with his brother.

64. pasakəl lia, ahuan lia.
    arrive   Asp night Asp
    到達   了   夜   了
    到達時天已黑了。
    When (they) arrived (there), it was night time.

65. m-idəm   ahuan.
    AF-sleep night
    睡   夜
    （在那兒）過夜。
    (They) slept (there) overnight.

66. ma-kuas namisiw ina,   "tia didua ma-laləŋ; dahu a ka-kan-ən."
    AF-tell his   mother   go there AF-live   many Red-eat-PF
    告訴   他的   母   去 彼處 住   多   吃的
    （他）告訴他媽媽，「搬到那邊去住；（那兒有）很多吃的。」
    (The boy) said to his mother, "Go there to live; (there is) plenty to eat."

67. namisiw a ina   ka,   "haw,   m-asuʔ-ay   yamini a balax. niam a
    his   mother Conj   all right AF-bring-Fut these   things we
    他的   母   Conj   好   要帶   這些   東西 我們

    balax ka, ta-aduʔ-aw   dini ka ta-susuʔ-aw."
    things we let's-leave-Ir here   let's-lock up-Ir
    東西 咱   留存   此地   咱們要鎖
    他媽說，「好，要帶走那些東西。我們有的東西就留在此地鎖起來。」
    His mother said, "All right. We shall take those things with us, (but) let's leave the (other) things of ours here (and) lock them up."

68. m-ukusa maki yamisiw.
    AF-go   with them
    去   跟   他們
    她就跟他們去了。
    (She) went with them.

69. pasakəl lia, ma-hata-hatan.
    arrive   Asp   AF-Red-laugh
    到   了   高興
    到了，大家很高興。
    (When they) arrived, (all) were happy.

70. ma-kawas   pa-tumala   isia,   "haw   ria-riak-an   dəkəl-ən   nisiw.
    AF-tell   Caus-listen that, she   fortunately good   picke up-PF you
    說,告   使聽   那,她   幸   好   被揀   你

    pa-kan-ən   nisiw [kaw]   haimisiw a ma-taru."
    Caus-eat-PF you   until   that   Sta-big
    使吃   你   到(閩語) 那麼   大
    生母說給她聽,「幸好被你揀到,又讓你養得那麼大。」
    (The boy's mother) said to her, "Fortunately (he) was picked up by you. He was raised by you until (he grew) so big."

71. "maki yami-an ma-laləŋ, ru-runuʔ-ay   rakihan ka maki isiw [ma]
    with us-Loc   Af-live   Red-separate-Fut son   with you   also
    跟   我們   住   分開   兒子   跟   你   也(閩語)

    riak."
    good
    好
    「要跟我們住,或另外孩子跟你(分開住)也好。」
    (You can) stay with us, (or) it will be fine for you to live separately with your own son.

72. rakihan   ka maawis. ini ma-laləŋ.
    child   skillful   not AF-rest
    孩   很能幹   不   停止
    這孩子很能幹,閒不住。
    The boy was very skillful. He would not stay idle.

73. m-ukusa binayu ma-tilikat ka, m-ara ayam, (m-ara) luxut. m-ukusa
    AF-go   mountain AF-set traps Conj AF-take bird   AF-take deer   AF-go
    去   山上   設陷阱   捉   鳥   捉   鹿(肉) 去

    raxuŋ ka, m-ara alaw."
    river   Conj AF-take fish
    河   捉   魚
    去山上設陷阱就捕獲鳥和鹿,去河裡就捕到魚。」
    (If he) went to the mountain to set up traps, (he) caught birds (and) deer. (If he) went to the stream, he caught fish.

74. "ru-runu   a yaku."
    Red-separate   I
    分開   我
    生母說,「我分開住好了。」
    I'd rather live separately.

Text 7. kiusun rahuay 被老鷹抓走 *Seized by an Eagle*

Narrated by Pan Jin-yu (female, 84) on April 17, 1997
Recorded in Auran, Puli by Paul Li
潘金玉（女，84 歲）口述、解說 (1997.4.17)
李壬癸記錄
地點：埔里愛蘭

1. ta-dudu-aw   paasukuan   laita.
   Let's talk   story   us
   咱講   故事   咱們
   咱們來講故事。
   Let's talk about a story.

2. uhuu-huuza   ka   nahada   dusa   mamais   mamaləŋ.
   Red-before   Top   exist   two   lady   man
   從前   有   二   女   男
   很久以前有男女兩人。
   In the long past there were a man and a woman.

3. parisan   adaŋ   a   rakihan   mamaləŋ.
   was born   one   Lig   baby   boy
   生   一   孩   男
   他們生了一個男孩。
   They had a baby boy.

4. m<a>-usaʔ-ay di karid-an   mu-kukusa lia la[1].
   AF-go-Fut   Loc swidden field-Nmz AF-work   Asp
   要去   旱園   工作   了
   他們到田裡去工作。
   They were going to the swidden field to work.

5. mausay   paxuruma   dələm,   xaidaŋ,   tukun   la.
   will go   plant   corn   bean   taro
   要去   種   玉米   豆   芋
   他們去種玉米、豆、芋頭。
   They were going to plant corn, beans and taro.

---

[1]   The sentence-final particle *la* is a loan from Taiwanese *la*.

6. taxu   kari-karid-an   ka,   mi-kita   hada   adaŋ   a   ma-taru   a   kahuy.
    arrive   Red-field-Nmz   Conj   AF-see   exist   one   Lig   Sta-big   Lig   tree
    到   園   看   有   一   大   樹
    他們到田裡時看到有一棵大樹。
    When they arrived at the field, they found that there was a big tree.

7. ruburubu   ka   nahada   ma-taru   a   batu.
    below   exist   Sta-big   stone
    下面   有   大   石
    下面有大岩石。
    There was a large rock under it.

8. liaka   ina   isia   ka,   pa-kizih-ən   pa-idəm-ən   di   batu   babaw   lia   ki
    then   mother   that   Caus-low-PF   Caus-sleep-PF   rock   above   Asp
    然後   母   那   解下   使睡   岩石   上面   了

    rakihan.
    child
    孩
    然後母親解下嬰兒，讓他在岩石上睡覺。
    Then the mother released the baby and let him sleep on the rock.

9. duila   mu-kukusa   lai   yasia   dusa.
    go   AF-work   Asp   they   two
    去   工作   了   他們   二
    他們兩人就去工作了。
    Those two people then left for work.

10. kaidi   babaw   kahuy   dida   ka,   hada   ma-taru   a   rahuay   la.
    stay   above   tree   that   exist   Sta-big   eagle
    在   上   樹   那   有   大   老鷹
    在那棵樹上有一隻大老鷹。
    There was a big eagle on the tree.

11. rahuay   ka   mi-kita   kaidi   ruburubu   ka   hada   mari-kazay   a   asay   xaimisiw.
    eagle   AF-see   stay   below   exist   MARI-move   what   that
    老鷹   看   在   下   有   動   什麼   那
    老鷹看見下面有什麼在動。
    The eagle saw something moving under it.

12. mi-kita   liaka   asay   xaimini   ka-kan-ən.
    AF-see   then   what   this   Red-eat-PF
    看   然後   什麼   這個   可吃
    牠看到了以為是什麼可以吃的東西。
    When it saw that and thought that there was something to eat.

13. liaka   kius-ən   asu-n   di   maanu   lia.
    then   seize-PF bring-PF Loc   far   Asp
    然後   挾   帶   遠   了
    然後（嬰兒）就被挾走了，帶到很遠的地方去了。
    Then the baby was seized and carried far away.

14. mata   di   xanixanisay   a   binayu   lia   xanixanisay   a   raxuŋ.
    from   how many   mountain Asp   how many   river
    從   多少   山   了   多少   河
    一山翻過一山，一條河又過一條河。
    It flew over several mountains and rivers.

15. liaka   m-aŋit   lia   ki   rakihan   lia.
    then   AF-cry   Asp   baby   Asp
    然後   哭   了   孩   了
    然後小孩哭了。
    Then the baby cried.

16. maxi-a-ʔaŋi-ʔaŋit   lia   ki   rakihan,   ma-taru   a   siŋax   lia.
    bring forth-A-Red-cry   Asp   baby   Sta-big   sound   Asp
    哭得凶   了   孩   大   聲   了
    小孩一直哭得很凶，聲音很大。
    The baby kept crying very loudly.

17. hada   ababaw   raa-rapun.
    exist   God   Red-take care of
    有   上天   照顧
    有上天在照顧。
    God was taking care of him.

18. liaka   mi-kita   lia   ki   rahuay,   uzay   ka-kan-ən   xaimini.
    then   AF-see   Asp   eagle   not   Red-eat-PF this
    然後   看   了   老鷹   不是   食物   這
    然後老鷹看見這並不是食物。
    Then the eagle found that it was not something to eat.

19. haiki   saw   a   rakihan   xaimini.
     seem   human   baby   this
     似乎   人   孩   這
     這似乎是嬰兒。
     It looked like a human being.

20. mi-kita   ruburubu   a   saw   m<a>u-kukusa.
     AF-see   below   people   AF-Prg-work
     看   下   人   在工作
     牠看見下面有人在工作。
     (The eagle) saw someone working down below.

21. kaidi   dida   m<a>u-kukusa   a   saw   ka   kaidan   sən   ki   laŋat.
     stay   that   AF-Prg-work   person   personal name   is said   name
     在   那   工作   人   人名   據說   名
     在那裡工作的人據說名叫 Kaidan。
     The person working there is said to be named Kaidan.

22. rahuay   ka   m<a>a-kinakaw   mu-habahar.
     eagle   AF-Prg-slow   fly
     老鷹   慢   飛
     老鷹慢慢地飛。
     The eagle was flying slowly.

23. taxu   di   kaidan   a   karikarid-   a   ka,   p<in>axuruma   dadas   rabax
     arrive   at   personal name   field   Conj   Prf-plant   sweet potato   leaf
     到   人名   園   種   地瓜   葉

     babaw   adu-ən   dida   ki   rakihan.
     above   put-PF   there   baby
     上面   放   那裡   孩
     到了 Kaidan 的菜園，把小孩放在他所種的地瓜葉上。
     Upon arrival at Kaidan's field, it left the baby on the leaves of sweet potatoes.

24. liaka   ma-raxiw   lia   ki   rahuay.
     then   AF-escape   Asp   eagle
     然後   逃   了   老鷹
     然後老鷹就逃走了。
     Then the eagle escaped.

25. talawas   lia   ki   kaidan   kita   sən   ka   rahuay   raa-razaw.
    raise head Asp   name   look   is said   eagle   Red-pass
    抬頭   了   人名   看   據說   老鷹   在通過
    據說 Kaidan 抬頭看見老鷹正在飛過去。
    It is said that Kaidan raised his head and saw the eagle passing over him.

26. tumala   rakihan   a   m-aŋit.
    hear   baby   AF-cry
    聽   孩   哭
    他聽見小孩的哭聲。
    He heard a baby crying.

27. "nima   rakihan   pai   mini?"
    whose   baby   Q   this
    誰的   孩   疑問   這個
    「這是誰家的小孩？」
    "Whose baby is this?" (he thought).

28. kitaʔ-ən   ka   rakihan   kaidida.
    see-PF   baby   over there
    看   孩   在那裡
    他看見了那個小孩。
    He saw the baby over there.

29. liaka   kalapuʔ-ən   ni   kaidan   lia.
    then   hold-PF   personal name Asp
    然後   抱   人名   了
    然後 Kaidan 把他抱起來。
    Then Kaidan held the baby in his arms.

30. kita   sən   ka   rubaŋ   mamaləŋ,   kaxa-saisim-an   rabəx   a   rakihan.
    see   said   young   boy   KAXA-love-LF   baby   child
    看   據說   年輕   男   可愛   嬰   孩
    據說一看是個男孩，很可愛的嬰兒。
    It is said that he found that it was a baby boy, a very lovely one.

31. asu-ən   di   nisia   xumak   lia.
    bring-PF his home   Asp
    帶   他的 家   了
    他把他帶回家了。
    He brought it home.

32. liaka "sasay naki pai mini? kuah a saa-pa-kan?"
    then how I Q this none IF-Caus-eat
    然後 如何 我 這個 沒 餵食
    「我怎麼辦？沒有餵他的食物！」
    "What shall I do? I have nothing to feed him with!" he thought.

33. liaka mu-dəŋədəŋ r<iŋ>xaw lia.
    then AF-cook Prf-congee Asp
    然後 熬 稀飯 了
    然後他就熬稀飯。
    Then he cooked rice gruel.

34. m-ula ka mu-dius taatiŋ a lamtak paka-lamik-ən pa-kan-ən.
    AF-frist AF-scoop little rice liquid Caus-cool-PF Caus-eat-PF
    先 舀 一點點 飯湯 使涼 餵
    他先舀出一點點飯湯來，使它涼了再餵食。
    He scooped out a little rice liquid, and cooled it in order to feed the baby with it.

35. pa-kan-ən lamtak ka mə-kan ki rakihan isia.
    Caus-eat-PF laquid AF-eat baby that
    餵 飯湯 吃 孩 那
    餵他飯湯，那嬰兒也吃了。
    He fed the baby with it, and the baby ate it.

36. ma-rixaw lia ki r<iŋ>xaw, duray-ən paka-ma-rixaw-ən, rimad-ən pahar.
    Sta-soft Asp Prf-congee grind-PF Caus-Sta-soft-PF mix-PF salt
    爛 了 稀飯 揉 使爛 摻 鹽
    他把稀飯揉爛了再加鹽巴
    He massed the rice gruel, softened it, and mixed it with a little salt.

37. pa-kan-ən mə-kan ki rakihan a isia.
    Caus-eat-PF AF-eat baby that
    餵 吃 孩 那
    餵他，那個小孩也吃了。
    He fed the baby with it, and the baby ate it.

38. nahada ababaw raa-rapun.
    exist above Red-take care
    有 上天 在照顧
    有上天在照顧。
    God was taking care of him.

39. adaŋ a dali, dusa a dali, puzah a adaŋ a apu.
one day two day come one old woman
一 天 二 天 來 一 老太婆
第二天來了一個老太婆。
On the second day, an old woman came along.

40. "kaidan, haiki nahada rakihan m-aŋit kaidi nisiw-an dini."
name seem exist baby AF-cry at your-place-Nmz here
人名 似乎 有 孩 哭 在 你住處 這兒
「Kaidan，你這裡似乎有小孩在哭。」
"Kaidan, there seems to be a baby crying here in your house."

41. kaidan ka, "d<in>əkən di naki a p<in>axuruma dadas a rabax.
name Prf-pick up I Prf-plant sweet potato leaf
人名 揀 我 已種的 地瓜 葉

    haiki k<in>ius rahuay adu sən di naki p<in>axuruma dadas rabax
    seem Prf-snatch eagle put is said I Prf-plant sweet potato leaf
    似乎 挾 老鷹 放 據說 我 種 地瓜 葉

    a babaw. kalapu asu-ən di naki a xumak. tata, sasay-ən pai yaku
    above hold bring-PF my home aunt how-PF Q I
    上 抱 帶 我的 家 姨 如何 我

    m-iba rakihan imini rəəzaw aku, ini mausay mu-kukusa? riax-i ka
    AF-hold baby this only I not will go AF-work find-Imp
    抱 孩 這 只 我 不 要去 工作 找

    naki aunu ta-u-xumak saa-rapun rakihan imini."
    I make Agt-house IF-take care child this
    我 做 妻 照顧 孩 這
Kaidan 說，「在我所種的地瓜葉子上揀到的，他似乎被老鷹挾來丟在我所種的地瓜葉子上。我就把他抱回家了。阿婆，我只抱著這嬰孩而不工作怎麼辦呢？替我找個老婆照顧這個小孩吧！」
Kaidan said, "I picked it up on the leaves of sweet potatoes. It seemed to have been seized and left on the leaves of sweet potatoes by an eagle. I brought it home. What shall I do if I have to hold this baby and cannot work? Please find me a wife to take care of this baby."

42. apu a isia ka, "haw lia. ədər, ini m-ara siw ka sasay-ən laula?"
old woman that good Asp true not AF-take you how-PF
婆 那 好 了 真 不 娶 你 如何 是好
老太婆說，「好吧！說真的，你不娶的話，如何是好？」
The old woman said, "Alright. It's true. What else could you do without marrying someone?"

43. liaka m-ukusa di namisiw a xumag- a taubarət, mu-riax adaŋ a rubaŋ
    then   AF-go   her   home   neighbor   AF-find one   young
    然後   去   她的   家   鄰居   找   一   年輕

    a mamais kalayu   sən   ki laŋat.
        lady   female name said   name
        女   女人名   據說   名
    然後她就到她家的鄰居找到一個姑娘，據說名叫 Kalayu。
    Then she went to her neighbors and found a young lady named Kalayu.

44. "tia, tia ta-kitaʔ-i kaxa-saisim-an adaŋ a saw   rəəzaw mə-dəkən adaŋ
    go go   let's look KAXA-love-LF one   person only   AF-pick up one
    去 去   咱看   可愛   一   人   只   揀   一

    a rakihan. tia mi-kita," lia ki apu   a isia.
        baby   go   AF-see   Asp   old woman   that
        孩   去   看   了   婆   那
    「去！去！咱們去看一個人揀到一個可愛的嬰兒。去看！」那個老太婆說。
    "Go! Let's go and look at a cute baby picked up only by someone. Go and look at it!" the old woman said.

45. liaka   mu-kusa mi-kita.
    then   AF-go   AF-see
    然後   去   看
    然後她們去看。
    Then they went there to look at it.

46. haw laila lia ki kalayu   isia.
    good thus   Asp   name   that
    好   那樣 了   女人名   那
    Kalayu 也很喜歡。
    Kalayu was also fond of the baby.

47. xasəbuza dali ka araʔ-ən lia. araʔ-ən di xumak lia.
    six   day   take -PF Asp take-PF   home   Asp
    六   天   娶   了   娶   家   了
    六天後他娶了她，娶到他家。
    Six days later, he married her. She moved to his home.

48. kalayu   iu   kaidan   ka,   "ta-ku-laŋad-aw   nita."
    name   and   name   let's-KU-name-Ir   we
    女名   和   人名   咱們取名   咱
    Kalayu 和 Kaidan 商量，「咱們給他取名吧！」
    Kalayu said to Kaidan, "Let's name him!"

49. "haw.   kulaŋad-ən   'tun'   tasiaw."
    good   name-PF   pine   maybe
    好   取名   松   可能
    好吧，就取名叫 Tun 吧！
    "Fine! Name him 'Tun'."

50. tun   ka   riak   a   kahuy   tubabaw,   matər   ka   a-tun   sən.
    pine   Good tree   tall   hard   pine said
    松   好   樹   高   硬   松   據說
    據說 tun（松）是好的樹，高大而又硬。
    It is said the term 'tun' refers to a good plant (pine tree), tall and hard.

51. dusa   mamais   mamaləŋ   saisim-an   atun.
    two   female   male   love-LF   name
    二   女   男   疼   人名
    夫妻兩人都疼 Atun。
    The couple loved Atun.

52. adaŋ   a   dali,   adaŋ   a   ilas,   adaŋ   a   kawas.   taxu   pasakən-ay   adaŋ   a
    one   day   one   month   one   year   till   arrive-Fut   one
    一   天   一   月   一   年   到   將到達   一

    kawas   ka,   ituku?-ən   saw   lia   ki   kalayu.
    year   pregnant-PF person Asp   female name
    年   懷孕   人   了   女人名
    一天過一天，一個月過一個月，一年過一年。快到一年時，Kalayu 懷孕了
    Day after day, month after month, year after year, in less than a year, Kalayu became pregnant.

53. mayaw   taxu   isida   ilas   ka,   parisan   lia   ki   kalayu,   parisan   adaŋ   a
    not yet   till   ten   month   was born   Asp   name   was born   one
    還沒   到   十   月   生   了   女名   生   一

    rubaŋ   mamaləŋ.
    young   boy
    幼小   男
    不到十個月，Kalayu 生了一個男嬰。
    Kalayu had a baby boy in less than ten months.

54. dusa rakihan mamaləŋ pialay ka riak.
　　two　child　　boy　　begin　　good
　　二　孩　　男　　　開始　　　好
　　兩個男孩開始時很好。
　　In the beginning it was nice to have both boys.

55. dusa mamais mamaləŋ, saisim-an dusa rakihan.
　　two　female　male　　love-LF　two　child
　　二　女　　男　　　疼　　　二　孩
　　男女兩人都疼兩個孩子。
　　The couple loved both children.

56. ma-taru lia ka ini aisiiyay lia ki ina.
　　Sta-big　Asp　　not　same　Asp　mother
　　大　　了　　不　相同　了　母
　　長大了母親就不同了。
　　As they grew up, the mother behaved differently.

57. ini xadu saisim-an atun, saisim-an p<in>arisan talima.
　　not much love-LF　name　love-LF　Prf-born　own
　　不 怎麼 疼　　人名 疼　　　生　　　自己
　　她不怎麼疼愛阿敦，只疼自己生的。
　　She did not love Atun, but loved her own child.

58. talima p<in>arisan a rakihan mə-kən risilaw a sumay, riak a
　　own　Prf-born　child　AF-eat　white　rice　good
　　自己　生　　　孩　吃　　白　　飯　　好

　　saa-kən: rumut, alaw, iu atun ka pa-kan-ən durun, rimad-ən taatih a
　　side dish　meat　fish　but　name　Caus-eat-PF　bran　mix-PF　a little
　　菜　　肉　魚　而　人名　使吃　　　糠　　摻　　一點

　　sumay, ŋ<in>api tuasəm a saa-kən.
　　rice　Prf-leftover　spoiled　side dish
　　飯　剩　　　酸臭　　菜
　　自己生的孩子吃白飯，好的菜：肉、魚，而阿敦只給他吃米糠加一點點飯，剩下
　　的酸臭的菜。
　　Her own child was fed with white rice and good food: meat and fish, yet Atun was fed with bran mixed with a little rice, leftover or spoiled food.

59. hada aba babaw raa-rapun.
exist father above Red-take care
有 父 上 在照顧
有上天在照顧。
God was taking care of him.

60. mə-kən ma-luhusu ki atun, bagət tubabaw.
AF-eat Sta-in that way name strong tall
吃 那樣 人名 強健 高
雖然阿敦吃的那些，卻長的強健又高大。
Despite what Atun ate, he was strong and tall.

61. p<in>arisan talima rakihan mə-kən riak, ma-kuris itəkn.
Prf-born own child AF-eat good Sta-thin short
生 自己 孩 吃 好 瘦 矮
自己生的孩子吃的好，卻又瘦又矮。
(Kalayu's) own child ate good food, yet he was thin and short.

62. liaka puzah lia ki taubarət, tata iu apu.
then come Asp neighbor aunt and old woman
然後 來 了 鄰居 姨 和 婆
然後鄰居的阿姨和老太婆來了。
Then the neighbors and the old woman came.

63. mu-kusa di m<a>a-hadas, mi-kita yamisiw k<a>a-kən ruŋun-un.
AF-go AF-Prg-have fun AF-see they Red-Prg-eat differently-PF
去 遊玩 看 他們 在吃 不同
她們去玩，看到他們吃的不同。
When they visited them, they found that (the kids) eating differently.

64. maa-kuas lia ki yasia.
Rec-talk Asp they
交談 了 她們
他們議論紛紛。
They talked about it.

65. adaŋ a dali liaka maa-kuas kani atun, "uzay p<in>arisan isiw a ina.
one day then Rec-talk Obl name not Prf-born you mother
一 天 然後 講 人名 不 生 你 母

d<in>əkən namisiw haisiw. aidu haka namisiw p<in>arisan a rakihan.
Prf-pick up their you name true their Prf-born child
揀 他們的 你 人名 才是真的 他們的 生 孩

yami mi-kita isiw ma-laləŋ dini ka haziah siw lahamin."
we AF-see you AF-live here not good you we
我們 看 你 住 此地 不好 你 我們

然後有一天她們對阿敦說，「你不是你母親生的，你是他們揀來的。Aidu 才是他
們親生的孩子。我們看你住在此地，我們認為對你不好。」

On a certain day, then they said to Atun, "She is not your own mother. You were picked up by them. Aidu is their own child. So far as we can tell, it is not good for you to keep staying here."

66. tumala ma-luhusu ma-kuas atun ka adu-ən di hinis apu a
listen Sta-in that way AF-talk name put-PF mind old woman
聽 那樣 講 人名 放 心 阿婆

k<in>awas a rahan.
Prf-say word
說 話

聽到她們那樣講，阿敦把老太婆的話放在心裡。

Atun listened to what the old woman had said and kept it in his mind.

67. taxaw ma-taru isit xasəbisupat kawas.
until Sta-big ten nine year
到 大 十 九 年

一直到他長大十九歲時。

Until he was nineteen.

68. adaŋ a dali, kuah di xumak ki ina. liaka ma-kuas di abaʔ-an, "aba,
one day none home mother then AF-talk father-Loc father
一 天 沒 家 母 然後 講 父 爸

mausay di mu-zakay talima daran." lia atun.
will go AF-walk own road Asp personal name
要去 走 自己 路 了 人名

有一天，趁母親不在家，他對父親說，「爸爸，我要去走自己的路。」阿敦說。

On a certain day, when his mother was not home, he said to his father, "Daddy, I would like to lead my own life," Atun said.

69. aba ka, "mausay di asay pai siw?"
tather will go where Q you
父 要去 何處 Q 你

父親問，「你要到哪裡去？」

Father asked, "Where would you like to go?"

70. "mausay taxu di asay a daxə ka, naki a laŋat. ini ma-rukat
    will go till   where land Conj   my   destiny not AF-go out
    要去 到   何處 地   我的   命運 不 出去

    talimaʔ a daran."
    own   Lig road
    自己   路

    「走到什麼地方都是我的命。不出去闖自己的路（也不行）。」
    "I shall go where my fate leads me to. (If) I don't work my way out, (it won't be good for me.)"

71. aba ka, taxi-bubuk a punu.
    father Top TAXI-lower   head
    父   低下   頭
    父親低下頭。
    The father lowered his head.

72. "haw," laila ki aba, "isiw ka uzay niam a p<in>arisan siw.
    good in that way fahter you Top not we   Prf-born   you
    好 那樣 父 你   不是 我們 生   你

    d<in>əkən niam di kari-karid-an rabəx a saw siw. kita sən
    Prf-pick up we Red-swidden field-Nmz baby person you look said
    揀 我們 旱田 嬰 人 你 看 據說

    naki ka, k<in>ius rahuay aduʔ-un di p<in>axuruma dadas dida
    I   Prf-snatch baby put-PF   Prf-plant sweet potato there
    我 挾 嬰 放 種 地瓜 那邊

    haw, usa riax-i p<in>arisan isiw a ina aba. aubin a dali ka,
    good go find-Imp Prf-born you   mother father later   day
    好 去 找 生 你 母 父 後來 日

    rii-riak-ay siw. hada aba babaw raa-rapun-ay isiw. aubin a dali
    Red-good-Fut you exist Dad above Red-take care-Fut you later day
    好 你 有 父 上面 將照顧 你 後來 日

    maxu-ria-riak siw ka, alu kitaʔ-i yamin." lai ki kaidan a isia.
    MAXU-Red-good you Conj come see-Imp we Asp name that
    好 你 來 看 我們 了 人名 那

    「好吧！」父親說，「你確實不是我們生的。你是我們在旱田裡揀回來的嬰兒。
    我看是老鷹挾來放在（我所）種的蕃薯那邊。好，去找你的生父母，將來你會過
    好日子。有上天照顧你。將來你過好日子，就來看我們。」
    "Alright," the father said. "You are not our own child. We picked you up in the field when you were a
    baby. I believe you were seized by an eagle and left in my sweet potato field. All right, go and find
    your own parents. You'll lead a good life. May God bless you. When you come by a good fortune,

come to see us," Kaidan said.

73. atun   ka   maxi-a-rəsə-rəsə.
    name   MAXI-Red-tears
    人名   流淚
    阿敦流淚。
    Atun shed tears.

74. aba   ka   mu-kusa   m-ara   a-uku-kusaʔ-ən   a   balax   tatak,   tadaw,   sauki,
    father   AF-go   AF-take A-Red-work-PF   tool   hoe   knife   scythe
    父   去   拿   工作   工具   鋤   刀   鐮刀

    yasam   iu   m-ara   tatiŋ   a   paray.
    axe   and   AF-take a little   money
    斧   和   拿   一點   錢
    父親去拿工作用具：鋤頭、鐮刀、斧頭，又拿了一點錢（給阿敦）。
    Father got some tools: a hoe, a knife, a scythe, an axe, and a little money and gave them to Atun.

75. "asu-i   ki   nisiw   a   sabusaw,   siatu."
    bring-lmp   your   coverlet   clothes
    帶   你的   被子   衣
    「帶你的被子和衣服。」
    "Take your coverlet and clothes."

76. "haw,"   laila   ki   atun.
    fine   in that way   name
    好   那樣   人名
    阿敦說，「好。」
    Atun said, "Yes."

77. dusa   aba   iu   rakihan   maa-ʔaŋi-ʔaŋit.
    two   father and   child   Rec-Red-cry
    二   父   和   子   哭
    父子兩人哭了。
    Both the father and the son cried.

78. atun   mu-xalit   aba   a   rima   pikadun   duila   lia.
    name   AF-lead   father   hand   set out   go   Asp
    人名   牽   父   手   出發   去   了
    阿敦拉著父親的手，就出發走了。
    Atun held his father's hand and set out.

79. aba   ka,   mi-kita   rakihan   zaa-zakay   m-aŋit   lia.
    father   AF-see   child   Red-leave   AF-cry   Asp
    父   看   子   正在離開   哭   了
    父親看著兒子走了，就哭了。
    The father saw the son leaving and cried.

80. adaŋ a   dali,   taxu   supad- a   dali,   mi-kita   adaŋ a   subut.
    One   day   till   four   day   AF-see   one   spring
    一   天   到   四   天   看   一   泉
    一天過一天，到第四天他看到泉水。
    Day after day, on the fourth day, he saw a spring.

81. "a,   riak   a   dalum   haimini,   tuxubəs   a   dalum.   imini   haka   riak."
    good   water   this   sweet   water   this   really   good
    好   水   這   甜   水   這   真的   好
    「啊！這裡的水好，水甜。這裡好。」
    "Yea, this is good water. It tastes good. This is really good."

82. mata di daya kita sən   ka   ma-taru a   subut.
    from   above look said   Sta-big   spring
    從   上方   看   據說   大   泉
    到上面（高處）他看到很大的水泉。
    He went up and saw a large spring there.

83. kita sən   ka   taparax a   kari-karit.
    look said   broad   Red-swidden field
    看   據說   寬闊   旱田
    據說（他）看到寬闊的旱田。
    It is said that he saw a broad swidden field.

84. nahada tubabaw a saa-patu-xumak ka   riak.
    exist   high   IF-build-house   good
    有   高   蓋房   好
    有較高的地方可以蓋房子。
    There was a higher place to build a house.

85. ta-patu-xumaʔ-ay   dini lia ku.
    Let's-build-house-Fut   here   Asp   I
    咱們蓋房   此地   了   我
    我就在這裡蓋房子吧。
    "Let's build a house here," (he said to himself).

86. m-ara   nisia   tadaw   mu-kusa   mu-tamak   kahuy,   mu-tamak   rahas   anu   paliŋ.
    AF-take   he   knife   AF-go   AF-cut   wood   AF-cut   for   wall
    拿   他   刀   去   砍   柴   砍   茅草   做   牆
    他拿刀去砍木柴，砍菅蓁（茅草）做牆壁。
    He cut trees with his knife and cut miscanthus for walls.

87. mu-tamak   dahu   lia,   səəsəkət.
    AF-cut   many   Asp   rest
    砍   多   了   休
    砍了很多了，他在休息。
    After he cut a lot, he was taking a rest.

88. liaka   puzah   adaŋ   a   rubaŋ   mamais,   nahani   m-iliw   dalum.
    then   come   one   young   lady   come   AF-carry water
    然後   來   一   年輕   女   來   挑   水
    然後一個姑娘來挑水。
    A girl came to fetch water.

89. mi-kita   liaka   haiki   p<a>atu-xumaʔ-ay.   mi-kita   rəəzaw.
    AF-see   then   seem   Prg-build-house-Fut look   only
    看   然後   似乎   要蓋房   看   只
    她看見他似乎要蓋房子。她只看了一下。
    She found that he was going to build a house. She simply took a look at it.

90. mu-kusa   talima   xumak   ma-kuas   nisia   ina.
    AF-go   own   home   AF-tell   her   mother
    去   自己   家   告訴   她的   母
    她回家告訴她母親。
    She went home and told her mother.

91. mu-kusa   mi-kita   lia   ki   ina   ka,   "rubaŋ   mamaləŋ,   sasay   pai   siw ?"
    AF-go   AF-see   Asp   mother   Conj young   man   what   Q   you
    去   看   了   母   年輕 男   什麼   Q   你
    她母親去看了，問他「年輕人，你在做什麼？」
    Her mother went to look at it herself, and said to him, "Young man, what are you doing?"

92. "p<a>atu-xumaʔ-ay   dini   aku."
    Prg-build-house-Fut here   I
    要蓋房   這裡   我
    「我要在這裡蓋房子。」
    "I shall build a house here."

93. "p<a>uzah di asay pai siw?"
    Prg-come   where Q   you
    來   何處   Q   你
    「你從哪裡來的？」
    "Where do you come from?"

94. atun ka,   "sasay-ən ma-kuas pai yaku?" "mata di maanu,   mu-zakay
    name   how-PF   AF-say   Q   I   from   far   AF-walk
    人名   如何   說   我   從   遠   走

    supad- a dali, haka taxu dini. mi-kita riag- a kari-karit   lahaku."
    four   day   true till here AF-see   good   Red-swidden field I
    四   天   真的 到   這裡 看   好   旱田   我
    阿敦（心裡想），「我要怎麼說呢？」他說，「從很遠的地方走了四天才到此地，
    我看到好的田園。」
    Atun thought, "What shall I say?" (Then he said), "I came from far away. It took me four days to get here. I found a good field here."

95. tata isia ka,   "riak. dini a daxə ka   bagət. paxuruma yadisaysay ka
    aunt that   good here land   fertile plant   what   Conj
    姨   那   好   此   地   肥沃   種   什麼

    riak."
    good
    好
    婦人說，「好！這裡的地很肥沃，種什麼都長的好。」
    The woman said, "Good, the land is fertile here. Whatever you plant, it grows well."

96. mi-kita atun a riag- a gagam.
    AF-see   name good   stature
    看   人名 好   身材
    她看見阿敦一表人才。
    She found Atun had a good stature.

97. liaka pa-dudu, "xaima   a saw   pai siw ?"
    then   PA-ask   how many   people Q   you
    然後   問   多少   人   Q   你
    然後她問道，「你幾個人？」
    Then she asked him, "How many people do you have?"

76

98. atun ka, "yaku talima rəəzaw."
   name I own only
   人名 主題 我 自己 只
   阿敦說，「我只有自己一個人。」
   Atun said, "Only myself."

99. tata isia ka, mi-kita atun a m<a>u-kukusa liaka mu-kusa talima xumak.
   aunt that AF-see name AF-Prg-work then AF-go own home
   姨 那 看 人名 工作 然後 去 自己 家
   那婦人看了阿敦工作之後就回家了。
   The woman saw Atun working and then went home.

100. ma-kuas ka nisia mamaləŋ mu-ʔasay mu-ʔasay riak haki ruban
    AF-tell her man AF-what AF-what good maybe young
    告訴 她的 男 什麼 什麼 好 可能 年輕

    mamaləŋ a isia.
    man that
    男 那
    她告訴她丈夫如此這般，那個青年如何如何似乎不錯。
    She told her husband so and so and that the young man seemed to be a good guy.

101. nisia rubaŋ mamais a laŋat ka sabuŋ sən.
    her young girl name Top name is said
    她的 年輕 女 名 女名 據說
    據說她的姑娘名叫 Sabuŋ。
    It is said that her girl's name was Sabung.

102. tumala nisia ina, aba maa-kuas,
    hear her father mother Rec-talk
    聽 她 父 母 交談
    她聽見父母交談。
    She heard of her parents discussing.

103. rubaŋ mamais a isia ka, adaŋ a dali, adaŋ a dali mu-bazu siatu,
    young girl that one day one day AF-wash clothes
    年輕 女 那 一 天 一 天 洗 衣

    m-iliw dalum di subudan dida.
    AF-carry water spring there
    挑 水 泉 那邊
    那姑娘每天在水泉那裡洗衣、挑水。
    The girl went to do laundry and fetch water from the spring.

104. sabuŋ a ina,   mu-kiliw adaŋ a apu,   "usa di nita subud- a
name   mother AF-call one   old woman go   we   spring
女名   母   叫   一   婆   去   咱   泉

k<in>ixid-an. hada adaŋ a mamaləŋ a isia. pa-kuas-i ta-baxaʔ-aw
Prf-nearby-Loc exist one   man   that tell-Imp   let's-give-Ir
旁   有   一   男   那 告訴   咱將給

anu nisia. haiki riak a mamaləŋ. pa-kuas-i na,"   laila   ki sabuŋ
for he   seem   good man   PA-tell-Imp please in that way name
為了 他   似乎   好 男   講   請   那樣   女名

a ina.
mother
母

Sabuŋ 的母親叫一個老太婆，「到咱們水泉的旁邊去，那裡有一個年輕人。告訴
他咱們有意（把女兒嫁）給他。他似乎是好青年。請對他講。」
Sabuŋ's mother called on an old woman and said to her, "Go to the place near the spring. There is
a young man there. Tell him that we would like to marry our daughter to him. He looks like a good
young man. Please talk to him."

105. "haw,"   laila   ki apu   a isia. mu-kusa di atun-an.
good   in that way   old woman that   AF-go   name-Loc
好   那樣   婆   那   去   男名
老太婆說，「好。」就到阿敦處。
The old woman said, "Yes," and went to Atun.

106. "haw." laila   ki atun a isia.
fine   in that way name   that
好   那樣   男名   那
那阿敦說，「好。」
Atun agreed (to the marriage.)

107. haw laila   liaka m-ara   lia.
fine in that way then   AF-take Asp
好   那樣   然後   娶   了
他們說好了就娶她了。
When all agreed, he married her.

108. dusa mamais mamaləŋ ma-hapət mu-kukusa di namisiw a kari-karit.
two   lady   man   Sta-diligent AF-work   their   swidden field
二   女   男   勤奮   工作   他們的   旱田
男女兩人在他們的旱田認真的工作。
Both the boy and girl worked hard on the swidden field.

109. paxuruma binayu   a mulasi,   paxuruma piaxun, dadas,   tawtaw,
     plant   mountain   rice plant plant   millet   sweet potato peanut
     種   山   稻   種   小米   地瓜   花生

     xalam,   yaadisaysay.
     vegetable various things
     蔬菜   各種

     在山上種稻、種小米、地瓜、花生、蔬菜等等。
     They planted rice, millet, sweet potatoes, peanuts, vegetables, etc.

110. imini ka atun a aba   p<in>akuas a rahan, "atun, aubin a dali
     this   name father Prf-talk   word   later day
     這   男名 父   講   話   人名   後來   天

     ka, rii-riak-ay siw. maxu-ria-riak-ay siw. m-ara   riak a mamais siw
          Red-good-Fut you   MAXU-Red-good-Fut you   AF-take   good   lady   you
     將會好   你   幸福   你   娶   好   女   你

     ka, rii-riak-ay,   riag- a karum-xumak."
          Red-good-Fut   good   family
     將會好   好   家庭

     這就是阿敦的父親說的話,「阿敦,日後你會好,你會幸福。你娶個好妻子,就
     會好,有好家庭。」
     This is what Atun's father had said to him, "Atun, you will lead a good life. You will have good luck.
     When you get a good wife, you will be fine with a good family."

111. taxaw   uhuni ka haiki nisia aba   p<in>akuas a rahan.
     untill now   seem   his   father Prf-talk   word
     到   現在   似乎   他的   父   講   話

     到現在似乎他父親所祝福的話都應驗了。
     Up to now all his father's words materialized then.

112. dusa ka maa-zəbəzəp mamais mamaləŋ.
     two   Rec-chest   woman   man
     二   合作   女   男

     男女兩人合作無間。
     The man and woman cooperated with each other.

113. parisan   rubaŋ mamaləŋ, rubaŋ mamais, maxu-ria-riak.
     was born   one   boy   one   girl   MAXU-Red-good
     生   一   男   一   女   健康

     他們生了一男一女,都很健康。
     They had a son and a daughter, both strong and healthy.

114. dadua lia.   taxaw dini ki naki a k<in>awas.
     all   Asp   up to here my   Prf-word
     全部   了   到   此   我的   話
     全部說完了。我的話到此為止。
     That is all. My story ends here.

Text 8. pinatula 捕鰻 *Catching an Eel*

Narrated by Pan Jin-yu (female, 86) on Jan.7, 1999
Recorded in Auran, Puli by Paul Li
潘金玉口述講解 (1999.1.7)，按此為五十年前事實的陳述
李壬癸記錄
地點：埔里愛蘭

1. ta-duduʔ-aw uhuza naki a baba mausay pa-tilikat di adaŋ a
   let's-talk-Fut before my Lig uncle will go set-a trap Loc one Lig
   咱講 從前 我的 舅 要去 放陷阱 一

   ma-taaru a luduk.
   Sta-big pond
   大 潭

   咱們要講從前我舅舅要到潭邊放陷阱。
   We shall talk about my uncle, who was going to set a trap by a big pond, in the past.

2. ludug- a k<in>ixid-an dahu a sabun, hayahay, xasi, rabəx
   pond Prf-nearby-Loc a lot grass stalks of miscanthus miscanthus tender
   潭 旁 多 草 茅莖 細茅草 嫩

   a hayahay.
   stalks of miscanthus
   茅莖

   在潭邊有青草、粗茅莖、細茅草、嫩茅草。
   Nearby the pond, there was a lot of grass, (two types of) miscanthus, and new growth of miscanthus.

3. naki a baba isia ka, mausay pa-tilikat, mu-razaw mata dida.
   my uncle that Top will go set-a trap AF-pass by from there
   我的 舅 那 要去 放陷阱 經過 從 那兒

   我舅舅要去放陷阱，打從那裡經過。
   My uncle was going to set traps, passing by that area.

4. mi-kita sabun isia ki naki a baba, kita sən ka haiki r<in>iux
   AF-see grass that Nom my uncle look said Conj seem Prf-slide over
   看 草 那 我的 舅 看 據說 好像 爬過

   əzəd- a daran.
   snake Lig road
   蛇 路

   我舅舅看到那些青草好像蛇爬過的路。
   My uncle found that the grass seemed to have been slid over by a snake.

5. naki a baba mi-kita sabun a imini haiki k<in>an əzət ka, ini
   my uncle AF-see grass here seem Prf-eat snake Conj not
   我的 舅 看 草 這兒 好像 吃過 蛇 不

   mə-kən sabun ki əzət.
   AF-eat grass snake
   吃 草 蛇

   我舅舅看到這些青草好像蛇吃過的，可是蛇卻不吃草。
   My uncle found that the grass seemed to have been nipped by a snake, yet a snake did not eat grass.

6. kita sən r<in>iux a daran ka xamaxam-ən ka kuiŋəx ki daran.
   lood is said Prf-slide over road touch-PF sticky road
   看 據說 爬 路 摸 粘粘 路

   他看爬行過的路，用手一摸是粘粘的。
   He looked at the path that had been slid over, and it was sticky when he touched it.

7. "kuiŋəx asay pai mini ha?"[1] maxa-kə-kəla ma-səzəm.
   sticky what Q this MAXA-Red-think Sta-long
   粘 什麼 Q 這 想 久

   「這個粘粘的是什麼？」他想了很久。
   "What is this sticky stuff?" he considered it for a long time.

8. haiki uzay əzət a daran. haiki r<in>iux tula a daran lia.
   seem not snake road seem Prf-slide over eel road Asp
   好像 不是 蛇 路 好像 滑行 鰻 路 了

   好像不是蛇的路，好像是鰻爬過的。
   It did not seem to be a path of the snake, but rather slid over by an eel.

9. riŋis-ən mi-kita taxaw rudug a k<in>ixid-an liaka kuah lia ki daran.
   check-PF AF-see pond Prf-nearby-Loc then none Asp road
   查看 看 到 潭 旁 然後 沒 了 路

   他尋查看一直到潭邊就沒有路了。
   He checked it up to the side of the pond and then he lost the track of the path.

---

[1] The form *ha* indicates a surprise or a question in mind. It may be a loan from Taiwanese *hã*, which indicates a surprise or question.

10. naki   a baba ka,   "uzay   əzət mini, tula haimini mə-kən   sabun, mə-kən
    my   uncle   not   snake this   eel this   AF-eat   grass   AF-eat
    我的   舅   不   蛇   這   鰻   這   吃   草   吃

    hayahay,"   lia ki naki a baba isia maxa-kə-kəla.
    stalks of miscanthus Asp Nom my   uncle that MAXA-Red-think
    茅莖   我的   舅   那   想

    我舅舅心裡想，「這不是蛇，這是鰻魚，才會吃青草和茅草。」
    My uncle thought, "This is not a snake, but rather an eel that will nip grass and miscanthus."

11. liaka   mu-pukupuk tamaku lia ki naki a baba isia.
    then   AF-smoke   tobacco Asp   my   uncle that
    然後   抽   菸   了   我的   舅   那

    然後我的舅舅就抽菸了。
    Then my uncle smoked.

12. "uzay   əzət," maxa-kə-kəla   mu-kusa di xumak lia.
    not   snake   MAXA-Red-think   AF-go   Loc home   Asp
    不是   蛇   想   去   家   了

    他想，「那不是蛇。」就回家了。
    "It was not a snake," he thought and returned home.

13. mu-riax   halipid- a kaxa xanixanisay, zupay-ən   kamalaŋ xanixanisay haiki
    AF-find   thin   iron   several   sharpen-PF sharp   several   seem
    找   薄   鐵   幾個   磨   利   幾個   好像

    tadaw.
    knife
    刀

    他找了幾根薄鐵把它們磨利了，像刀一樣地利。
    He looked for several thin pieces of iron and sharpened them until they became as sharp as knives.

14. du-dusaʔ a dali a ka mu-kusa inaŋ sibad-ən   di r<in>iux   a
    Red-second day   Top   AF-go   again put into order-PF   Prf-slide over
    第二   天   去   再   排好   滑行

    daran a isia.
    road   that
    路   那

    第二天他再去把它們（薄鐵）排好在（鰻魚）滑行的路上。
    On the second day, he went there again to lay them on the path that had been slid over.

15. sibad-ən   xanixanisay haiki tadaw a isia lia.
    put in order-PF several   like knife   that Asp
    排放   幾個   像   刀   那
    他排放了幾根像刀一樣（的鋒利的鐵片）。
    He laid several pieces (of thin iron) as sharp as knives.

16. sibad-ən   sarawan ka nahaniʔ-ay.
    put in order-PF tomorrow   come-Fut
    排放   明天   要來
    排好了明天要再來。
    Having laid them, he would return the next day.

17. mausay mu-sibat   isia ka m-asu   abu lia.
    will go AF-put in order then   AF-bring   ash Asp
    要去   排   那時   帶   灰   了
    他要去排放（薄鐵片）時帶了灰。
    When he was going to lay them, he brought ashes with him.

18. taxu hayahay   a dida ka di daran habuʔ-ən   abu la.
    till stalks of miscanthus   there   road sprinkle-PF ash
    到   茅莖   那裡   路   撒   灰
    他把灰撒在要到茅草那裡的路上了。
    He sprinkled ashes on the path leading to the miscanthus.

19. abu ka ma-tupaŋ   taxaw dida ka ini mu-riux   lia.
    ash   Sta-unsmooth   there   not AF-slide over Asp
    灰   澀   到   那兒   不   滑行   了
    灰使到那裡的（路）澀澀的，就不能滑行了。
    The ashes were unsmooth and they were hard to slide on.

20. taxu-riupuŋ   dida lia.
    TAXU-roll over there Asp
    翻滾   那兒 了
    牠在那裡翻滾了。
    (The eel) rolled over it.

21. kita sən ka ma-taru   a tula ka dida lia.
    look said   Sta-big   eel   there
    看   據說   大   鰻   那裡
    他看好大的鰻魚在那裡。
    He found a big eel there.

22. mu-riux   ka   kəxəd-ən   tadaw   lia   ki   nisia   tian.
    AF-slide over   cut-PF   knife   Asp   Nom   its   belly
    滑行   割   刀   了   主   牠的   腹
    牠滑行時腹部被刀子（磨利的薄鐵片）割傷了。
    As it was sliding (over the path), its belly was cut by the sharp knives.

23. mata   di   abu   ka   ini   mu-riux   lia.
    from   ash   not   AF-slide over   Asp
    從   灰   不   滑行   了
    有灰的地方牠無法滑行了。
    It could not slide where there were ashes.

24. taxu-riu-riupuŋ   dida   lia.
    TAXU-Red-roll over   there   Asp
      翻滾   那裡   了
    牠一直在那裡翻滾了。
    It kept rolling over there.

25. mi-kita   ki   naki   a   baba   isia   ka   tula   haimini,   ma-taaru[2]   a   tula   kaidini.
    AF-see   my   uncle   that   Conj   eel   this   Sta-very big   eel   here
    看   我的   舅   那個   鰻   這   很大   鰻   在這兒
    我那個舅父看見這就是鰻魚，好大的鰻魚在這裡。
    My uncle found that it was an eel, a very big eel.

26. ma-hatan   lia   ki   naki   a   baba   isia.
    AF-laugh   Asp   my   uncle   that
    笑   了   我的   舅   那
    我舅舅笑了。
    My uncle laughed.

27. nahaza   saa-rubus.   liaka   rubus-ən   lia.
    exist   IF-bag   then   put into a bag-PF   Asp
    有   麻袋   然後   裝袋   了
    他有麻袋。然後他把牠裝在麻袋裡。
    He had a bag, and then he put it into the bag.

---

2   Intensity of a stative verb, such as *ma-taru* 'big' is indicated by vowel-length of the first vowel of the
    root, namely *ma-taaru* 'very big'.

28. liaka   apaʔ-ən   asu-un   di   xumak   lia.
    then   carry-PF   bring-PF   home   Asp
    然後   揹   帶   家   了
    然後他把牠揹回家了。
    Then he carried it home on his back.

29. naki   a   tata   ka   mu-kusa   di   naamisiw   a   rətən   maa-kuas   lia.   maa-kuas
    my   aunt   AF-go   their   village   Rec-tell   Asp   Rec-tell
    我的   舅媽   去   她們   村   告訴   了   告訴

    kani[3]   saw.
              people
              人
    我舅媽去告訴她村（蜈蚣崙）中的人了。
    My aunt went to tell the other villagers.

30. maaka-hata-hatan   dadua   lia.
    Rec-Red-happy   all   Asp
    高興   大家   了
    大家都很高興。
    All of them were pleased.

31. halupas   iu   ma-taru   lia   ki   tula.
    long   and   Sta-big   Asp   Nom   eel
    長   和   大   了   鰻魚
    鰻魚又長又大。
    The eel was long and big.

32. naki   a   baba   isia   ka   sənaw-ən   paka-ma-səzaw-ən.
    my   uncle   that   wash-PF   Caus-Sta-clean-PF
    我的   舅   那   洗   弄乾淨
    我那個舅舅把牠洗乾淨了。
    My uncle rinsed it and cleaned it.

33. puzah   mi-kita   a   saw   ka   xizib-ən   baxaʔ-ən.
    come   AF-see   people   cut-PF   give-PF
    來   看   人   切   給
    來看的人都切給他（一些鰻魚肉）。
    Everyone who came to look at it was given a piece (of the eel).

---

[3]   The form *kani* is an oblique marker for a following person.

86

34. naki   a   ina   mamah   mu-baxa yamin tula rumut.
    my   mother brother   AF-give   we   eel   meat
    我的   母   兄   給   我們   鰻魚   肉
    我舅父給了我們鰻魚肉。
    My older maternal uncle gave us some eel meat.

35. isia   ka   yaku   ka   tatiŋ.
    then   I   young
    那時   我   小
    那時我年紀小。
    I was still very young then.

36. xaima   kawas   ka   ma-mərək   aku.
    How maney   age   Sta-unknown I
    幾   歲   不知   我
    我不知幾歲。
    I don't know how old I was.

B. Kaxabu Text Recorded by Paul Li

Text 9. 遷移到埔里 *Moving to Puli*

Narrated by Pan Jun-nai (male, 83) on Jan.16, 1988
Recorded in Shou-cheng, Puli by Paul Li
潘郡乃（男，83歲）口述、解說 (1988.1.16)
李壬癸記錄
地點：埔里鎮守城份

1. kaluʔ kaxabu a ahan mu-kawas.
   use   word AF-talk
   用   話,口 講
   以下我用四庄話來講。
   (I'll) talk in Kaxabu.

2. ta-duduʔ-i nu[1] ʔuhuzaʔ naita.
   let's-tell-Imp   ancient us
   講,論起   古代   咱
   咱們來談咱們古時侯的事。
   Let's talk about our past.

3. sii tabaʔ ki niam a xumak, kaxuʔ maxa-luak ʔisia lia ki mu-puzah
   at village we Lig home until become-poor then Asp   AF-come
   在 村   我們   家   到   變貧   那時 了   來

   purisiaʔ.
   place name
   埔里社
   在村子裡我們的家，到了貧窮之時，（我們）就到埔里來了。
   Our families in the village became so poor that we moved to Puli.

4. kaxuʔ ʔadaŋ a nak mu-puzah lia ki huahu.
   till   one   period AF-come Asp   Japanese
   到   一   段   來   了   日本人
   一段時期之後，日本人來了。
   After a certain period of time, the Japanese came.

---

[1] The function of the functin word *nu* in this sentence is not clear. It may not be a genitive marker, as illustrated in Li and Tsuchida (2001:216). Cf. also the *nu* in the ritual songs of *ayan*; see B in Part Two.

5. ʔisiaʔ lia ki maapapuihiat, midaahin.
   then Asp   struggle   frighten
   那時 了   拼命   驚怕
   那時大家拼命，很怕（被日本人所殺）。
   At that time (the people) were struggling, as they were very frightened.

6. ʔisiaʔ lia siaʔ kaxuʔ ki ma-lələt lia siaʔ/ka xəsət.
   then Asp that till   AF-obey Asp then   quiet
   那時 了 那 到   服從   了 那時   安靜
   那時服從了（日本人），（大家）才安靜下來。
   Then they followed (the regulations of the Japanese), and then they bacame quiet.

7. xəsət lia siaʔ huahu paka-yak u sauʔ.
   quiet Asp that Japanese Caus-good   people
   安靜 了 那   日本人   使好   人
   安靜下來時，日本人使人好（照顧人）。
   As they became quiet, the Japanese were nice to them.

8. misiuʔ lia ki maki zaaxuʔ maa-taŋis.
   then Asp and   aborigines Rec-fight against
   那時 了   和,與 生番   對抗,打仗
   那才和生番對抗／打仗。
   Then they fought against the mountain aborigines.

9. mu-puzah zaaxuʔ nahaniʔ m(u)-tahay sauʔ.
   AF-come   aborigines come   AF-kill   people
   來   生番   來   殺   人
   生番來要殺人。
   The mountain aborigines came to kill (Pazih) people.

10. mu-puzah zaaxuʔ, huahu ki maa-taus/maa-taŋis. disiwdisiw nahazaʔ saaʔ.
    AF-come   aborigines Japanese Rec-fight   everywhere exist
    來   生番   日本人   相鬥/對抗   到處   有
    idaahin.
    fear
    怕
    生番來了，日本人和他們打仗。到處有得怕。
    When the mountain aborigines came, the Japanese fought against them, and there was fear everywhere.

11. ma-hata-hatan   lia   ki   purisiaʔ   sauʔ,   yak   a   p<a>a-laləŋ-an.
    AF-Red-laugh   Asp   place name   person   good   Prg-live-Nmz
    高興   了   埔里   人   好   住

    埔里人很高興，埔里是個好住處。

    The people in Puli were then happy, as Puli was a nice place to live.

C. Pazih Texts Recorded by Shigeru Tsuchida

Text 1. 兩個傻人 *Two Stupid Men*

Narrated by Taruat (female, 78)
Recorded in Auran, Puli in November 1969 by S. Tsuchida
潘詹梅（女，78 歲）口述，解說
土田滋記錄　　1969 年 11 月
地點：埔里愛蘭

1. uhuni　　ka　　d<a>u-du-ay　　paa-suku-an.
   now　　　Top　　AF/Prg-tell-Fut　old-story
   現在　　　　　　要講　　　　　　故事
   現在我要講故事。
   Now, I'll tell (you) an old story.

2. m<a>aka-kawas-ay　uhuza　　a　　saw.
   AF-Prg-talk-Fut　　　　　ago　　Lig　person
   講　　　　　　　　　　　古時　　　　人
   （我）要講古時候的人。
   I shall talk about ancient people.

3. dusa　　maatu-batan.
   two　　　AF/Rec-be friends with each other
   二　　　　做　　　朋友
   他們兩人是朋友。
   The two were friends with each other.

4. masi-karum　　binayu.
   AF-enter　　　　mountain
   進入　　　　　　山
   他們到山上去。
   (They) went into the mountains.

5. "tia,　　t-ara-i　　　　　　　luxut."
   now!　　PF/let's-catch-Imp　deer
   　　　　咱們捉吧　　　　　　鹿
   去吧，咱們去捕鹿吧！
   "Now, let's catch deer!"

6.

dusa	a	batan,	mu-kusa	masi-karum	di	binayu,	riak	a	m-ara	turu
two	Lig	friend	AF-go	AF-enter	Loc	mountain	good	Lig	AF-take	three
二		朋友	去	進入		山	好		捕	三

a	luxut.
Lig	deer
	鹿

兩個朋友到山上去，幸運地捕到了三隻鹿。

The two friends, going into the mountains, fortunately caught three deer.

7.

ma-hata-hatan	laiki	dusa	a	yaasia	i.
AF-Red-laugh	thus	two	Lig	those	
高興	那樣	二		他們	

他們兩人都很高興。

Those two were therefore very happy.

8.

"tia,	taa-rukad-i	di	daran	a	dua	ka,	tia	ta-dusa-aw."
now	let's-go out-Imp	Loc	path	Lig	yonder	Conj	now	let's-divide-Fut
咱們出去吧		路			那邊			咱們分

好吧，咱們出去到那邊路上去分吧！

"Now, let's go out to the path over there and let's divide them into two!"

9.

ma-rukat	di	daran	lia.
AF-go out	Loc	path	Asp
出去	路		了

他們出去走到了路上了。

(They) went out to the path.

10.

m-ara	turu	a	luxut	ka,	dusa	a	saw.
AF-catch	three	Lig	deer	Conj	two	Lig	person
捕	三		鹿		二		人

他們捕到了三隻鹿，卻只有兩個人。

(They) caught three deer, but (there were) two people.

11.

duu-dusa	luxut,	ma-mərək	mu-dusa.
Red-halve	deer	Sta-unable	AF-divide into two
分成兩份	鹿	不能	分

他們要把鹿分成兩份，可是辦不到。

(They) tried to divide the deer into two, but couldn't do it.

12. huruhur-un   dua   dini   laiki adadumud- a   luxud-   a   isia ə.
    drag-PF   that yonder here   thus   only one   Lig   deer   Lig   that eh
    拖   那邊   這裡   那樣   只有一隻   鹿   那
    那一個人把那第三隻鹿拖到他那邊去。
    So that man here dragged the third deer (to himself).

13. huruhur   sən   di   adang   a   dakal ka,   "nisiw   ka   dusa lia, naki   ka
    drag   said   Loc   one   Lig front Conj   yours   Top   two   Asp   mine   Top
    拖   據說   一   前   你的   二   我的

    adadumut."
    only one
    只有一隻
    當他拖到他面前時，另一個人說道，「你的有兩隻，而我的卻只有一隻。」
    When he dragged it to the front of him, (the other said,) "Yours is two now, but mine is only one."

14. adaŋ   a   isia lia, huruhur   sən   di   nisia a   dakal lia ka,   "isiw   ka
    One   Lig that Asp drag   said   to   his   Lig front Asp Conj you   Top
    一   那   Asp 拖   據說   他的   前面 了   你

    dusa, yaaku   ka   adadumut,"   laiki   maa-kawas.
    two   I   Top only one   thus   AF-speak
    二   我   只有一隻   那樣   商談
    當另一個人把它拖到他那邊去，另外一個人就說，「你有兩隻，可是我卻只有一隻。」
    When another guy dragged (the deer) to the front of him, (the other) thus said, "You (have) two, but I (have) only one."

15. "aa,   nita   a   mu-dusa   ka,   ini   ma-ləkət lia. sasai-n[1]   lia?"
    oh   ours   Lig AF-divide Top   not   MA-right Asp   what to do-PF Asp
    咱們   分   不   對   怎麼辦
    「哎呀，我們的分法不對。怎麼辦呢？」
    "Oh, our way of dividing is not right. What should we do?"

16. maa-xakəkəla.
    AF/Rec-think
    想
    他們一起想。
    (They) thought with each other.

---

[1]   The form *sasai-n* 'what to do-PF' is also realized as *sasaiʔ-ən*; see Li and Tsuchida (2001:269).

17. tuutua²   nahada   maaxi-bariw   ma-kələm   a   alaw   in-iliw   a
       just then   there is   AF-sell   Sta-salty   Lig   fish   Prf-carry on pole/PF   Lig
       碰巧   有   賣   鹹   魚   挑

       saw   raa-razaw.
       person   AF/Red-pass
       人   經過
       碰巧那時候有一個挑著鹹魚在賣的人路過。
       Right at that moment a man who sold salted fish carried on the pole happened to pass by.

18. mi-kita   nasia   duu-dusa   luxut.
       AF-see   their   Red-two   deer
       看   他們   分成兩份   鹿
       他看見他們在分鹿。
       He saw them dividing the deer into two.

19. pa-kizih   la   nisia   a   in-iliw   laiki   saw   a   isia   i.
       Caus-descend   Asp   his   Lig   Prf-carry on pole/PF   thus   person   Lig   that
       放下   他的   挑   那樣   人   那個
       那個人放下了挑在扁擔上的東西。
       That man put down what he was carrying on the pole.

20. riak   ka,   ara   sən   laiki   adaŋ   a   luxut,   huruhur   sən   di   nisia   a   dakal.
       good   Top   take   said   thus   one   Lig   deer   drag   said   to   his   Lig   front
       好   拿   據說   那樣   一   鹿   拖   據說   他的   前面
       幸而他把第三隻鹿拖到他的前面去。
       It was good that he took one deer and dragged it to his front.

21. "ma-luhuni   ka   riak."
       AF-do like this   Conj   good
       這樣做   好
       「這樣就好了！」
       "If we do like this, it'll be good."

22. "aa,   riak,   riak,   riak.   ma-luhusu   ka   riak."
       Ah   good   good   good   AF-do like that   Conj   good
       好   好   好   那樣做   好
       「啊，好極了，那樣就好了！」
       "Ah, good, good, good! If we do like that, it is good."

---

2   The form *tuutua* is a loan word from Taiwanese *tutu-a* 'just right, just at that moment'.

23. "aa,   ina mu-puzah mu-ula isiw ka,   ini tahayak niam   a
     Ah,   if   AF-come   AF-lead you Conj   not tired   we/Gen Lig
           若   來   先   你   不 累   我們

duu-dusa. riak, riak, riak."
Red-two   good good good
分   好   好   好

「要是你早一點來的話，我們就不必分得這麼累了。好極了！」
"If you had come here earlier, we would not have become tired out with our dividing them. Good, good, good!"

Text 2. 母豹之愛 *The Great Motherly Love*

Narrated by Taruat (female, age 78)
Recorded and transcribed by Shigeru Tsuchida in November 1969
Interpreted by Pan Jin-yu and translated by Paul Li in 1997
潘詹梅（女，78 歲）口述
土田滋記錄，1969 年 11 月
潘金玉解說，李壬癸翻譯，1997 年

1. uhuni   ka   d<a>uduʔ-ay   nu   uhuza   a   paa-suku-an.
   now   Conj   Prg-tell-Fu   ancient   old-story
   現在   要講   古時   故事
   現在要講古時的故事。
   Now (I) shall talk about an old story.

2. uhuza   ka   nahada   adadumud-   a   saw.
   ancient Conj   exist   one   Lig   person
   古時   有   一   人
   從前有一個人。
   There was a person in the past.

3. tausay   maa-hadas   bii-binayu   na,   maa-xakəkəla   sukarum   la   di   binayu.
   let's go MAA-travel   Red-mountain   AF/Rec-think   enter   Asp   in   mountain
   去吧   遊玩   山   想   進去   山
   他想到山上去玩，就到了山中了。
   He was going to travel to the mountains and he did.

4. pulalawa   riak   a   marukad-   a   raŋaraŋ   a   rakihan   lia   hinauriak.
   a while   good   Lig   come out   Lig   leopard   Lig   baby   Asp   pretty
   一會兒   好   出來   豹   子   了   漂亮
   才一會兒的功夫，出來了一隻漂亮的小豹子。
   In a moment a pretty baby leopard came out.

5. kalapuʔ-un   nia   sən   di   nisia   dakal   lia.
   hold-PF   Asp   said   in   his   front   Asp
   抱   了   據說   他的   前   了
   據說他把牠抱起來在他的胸前。
   It is said that he held it in his arms.

6. ma-hata-hatan pulalawa, ah tumala di binayu a pudadək a daxə lia.
Sta-Red-laugh a while   hear L mount Lig steps Lig land Asp
高興   一會兒   聽   山   腳步聲,踏   地   了
他才高興了一會兒，就聽見山上腳步聲。
He was pleased for a while before he heard of the steps in the mountain.

7. m-aɲit laiki raŋaraŋ a xipu a isia i, rii-riax nisia rakihan nia
AF-cry thus leopard Lig female Lig that Red-seek her child Asp
哭 如此 豹   雌   那   在找 她的 孩子 了

mu-sazək nu saw a baŋazi lia.
AF-smell   person Lig odor Asp
聞   人   味道 了
那隻母豹哭叫著，正在找牠的孩子，聞到了人的氣味。
The mother leopard cried, was looking for her baby and smelled the odor of a man.

8. "ah, aidi asay ki naki a rakihan lia?"
Oh! stay where Nom my Lig baby Asp
啊 在 何處   我的   孩子
「啊！我的孩子在哪裡呢？」
"Where is my baby?"

9. kialih kialih lia.
near near Asp
近 近 了
牠愈來愈接近了。
It was getting closer and closer.

10. ma-ŋəsəl lai ki saw a isia i.
Sta-frighten Asp Nom man Lig that
怕 了   人   那
那個人怕了。
The man was frightened.

11. xatukul di puŋu kahuy lia.
climb on trunk tree Asp
爬上去   樹幹 樹 了
他爬到了樹上。
He climbed a tree.

12. "aa mu-puzah lia ka ka-kan-ən namisiw lia -ku?" la ma-ŋəsən.
    Oh! AF-come Asp Conj Red-eat-PF by it Asp I Sta-afraid
    　　來　　了　　吃　　牠　　我　　怕
    「啊！如果牠來了，我一定會被吃掉。」他很怕。
    "Oh! It has comes, I'll be eaten up by her," he was afraid.

13. ma-xatukul di puŋu kahuy lia.
    AF-climb on trunk tree Asp
    爬上去　　樹幹　樹
    他爬到樹上了。
    He climbed a tree.

14. pulalawa lia ka pasakən lai ki raŋaraŋ a isia i.
    a while Asp Conj arrive Asp Nom leopard Lig that
    一會兒　了　　到達　　　豹　　　那
    一會兒功夫，那隻豹就到了。
    In no moment the leopard arrived.

15. talawas na mi-kita namisiw a rakihan aidi babaw kahuy lia ka,
    raise head AF-see her Lig baby at above tree Asp Conj
    抬頭　　看　牠的　　小孩　在　上　樹
    m-aŋit ma-taru a m-aŋit lia, mu-huni lia.
    AF-cry Sta-big Lig AF-cry Asp AF-cry loudly Asp
    哭　大　　哭　了　響亮
    牠抬頭看見牠的小豹子在樹上，牠就大聲地嚎叫。
    Raising her head, she saw her baby on the tree and cried. She cried very loudly.

16. ma-sədər di puŋu kahuy.
    AF-turn around on trunk tree
    繞著轉　　樹幹　樹
    牠繞著樹頭轉。
    She turned around the tree.

17. pulalawa lia ka ŋaraŋar-ən laiki g<a>irigir u puŋu kahuy lia.
    a while Asp Conj bite-PF thus Prg-saw trunk tree Asp
    一會兒　了　　啃咬　　如此　鋸　　樹幹　樹　了
    過一會兒，牠啃咬樹頭想要把它咬斷。
    In a moment she bit crunching the trunk of the tree.

18. saw a isia lia ka aidi babaw puŋu kahuy ma-ŋəsən lia.
　　man Lig that Asp Conj stay above trunk tree Sta-frighten Asp
　　人 　那 　　　 在 上 樹幹 樹 怕 　　　了

那人在樹上很害怕。
The man on the tree was frightened.

19. "ma-urit laiki puŋu kahuy lia ka ka-kan-ən nimisiw lia -ku,"
　　 Sta-fall down thus trunk tree Asp Conj Red-eat-PF her Asp I
　　 倒 　 如此 樹幹 樹 了 吃 　 牠 　 我

　　ma-ŋəsən lia.
　　Sta-frighten Asp
　　怕 　　了

「樹倒下去的話，牠會吃我。」他很害怕。
"If the tree falls down, I'll be eaten up by her," he was afraid.

20. pulalawa lia ka ma-sədər inah lia ka masi-buri-burit di
　　a while Asp Conj AF-turn around again Asp Conj MASI-Red-turn around
　　一會兒 　　　 繞著轉 　又再 　　　　 轉

　　puŋu kahuy lia ka, laləŋ laila, m-ituku lia, ma-laləŋ lia.
　　trunk tree Asp Conj stop 　 AF-sit Asp AF-stop Asp
　　樹幹 樹 了 　停 　　 坐 　 停

過了一會兒，牠繞著樹頭轉，又繞著樹頭轉，然後停下來，坐著了，停止了。
For a while she turned around and then kept turning around the tree, then she stopped, sat there and stayed motionless there.

21. xutaxaʔ-ən, ini mari-kazay.
　　wait-PF not AF/MARI-move
　　等 　　 沒 動

等了（一會兒，牠仍然）沒有動靜。
He waited, but she did not move.

22. saw a isia aidi babaw kahuy ka, rikat la paŋa kahuy, təʔəŋ
　　man Lig that stay above tree Conj break Asp branch tree throw
　　人 　那 在 上 樹 　　 折 　 樹枝 樹 投擲

　　sən ki daurik, ini mari-kazay.
　　said Nom eye not MARI-move
　　據說 眼 沒 動

那個人就在樹上折了樹枝投擲牠的眼睛，但牠沒動。
The man on the tree broke a branch and threw it at her eyes, but she did not move.

23. ara   la   minah,   təʔəŋ   sən,   ini   mari-kazay.
    take Asp   again   throw   said   not   MARI-move
    拿   再   丟擲   據說   沒   動
    他再拿（樹枝）丟擲，牠仍然不動。
    He took (a branch) again and threw it at her, but she still did not move.

24. mata-turu   xaziŋ-ən   di   nisia   puŋu,   ma-laləŋ   ini   mari-kazay   lia.   purihat   lia.
    times-three throw-PF   to   her   head   AF-stop   not   MARI-move   Asp   die   Asp
    第三次   丟擲   牠   頭   停   沒   動   了   死   了
    第三次丟擲牠的頭，牠仍然靜止不動。原來牠已死了。
    The third time he threw (a branch) at her head, and she did not move. She had died.

25. kita sən   purihat lia,   ma-laləŋ   ini   mari-kazay.   mi-kizih   laiki   saw
    see   said die   Asp   AF-stay   not   MARI-move   AF-come down   thus   man
    看   據說 死   了   停   沒   動   下來   如此   人

    a   isia   i.
    Lig   that
          那
    看牠死了不動，那人就下來了。
    He found it dead, staying (there) without moving. The man came down (the tree).

26. kita sən,   xamaxam   sən   isia   ma-laləŋ.   aa   purihat lia.
    look said   touch   said she   AF-stop   die   Asp
    看   據說   摸   據說 牠   停   死   了
    看牠，摸牠，牠都靜止不動，已經死了。
    He looked at her, touched her, and she did not move. She has died.

27. isia   laiki   saw   a   isia   i,   araʔ-ən   laiki   raŋaraŋ   a   isia   ka   apaʔ-ən
    that   man   Lig   that   take-PF   thus   leopard   Lig   that   Conj   carry-PF
    那   人   那   拿   如此   豹   那   揹

    di   aubil   lia.
    at   behind Asp
         後面   了
    那個人把豹揹在後面。
    Then that man took the leopard and carried it on his back.

28. m-ukusa   di   m<a>a-sikarum-ay   di   nimisiw   a   ratən   lia.
    AF-go   at   AF-Prg-enter-Fut   at   his   Lig   village   Asp
    去   進入   他的   村莊   了
    他回到村子裡。
    He left and entered his village.

29. kita   laiki   saw   ka,   "asay pai misiw? asay ki   m-ara   raŋaraŋ pai siw?
    see   thus   people   Conj   what Q   that   how   AF-take leopard Q   you
    看   如此   人   什麼 那   如何   捉拿   豹   你

    ki   ini   mati-patus,   ini   mati-rawil   ka,   [tai] paara isia a   raŋaraŋ?
    not carry-gun   not   carry-arrow   Conj   catch   that Lig leopard
    沒   帶槍   沒   帶箭   捉   那   豹

    apaʔ-ən ki   azaŋ, ibaʔ-ən ki   adaŋ.
    carry-PF Nom one   hold-PF   Nom one
    揹   一   抱   一

村中的人看見時，問他，「那是什麼？你如何捉到豹子？你沒帶槍，沒帶弓箭，
怎麼捉到豹子？還揹一隻，抱一隻？」

When the villagers saw him, they asked, "What is that? How did you catch the leopards? You didn't carry a gun or arrows, yet you caught the leopards. You carried one on the back and held one in your arms."

30. m-ukusa laiki nimisiw a   rətən   a   saw,   mi-kita lia, dahu a   saw
    AF-go   thus   his   Lig village Lig people   AF-see   Asp   many Lig people
    去   他的   村莊   人   看   了   多   人

    di   namisiw a   xuma   lia.
    at   his   Lig house Asp
         他的   家   了

他村中的人去看，很多人到他家（去）。

The man's villagers went to look at them, and many people went to his house.

31. kita sən,   "aa asay ki   na   ma-gizəm   a   saw pai siw?"
    look said   oh   what Nom   Sta-capable   Lig man Q   you
    看   據說   怎麼   強健,能幹   人   你

他們看了說，「你怎麼這麼能幹？」

They looked at them and said, "How come you are such a capable man?"

32. m-ara   raŋaraŋ laila isia laiki saw   dahu a   m-ukusa mi-kita lia.
    AF-take leopard so   he   thus   people many Lig AF-go   AF-see   Asp
    捉   豹   那樣   他   如此   人   多   去   看   了

那人捉到豹子，很多人去看。

He caught the leopards, and many villagers went to take a look.

33.
nahada	kii-kita	saw	a	takarad-	a	isia	lia	ka,	"ii	maana.
have	Red-look	people	Lig	doctor	Lig	that	Asp	Conj		wait
有	看	人		醫生		那				且慢

ta-padudu-ay	isiw	naki.	riak	say?	ta-burax-aw	naki	nimu	[nisiw]	a
let's-ask-Fut	you	I	good	Q	let's-dissect-Fut	I	your	your	Lig
讓我看	你	我	好		咱解剖	我	你們的	你的	

in-ara	a	raŋaraŋ	a	imini.	riak	say?"
Prf-catch	Lig	leopard	Lig	this	good	Q
捉		豹		這	好	

去看的人當中有個醫生，他說，「且慢！我要向你請教一下，好嗎？我要解剖你捉到的豹子，好嗎？」

Among the ones looking at (the leoaprds), there was a doctor. He said, "Wait a minute. I'd like to ask your permission. I'd like to dissect the leopard you caught. Is that alright?"

34.
saw	a	isia	ka,	"haw,	burax-i!	ta-kita?-aw	mu-?asay	ki	ma-luhuni,"
man	Lig	that	Conj	fine	dissect-Imp	we-see-Fut	AF-what		AF-this way
人		那		好	解剖	咱們看	怎麼		這樣

laila.
in that way
那樣

那人說，「好，你解剖吧！咱們要看看怎麼會這樣」

The man said, "Fine! Dissect it! Let's see why that is so."

35.
riak	a	burax-ən	u	takarad-	a	isia	laiki	raŋaraŋ	a	isia	i.
good	Lig	dissect-PF		doctor	Lig	that		leopard	Lig	that	
好		解剖		醫生		那		豹		那	

好在那個醫生解剖了那隻豹子。

It's good that the doctor dissected the leopard.

36.
kita	sən	laiki	di	rizik	a	babu	a	imisiw	ka,	kipud-un	u	sələm
look	said	thus	in	inside	Lig	heart	Lig	her	Conj	wrap-PF		fat
看	據說	如此		裡面		心		牠的		包		脂肪

laiki	babu	a	isia	i	ki	purihat.
thus	heart	Lig	her			die
如此	心		牠的			死

據說看見牠裡面的心被脂肪包住才死的。

It is said that he found that her heart was wrapped up by fat, and she died of it.

37. ma-luhuni haimini, saisim-an a rakihan.
    AF-this way this love-LF Lig baby
    這樣 這個 疼 子
    就是這樣子，牠為了疼孩子。
    This is the reason: she loved her baby (too much).

38. maaxa-razaw maxa-kə-kəla lai lia, imisiw laiki kipud-un u sələm laiki
    MAAXA-exceed MAXA-Red-think Asp she thus wrap-PF fat thus
    過份 想 牠 如此 包 脂肪 如此

    babu imisiw laiki p<a>urihad-ay lia.
    heart her thus Prg-die-Fut Asp
    心 牠的 死
    他過份想念（小豹），因此脂肪包心而死了。
    She thought so much of her baby that her heart was wrapped up by fat and she died of it.

39. ki takarad- a isia m<a>a-kuas i, "ma-luhuni ki nita x<in>a-kə-kəla
    Nom doctor Lig that Prg-AF-talk AF-this way Nom our XA-Prf-Red-think
    醫生 那 講 這樣 咱的 想

    maaxa-razaw laiki p<a>urihad-ay lia."
    MAAXA-exceed thus Prg-die-Fut Asp
    過份 死 了
    那個醫生說，「咱們急得太過份，就會死掉。」
    The doctor said, "If we are too worried like this, we may die."

Text 3. 釣大魚 *Catching A Big Fish*

Narrated by Pan Wan-ji (male, 87)
Recorded by Shigeru Tsuchida in 1969
Interpreted by Pan Jin-yu and translated by Paul Li in 1997.
潘萬吉（男，87 歲）口述
土田滋記錄，埔里愛蘭，1969 年 11 月
潘金玉解說，李壬癸翻譯，1997 年

1. ta-duduʔ-aw rahan hakəhakəzəŋ paa-subil.
   let's-talk-Fut story ancestors pass-down
   咱講 話 祖先 留下
   咱們講祖先流傳下來的話。
   Let's talk about an old story passed down by the ancestors.

2. iu ki rubaŋ u mamaləŋ isia la i, damuri rarəsət.
   and Nom young Lig man that already personal name
   並 年輕 男 那個 人名
   有一個男青年名字叫 Damuri Rarəsət。
   There was a young man named Damuri Rarəsət.

3. maa-kuas namisiw ina aba, "mausay aku mu-ririx daxə di asay
   Rec-tell his mother father will go I AF-search land at where
   講 他們的 母 父 去 我 探巡 土地 在 何處

   puupuh raxuŋ."
   origin river
   源頭 河
   他對他的父母說，「我要去探看地方，哪裡才是溪流的源頭。」
   He said to his parents, "I shall go and search for the land where the river orginates."

4. isia laiki m-a-usaʔ-ay lia.
   then thus AF-Prg-go-Fut Asp
   那時 如此 要去 了
   他說了就要走了。
   Then he left.

5. m-a-apaʔ-ay buzux rawil lia.
   AF-Prg-carry-Fut bow arrow Asp
   揹 弓 箭 了
   他要揹弓箭了。
   He was carrying a bow and arrows.

6. mausay   la   isia.
   will go   Asp   he
   要去   了   他
   他要去了。
   He was going.

7. duila lia mata di zaxi-zaxi, mata di dapi-dapi, mata raxu-raxuŋ.
   go   Asp from at Red-bushy   from at Red-cliff   from   Red-rivers
   去   了   經過 Loc 崎嶇不平   經過   懸崖   經過 河
   他去了，經過崎嶇不平，經過懸崖，經過一條溪又一條溪。
   He walked on bushy places, along cliffs and crossed rivers.

8. tuhuliŋ   ma-rizaux ma-xatukul   p<a>a-sakəl-ay di puupuh   raxuŋ.
   thrubush   AF-go down AF-climb   PA-Prg-arrive-Fut at origin   river
   爬藤,雜草叢生 下去,下坡 上坡   將到達   源頭   河
   沿路雜草叢生，上坡下坡，快到溪的源頭了。
   He went through bushes, descended and ascended mountains and finally arrived at the origin of the river.

9. kii-kitaʔ-ay ma-ngayah rumaw ilia.
   Red-see-Fut Sta-blue   lake   Asp
   在看   綠   潭   了
   在看綠色的水潭。
   He was looking at a blue lake.

10. "haw lia maa-baza asay pai dini   lia."
    good Asp AF-know where Q here   Asp
    好   了 知   什麼   此地 了
    「好了，（我）知道此地是什麼地方了。」
    "Good! I know now where this is."

11. ma-rikazay a dalum. "imini lia."
    AF-move   water   this   Asp
    動   水   這   了
    水在動。（他說，）「是這裡了。」
    The water was moving. "That's it!"

12. ki   rubang mamaləŋ isia   i, taadəpəday mana-ria-riak, kii-kitaʔ-ay
    Nom young   man   that   do-well   MANA-Red-good Red-see-Fut
    年輕   男   那個   仔細看   好好地   看

    tuua kuadəŋ   ma-taru a   alaw.
    just surprising Sta-big Lig fish
    剛巧 驚訝   大   魚
    那年輕人仔細看著，正好看到令人驚奇的大魚。
    The young man was looking at the lake very carefully, and he saw a surprisingly big fish.

13. isia   laiki paa-kizih-ay in-apa   a   buzux rawil.
    then   Caus-low-Fut Prf-carry Lig bow   arrow
    那時   如此 放下   揹   弓   箭
    他放下了所揹的弓箭。
    So, he put down the bow and arrows carried on his back.

14. isia   laiki kaa-kauŋ-ay   lia.
    then   thus   Red-draw a bow-Fut Asp
    那時   如此 正要以弓射   了
    他正準備要用弓射。
    Then he drew a bow to the full.

15. i   rakad-ən nia irumaʔ-ən lia.
      shot-PF   Asp found-PF   Asp
      射   了   找到   了
    他射了牠也找到了牠。
    He shot it and got it.

16. haw   lia mi-xabaxap paxu-riupuŋ   lia.
    good Asp AF-float   PAXU-turn over   Asp
    好   了 浮   翻來翻去   了
    好了，（魚）浮起來翻來翻去。
    (The fish) floated and turned over its body.

17. asaila, duasaila.   ara,   pi-dəkədək lia. ini   kitaʔ-an   nia.[1]
    what   what happened oh!   Pl-sink   Asp not see-LF   Asp
    什麼   怎麼了   哎呀 沉下去   了 不 見   了
    怎麼了？哎呀！（魚）沉下去了，不見了。
    What? What happened? (The fish) sank and became invisible.

---

[1] The initial of the aspect marker *lia* is assimilated to the preceding consonant *n* as *nia*.

18. "anuy aa   kuadəŋ   a   alaw a   imini," isia lia ki   mati-zəŋəd- a
    pity surprising Lig   fish Lig this   then Asp Nom MATI-regret   Lig
    可惜 意外   魚   這   然後   心中難過

    maxa-kəla   lia.
    MAXA-think   Asp
    想   了
    「可惜這條魚！」他心中（難過地）想道。
    "What a pity! This was such a big fish!" he regretted in his mind.

19. kita-kita?-ən kuah.   pi-itul   kuah, pi-zaux   kuah.
    Red-see-PF   none   go-up   none   go-down   none
    看   沒   往上游   沒   往下游   沒
    一直看都沒有，往上游沒有，向下游也沒有。
    He kept watching, but there was none. Neither upstream, nor downstream.

20. dua   mata   asay   lia.
    go   from   where   Asp
    去   經過   何處   了
    不知道哪裡去了。
    Where has it gone?

21. alaw isia lia ka, mi-dəkədək lia.
    fish   that Asp Top AF-sink   Asp
    魚   那   了   沉   了
    那條魚大概沉下去了。
    That fish must have sunk to the bottom.

22. haw   lia xutaxa?-ən kuah   lia.
    alright Asp wait-PF   none   Asp
    好   了   等   沒   了
    罷了！等不到了。
    Alright, it's useless to wait any more.

23. isia   laiki   m<a>a-tabilih-ay   lia. maatabilihay di   xuma.
    then   AF-Prg-return-Fut   Asp   return   at   home
    那時   回去   了   回去   家
    他要回去了，回家去。
    So, he was going home.

24. maaka-kita?-ay   ina   aba.
    Rec-see-Fut   mother   father
    相見   母   父
    要見他的父母。
    He was going to see his parents.

25. "haw   mu-puzah   lai   siw   say?"
    fine   AF-come   Asp   you   Q
    好   回來   你
    他們問，「你回來了？」
    "So have you come home?" they asked.

26. rubang   mamalən   isia   i,   "haw   mu-puzah   lia   -ku."
    child   man   that   fine AF-come   Asp   I
    年輕   男   那   好   回來   了   我
    年輕人說，「是，我回來了。」
    The young man said, "Yes, I've come home."

27. "saasay   lia,   haw   ha   i.   pana?-ən   naki   lia   alaw   a   isia   i   aidi
    what   Asp   shot-PF   by me   Asp   fish   that   at
    什麼   了   射   我的   了   魚   那   在

    ma-ŋayah   a   rumaw   puupuh   a   dualia   i.   iruma?-ən   nia,   kita?-ən,   ini
    AF-green   Lig   lake   origin   Lig   there   search-PF   Asp   look-PF   not
    綠   潭   源頭   那邊   找   看   沒

    kita?-ən.   idəkədək   lia.   isia   lia   kuah   lia.   naki   a   maxa-kə-kəla
    seen-PF   sink   Asp   that   Asp   none   Asp   my   Lig   MAXA-Red-think
    見   沉   了   那   沒   我的   想

    sasai?-ən   nia   ma-luhuni   a   lia   imini   a   lailaki   yaku."   isia   laiki.
    what-PF   Asp   AF-this way   Asp   this   Lig   I   he   so
    怎麼辦   這樣,如此   這   我   他   如此
    「不知何故，我在那邊碧潭中（溪的源頭）射到了魚，找到了，看到了，又看不
    見了，沉下去了，牠就沒了。我想如何是好？如此這般我這樣。」他如此說。
    "What should I do? I shot the fish in the green lake, which is the source of the stream. I found it and
    saw it. It then disappeared. It sank and was gone. What shall I do? I'll do in this way," he thought.

28. hao   lia   kai-hinis   lia   ki   rubaŋ   mamalən   a   isia   hinis   a?i.
    fine   Asp   stay-mind   Asp   Nom   young   man   Lig   that   heart
    好   想   那   年輕   男   那   心
    那少年心中在想。
    The young man kept thinking in his mind.

29.
kaxu	adaŋ	a	ahuan,	duu-dusa	ahuan.	duudusa	dali	a	isia	laiki.
till	one	Lig	night	two	night	two	day	Lig	that	so
到	一		夜	二	夜	第二	天	那		如此

"mausay	liaku.	mausay	haku."
will go	already-I	will go	I
要去		要去	我

一夜、二夜，過了兩天。「我要去了。我要去」

One night, two nights, and two days passed. "I shall go. I shall go."

30.
maa-kuas	ina	aba,	"mausay	mu-ririx	daxə	inah.	mausay
Rec-tell	Mom	Dad	will go	AF-search	land	again	will go
告訴	母	父	要去	巡	地方	再	要去

pi-zaux	raxuŋ."
go-down	stream
下去	河

他告訴他父母，「我要再去查看地方。我要往河下面去。」

He said to his parents, "I'm going to look for a land again. I'm going down to the stream."

31.
hakə-hakəzəŋ	pasubil	rahal	ka,	"p<ii>na-luxut,	p<ii>na-ʔalaw,	ini	pitul
Red-old	leave	word	Top	catch-Prf-deer	catch-Prf-fish	not	go up
老人	留下	話		捕鹿	捕魚	沒	上

ha,	ini	ma-xatukul	ha,	pi-zaux	dadua	ha,"	laiki	namisiw	a	maa-kuas.
not	AF-climb		go-down	all		thus	their		Lig	Rec-say
沒	爬上去		下去	全體		如此	他們的			講

（這些是）祖先留下來的話，「（他去）捕鹿、捕魚，沒有上坡，沒有爬高，都只是下坡。」他們如此講。

The ancestors have left us with these words, "A deer which was hit and wounded, or a fish which was hit and wounded, never goes up, nor climbs, but it goes down all the way," thus they said.

32.
"haw	ha	i.	ta-ririx-aw	mata	rahut."
fine			we-check-Fut	from	downstream
好			咱找	從	下游

「好吧！咱們到下游去查看吧！」

"Alright. Let's go and search for (the fish) downstream."

33.
isia	laiki	m-a-usaʔ-ay	lia.
he	thus	AF-Prg-go-Fut	Asp
他	如此	要去	了

他那樣就要去了。

Then he went.

34. p<a>ikadul-ay m-a-asuʔ-ay suazi u wazu ta isia lia i.
Prg-set out-Fut AF-Prg-bring-Fut young Lig dog our that Asp
出發　　　　帶　　　　　小　　狗　咱　那

他要出發，要帶狗（和他一起去）那樣子。
He was to set out and bring along his pet dog with him.

35. m-a-usaʔ-ay lia. pi-zaux lia. duilader² lia isia laisia.
AF-Prg-go-Fut Asp go-down Asp go-really Asp he
要去　　　　了　　下去　　了　真的去　　　他

要去了，下去了，真的去了。
He was leaving and going down the stream. He really did.

36. nahada ni saw a kapadal.
have people piled stones
有　　　　人　　　　堆、疊石頭

有人疊石頭的地方。
There were stones piled by people.

37. "asay pai mini lia" isia laiki.
what Q this Asp he thus
什麼　　　這　　　　他　如此

「這是什麼？」他說。
"What is this?" he said.

38. p<a>i-zaux-ay kii-kitaʔ-ay.
Prg-go down-Fut Red-see-Fut
下去　　　　看

他要下去看。
He was going down to look at it.

39. ara, masia pa-karax-an ka nahada nu saw a xuma rikibul ilia.
Excl that Caus-broad-LF Top have by person Lig house granary Asp
那　溪口　　　　　　有　　　人　　　家　小穀倉

---

² The form *duilader* is derived from *duila* 'to go' + *eder* 'really'.

nahada	tarantaw	ilia.
have	ditch	Asp
有	水溝	

那溪流下游的地方有人的家、小穀倉。也有水溝。

Oh! There was a granary hut of some family in the broad space down the stream. There was a ditch (around it).

40.
haw	laiki	alaw	isia	a	pi-zau-zaux	lia	ka	asikis-an	lia.	uka	nu
fine	thus	fish	that	Lig	go-Red-down	Asp	Conj	painful-LF	Asp	other	by
好	如此	魚	那		下去			痛		其他	

saw	a	sən	nia.	ma-rizaw(at)	mu-laŋuy	mu-zakay	lia.
saw	a	said	Asp	Sta-dizzy	AF-swim	AF-walk	Asp
people	Lig	said	Asp				
人		據說		游	走	了	

呀！那條魚一直流下來了。牠痛，如人們所說的，歪歪斜斜地游走。

When the fish went down, it was painful, as people said. It was swimming away unsteadily.

41.
haw	lia	padadər	di	namisiw	a	suŋut	namisiw	a	x<in>utu	a
fine	Asp	get hooked	at	their	Lig	bridge	their	Lig	Prf-pile	Lig
好		鉤住		他們的		橋	他們的		堆	

batu	lai	ki	alaw	a	isia.
stone	Asp	Nom	fish	Lig	that
石頭			魚		那

那條魚剛好被橋下石墩（石頭堆）阻擋住了。

The fish was hooked by the piled stones under the bridge.

42.
maa-baza	hayaku.
AF-know	I
知道	我

我怎麼知道？

How would I know? (I did not expect it.)

43.
kaw	ki	rubaŋ	mamais	isia	lia.
then	Nom	young	lady	there	Asp
		年輕	女	那	了

那時後那裡有位年輕女子。

Then, a young lady was there.

44.
m<a>a-ka-kawas-ay	lia.
AF-Prg-Red-talk-Fut	Asp
交談	了

她要談話了。

She was going to talk.

45. maa-kita   lia.
    Rec-look   Asp
    互望   了
    他們相見了。
    They looked at each other.

46. maa-ka-kawas-ay lia ki   maa-bazaʔ-ay lia.
    Rec-Red-talk-Fut Asp Nom   Rec-know-Fut   Asp
    相談   了   知道   了
    他們彼此交談、相識了。
    They talked to each other and got acquainted with each other.

47. "m<a>a-baza haita padadər di asay? ini ma-mərək aku," isia lia, haw lia.
    AF-Prg-know we   hook   at where no Sta-unknown I   thus   good Asp
    知道   咱   勾住   何處 沒 不知   我   如此   好   了
    「我怎麼知道魚在哪勾住了呢？不，我不確定（是否這女孩拿走了那條魚）。」
    （男子如此自問）
    "How would I know where the fish was hooked? No, I'm not sure (if this girl took it)," thus he asked himself.

48. mu-riax   kaxu dida, kuah lia.
    AF-find   up to there none Asp
    找,尋回   到   那   沒有 了
    他找到那邊，但沒找到。

    He checked up to there, but there was no (fish).[3]

49. aa   baabaw lia, ma-akux lia.
         above   Asp Sta-hot   Asp
         上面   熱(天氣)
    日正當中，天氣很熱。
    (The sun) was up above, and it was hot.

50. isia   laiki, "naki   a   m<a>a-xatukul-ay di punu kahuy. dua nima xuma
    then   thus   my   Lig AF-Prg-climb-Fut at trunk tree   there whose house
    那時   如此   我的   要往上爬   樹幹 樹   那邊 誰的 家

---

[3] It seems that the informant started telling another plot from 48 on. Thus , the sentences 36 through 47 should be deleted. However, because they are still valid as sentence examples, they are left here as they appear in the original text.

pai	ni.	rikibul	a	mini	ha,	umamah,	tarantaw."
Q	here	granary	Lig	this		rice field	ditch
這裡	穀倉		這		田		水溝

他說，「我要爬上樹頭。那是誰的家？有穀倉、田和田溝。」
He said, "I shall climb the tree. Whose house is that? There is a granary hut, a rice field and a ditch."

51.
kaxu	isia	lia.	aubil	a	isia	mu-razaw	dali	isia,	nahani	laiki	rubaŋ
till	thus	Asp	later	Lig	he	AF-pass	day	that	come	thus	young
到	如此	了	然後		他	過	天	那	來	如此	年輕

mamais	isia,	ma-iliw-ay	dalum	laila.
lady	that	AF-carry-Fut	water	in that way
女	那	挑	水	那樣

到那時，後來過了一天，一年輕女子來挑水。
Until later, the next day, a young lady came to carry water.

52.
isia	lia	baa-bazuʔ-ay	siatu,	səə-sənaw	xalam,	m<a>a-bazaʔ-ay	ta.
then		Red-wash-Fut	clothes	Red-wash	vegetable	AF-Prg-know-Fut	we
然後		要洗	衣服	洗	蔬菜	有待瞭解	咱

然後她要來洗衣服或要來洗菜呢？咱們並不知道。
Then, she was going to wash clothes or vegetable. We don't know.

53.
isia	laiki	haw	lia.	kaw	isia	ki	suazi	wazu	baazi	raru.
she	like this	good		then		Nom	little	dog	companion	大概
她	像這樣	好	了	到			小	狗	同伴	perhaps

他帶了一隻狗作伴。
He was bringing along a little dog with him as his companion.

54.
nahani	laiki	rubang	mamais	p<a>uzah	di	namisiw	a	xuma	ka	disiw.
come	like this	young	lady	Prg-arrive	at	their	Lig	house	Conj	there
來		輕	女	來		她們的		家		那裡

女子正從她們的家來到那裡
The girl was getting there from her own house.

55.
haw	lia	i,	ma-riwiriw	ha	i,	puŋaŋus	ha	i,	kaw	ki	rubang
fine	Asp		AF-wag tail			whine			arrive	Nom	young
好			搖尾			狗的聲音			到		年輕

mamais	isia	lia	ka	laləŋ	laila	i.
lady	that	Asp	Conj	rest	in that way	
女				休息	那樣	

（狗）搖尾巴並發出聲音，那女子到那裡休息。
The dog wagged its tail, whining, and the girl got there to rest.

56. "nima   wazu?" laila   a   isia laiki   wazu a   suazi a wazu a
    whose   dog   in that way Lig that in this way dog Lig little a dog Lig
    誰的   狗   那樣   那   如此   狗   小   狗

    ma-riwiriw   lia.
    AF-wag tail Asp
    搖尾巴   了
    她問，「誰的狗？」那隻狗在搖尾巴。
    "Whose dog?" she said, and the pet dog was wagging its tail.

57. haw   i   lia. kialih kialih ma-riwiriw   lia.
    fine   Asp near   near   AF-wag tail Asp
    好   了   近   近   搖尾巴   了
    好了，狗搖著尾巴一直接近。
    Fine, (the dog) was getting closer and closer while wagging its tail.

58. duasaasay ki   rubang mamais talawas   laila.
    what to do Nom   young   lady   raise head in that way
    做什麼   年輕 女   抬頭   那樣
    女子不知要做什麼。她抬頭了。
    The girl didn't know what to do, and raised her head.

59. "kii-kita   yaku. yaku ka   ta-kita?-aw   naimu   lahaiki yaku."
    Red-look I   I   Conj we-see-Fut   you   I
    正在看 我   我   要看   你們   我
    （男人想道）「她正在看我。我也要看你們。」
    "(She's) looking at me. I'm also going to look at you," (the young man thought).

60. "haw haw, alu   rizaux. ima pai siw? p<a>uzah   di asay?" laiki
    alright   come go down who   you Prg-come   where in this way
    好   好   來   下來   誰   Q   你   來   何處   如此

    rubang mamais imisiw.
    young   lady   that
    年輕   女   那個
    「好，好，下來！你是誰？從哪裡來的？」那個女子問道
    "Alright, come down. Who are you? Where do you come from?" the girl asked.

61. isia   lia m<a>a-rizaux   lia.
    then   Asp AF-Prg-come down   Asp
    然後   了   下來   了
    然後他就下來了
    Then he was coming down.

114

62. maa-ba-baxaʔ-ay rahan rubaŋ mamalən isia i.
    Rec-Red-give-Fut word young man that
    應答 話 年輕 男 那
    少年人要應答。
    The young man was to respond.

63. "haw ha i. saasay pai siw laila?"
    alright what you in that way
    好 什麼 Q 你 那樣
    「你要做什麼？」（女孩問）
    "Alright, what are you up to?" (the girl asked).

64. "haw lia maluhuda maluhuda hayaku siidua mu-ririx daxə mata puupuh
    fine Asp thus thus I go AF-check land toward origin
    好 因此 因此 我 去了 巡察 地 向 源頭

    raxuŋ.
    river
    溪
    「我去探看過溪的源頭。
    "Alright, I went checking traps and searching for the source of the river in this way and in that way."

65. kii-kitaʔ-ay ma-ŋayah a rumaw. kii-kitaʔ-ay ma-taru a alaw.
    Red-see-Fut AF-blue lake Red-see-Fut Sta-big Lig fish
    看 青 Lig 潭 看 大 魚
    看到碧潭。看到大魚。
    I saw a blue lake, in which I saw a big fish.

66. isia laiki naki a paa-kizih-ay buzux u rawin.
    then in this way my Lig Caus-low-fut bow and arrow
    那時 如此 我的 解下,放下 弓 和 箭
    那時我解下弓箭。
    Then I released my bow and arrows.

67. s<a>ihərəʔ-ay lakad-ən naki lia. irumaʔ-ən lia.
    Prf-draw bow-Fut shoot-PF by me Asp found-PF Asp
    拉弓 被射中 我 了 找到 了
    我拉弓射了牠，也找到了。
    I drew my bow and shot at it. I hit the target.

68. mi-dəkədək   mi-xabaxap.   haw   ha   i   irumaʔ-ən   nia.
    AF-sink   AF-float   alright   found-PF   Asp
    沉   浮   找到
    沉下去又浮起來，找到了。
    It sank and floated. I found it.

69. m<a>a-baza   mi-dəkədək   lia   ka   ini   kitaʔ-ən   lia.
    AF-Prg-know   AF-sink   Asp   Conj   not   see-PF   Asp
    不知   沉   了   沒   看   了
    我不知道牠會沉下去，再也看不到牠了。
    I did not know it sank, and couldn't find it.

70. kaxu   uhuni   duu-dusa   a   dali.
    till   now   Red-two   day
    到   現在   第二   天
    到今天過了二天了。
    As of today, it's been two days.

71. imini,   isia   laiki   naki   a   minah   a   ta-usay   taxu-bilih.
    this   then   in this way   my   again   Lig   let's-go TAXU-return
    這   那時   如此   我的   再   要去   回去
    我要再回去（看看）。
    In this way, I'll go and return again.

72. nu   hakə-hakəzəŋ   maa-kuas   ka,   'luxut   piina,   alaw   piina,
         Red-ancestor   Rec-tell   Conj   deer   hit and wounded   fish   hit and wounded
         長輩   講   鹿   魚
    ini   pitul   ha   pi-zaux   ha' ka,   ini   ma-luhuni.
    not   go up   go-down   not   AF-do in this way
    沒   上去(游)   下來   沒   如此,這樣
    根據長輩所說，「如果鹿或魚被打中且受傷了，（牠們）絕不會往上逃，而是往
    下游去。」是不是就像這樣呢？
    According to our ancestors' saying, 'if a deer is hit and wounded, or a fish is hit and wounded, it never goes up, but it goes down,' isn't it like this?

73. haw   ha   i   haləkat   laiki   yaku.   ta-silaməd-ay   p<a>i-zaux-ay   raxuŋ.
    right   just recall   in this way   I   let's-learn-Fut   Prg-go down-Fut   river
    好   憶起   如此   我   下去   溪
    啊！我想起來了。咱們嘗試下去溪中試試看吧！
    Right, it just occurred to me that I should learn to go and see downstream. Then I went downstream.

74. kii-kitaʔ-ay nimu   a xuma kabad-an   a pii   a tarantaw.
    Red-look-Fut your   Lig home paved with boards Lig   Lig ditch
    看   你們的   家   鋪木板   [土卑]   水溝
    我看到你家和鋪有木板的水溝。
    I saw your house and a ditch paved with boards.

75. pakadini mi-kita nimu   a xuma lia. isia laiki.
    from-here AF-see   your   Lig home Asp then in this way
    從這裡   看   你們的   家   了   那時 如此
    （我）到這裡就看到了你們的家了，就這樣。
    When I came up to here, I saw your house. It was like this.

76. haayuu   duila mata asay? haw ha i.
    oh   go   from where
    哎呀   去   從   何處
    哎呀！（魚）到哪裡去了？
    Oh! Where has (the fish) gone?

77. ta-səkəd-i   na laha   yaku m<a>a-baza. mata di dini."
    let's-rest-Imp uncertain I   AF-Prf-know   from   here
    咱休息   不確定 我   不知   從   此地
    我想該休息了吧！我不知不覺就來到這了。」
    Let's take a rest, I thought. I came up to here without knowing it." (thus the young man said).

78. "huu, ma-luhusu   haisiw aai lia."
    oh   Sta-in that way you   Asp
          如此   你
    「你原來如此。」（女子說）
    "Oh! You were like this, I see." (She said).

79. maa-ba-baxa   rahan lia.
    Rec-Red-give   word Asp
    交談   話   了
    他們交談了。
    They talked to each other.

80. "haw lia. tia, tia ta-pahadas-i,   tia niam a xuma disiw i m-ituku."
    fine Asp go go let's-have fun-Imp go our   Lig home there   AF-sit
    好   了 去 去 咱們遊玩吧   去 我們的 家   那裡   坐
    「好了，咱們去玩吧！到我家那去坐坐。」
    "Alright now. Let's go to our house and sit there and have fun!" (she said).

81. mausay,   p<a>a-sakəl-ay namisiw a   xuma.
    will go   PA-Prg-arrive-Fut their   Lig home
    要去   將到達   他們的   家
    他們快到她家了。
    They were going and arriving at their house.

82. "palaləŋ   dini   na   siw   i. tausay[4]   maa-kuas niam a   ina   aba,"
    stay   here   you shall go Rec-tell   our   Lig mother father
    留   這裡   你   要去   告訴   我們的   母   父

    laiki   u   rubaŋ mamais   isia.
    如此   年輕   女   那個
    in this way   young lady   that
    「你就待在這裡。（我）要告訴我的父母去，」那女子如此說。
    "You stay here! I'll go and talk to my parents," the young girl said.

83. "alu   si,   saasay pai sia? p<a>uzah asay? ima?"
    come please what   Q   he   Prg-come where who
    來   什麼   他   來   何處   誰
    「叫他來！他在做什麼？從哪裡來？他是誰？」（她父母說）
    "Please tell him to come. What is he doing? Where did he come from? Who is he?" (asked her parents)

84. "m<a>a-baza yaku,"   laiki rubaŋ mamais   a   isia   i.
    AF-Prf-know I   thus   young lady   Lig that
    不怎麼知道 我   如此   年輕   女   那個
    「我不清楚。」那年輕女孩如此說。
    "I don't know," thus the young girl said.

85. asuʔ-un   nia mata namisiw a xuma lia.
    carry-PF Asp to   their   home Asp
    帶   了   向   她們   家   了
    她把他帶到她們家了。
    He was taken to their house.

---

4   The form *tausay* < *ta-usaʔ-ay* 'we-go-Fut', e.g., *tausaʔay lia-ku* 'I'm going'.

86. "haa, haa, haa, sikarum, sikarum. ima pai siw?" isia laiki.
   oh   oh   oh   enter   enter   who Q you   thus
                    進來   進來   誰   你   那樣

   「進來，進來。你是誰？」（她父母）如此對他說

   "Oh, come in, come in. Who are you?" they said.

87. m<a>aka-kawas-ay, "yaku ka damuri rarəsət sən yaku i," isia lia,
    AF-Prg-Red-talk-Fut   I Conj personal name said I   thus Asp
    講   我   人 名   據說 我   那樣

    haw lia.
    good Asp
    好

    「我的名字叫作 Damuri Rarəsət。」

    He was to say, "I am called Damuri Rarəsət," he said like that.

88. maa-kawas lia, maa-baxa rahan nia.
    Rec-tell   Asp Rec-give words Asp
    講話   了   交談   話   了

    他們就交談了。

    They talked to each other.

89. maa-paha-pahatan.
    Rec-Red-laugh
    笑

    他們笑了。

    They laughed.

90. "p<a>uzah di asay pai siw?"
    Prg-come   at where Q   you
    來   何處   你

    「你從哪裡來的？」

    Where did you come from?

91. "yaku ka p<a>uzah di miadua raxuŋ a binayu a dua yaku i.
    I   Conj Prg-come at over there river Lig mountain Lig yonder I
    我   來   那邊,對岸 溪   山   我

    ini maanu waadəŋ." isia laiki.
    not far   no concession thus
    不 遠   不讓步   如此

    「我從溪對岸那邊的山上來的，並不太遠。」他如此說。

    "I came from the opposite side of the river and the mountain over there, not far away." he said.

92. "haw lia. palaləŋ   dida."
    good Asp live   there
    好   了   住   那兒
    「好了，你就住在那兒。」
    "Good, you live there!" (her parents said.)

93. m<a>aka-kawas-ay lia.
    AF-Prg-Red-talk-Fut Asp
    互相講話   了
    他們交談了。
    They talked to each other.

94. saasay, saasay la maa-baxa rahal lia.
    what   what   Asp Rec-give words Asp
    什麼   什麼   交談   話
    他們討論要做什麼。
    They talked over what to do.

95. isia   laiki, haw   ha i. maa-paha-pahatan.
    they   thus   good   Rec-Red-laugh
    他們   如此   好   大家笑
    好，好，大家笑。
    They were happy like this.

96. aa iruma?-ən a   marinu   lia, hakə-hakəzəŋ   maa-kuas, iruma?-ən a
        find-PF   Lig weak point Asp old men   Rec-say   find-PF   Lig
        找到   弱點   了   長輩   說   找到
    marinu   lia. haw ha i.
    weak point   Asp   good
    弱點   好
    我們的長輩所說，他終於找到弱點（這女孩）了。這樣很好。
    He found (the girl) finally after all, as our ancestors said. It was good.

97. "nita m-ula   mə-dəkəl   ki alaw a   imini. ma-taru   a   alaw. padadər
    we   AF-first AF-pick up fish Lig this Sta-big   Lig fish   hook
    咱   先   揀   魚   這   大   魚   勾住
    dida   ki   rawil   a   imini." isia laiki.
    there Nom   arrow   Lig this   he   thus
    那兒   箭   這   他   如此
    「我先揀到這條大魚了。這支箭在那兒勾住大魚了。」他這樣講。
    "I first picked up this fish. A big fish. It has been hooked with this arrow," he said like this.

98. "haw   ha.   ituku,   ikuku."   maa-baxa   rahan   nia.   maa-paha-pahatan.
　　good   sit   sit   Rec-give   words   Asp   Rec-Red-laugh
　　好　　坐　　坐　　交談　　話　　Asp   大家笑

「好！請坐，請坐！」他們高興地交談著。

"Good! Sit down, sit down!" They talked to each other and were laughing.

99. kawki   rakihan   mamaləŋ   a   isia i,   ma-sika-sikad-   a   ka-kitaʔ-ən   a
　　but   child   male   Lig   that   Sta-Red-shy   Lig   look like-PF   Lig
　　但　　子　　男　　　　那　　不好意思　　　看起來

gagam.
the like
樣子

但那青年看起來不太好意思的樣子。

But that young man seemed to be shy.

100. kawki   ina   aba   yaasia i,   hii   ki   rubaŋ   mamais   a   isia i,
　　 but   mother   father   they   　　Nom   young   lady   Lig   that
　　 但　　母　　父　　他們　　　　　年輕　　女　　　那

mi-kita,   maa-puhinis   a   ka-kitaʔ-ən   a   gagam   isia   lia   a i,   ka-kita-ən
AF-see   Rec-fall in love   Lig   look like-PF   Lig   the like   he   Asp   　　look-PF
看　　中意　　　　看起來　　　　樣子　　他　　　　　看

a   gagam.
Lig   the like
　　樣子

那年輕女孩的父母看得出來，她看起來已中意他的樣子了。

But her parents found that the young girl seemed to have fallen in love with him.

101. haw   mini   a   ma-sikuari   isia   ma-sikuari   isia   lia   a,   maa-puhinis   a
　　 good   this   Lig   AF-fall in love   she   AF-fall in love   he   Asp   　　Rec-fall in love   Lig
　　 好　　這樣　　中意　　她　　中意　　他　　　　　中意

gagam   lia.
the like   Asp
樣子

這樣，她愛他，他愛她，他們彼此中意。

In this way, she loved him, he loved her, and they seemed to have fallen in love with each other.

102. isia   laiki,   "alaw ma-taru   padadər a   buzux," ka   laiki namisiw a
     they   thus   fish   Sta-big   hook   Lig arrow   Conj thus   they   Lig
     他們   如此   魚   大   勾住   　 箭   　 如此   他們   　

maa-kuas.
Rec-talk
講

「大魚被箭勾住了，」他們這樣說。

"(There was) a big fish hooked by an arrow," thus they talked to each other.

103. kawki rubaŋ   mamaləŋ a   isia ka,   "haw   ka   ta-kita?-aw naiki
     but   young   man   Lig that Conj good   Conj we-look-Fut my
     但   年輕   男   　 那   　 好   　 咱們看   我的

rawin niani," isia laiki.
bow   that   he   thus
弓   那   他   如此

但那青年說，「好，咱們看我那把弓吧！」

But that young man said, "Alright, let's take a look at my bow!"

104. "usa, ara?-i   aidi punia   a   mulasi ləzək-ən   di mulasi a   dida   i."
     go   take-Imp   at   granary Lig rice   stick into-PF at rice   Lig there
     去   拿   在   穀倉   穀   穿插   穀   那裡

isia laiki, m-ukusa m-ara   lia. pa-kita   sən   lia.
they thus   AF-go   AF-take Asp   Caus-see is said Asp
他們 如此   去   拿   了   使看   據說   了

「去拿那把插在穀倉那邊的弓箭。」他們這樣說，她就去拿來給他看了。

"Go and take what is planted into the rice in granary there." She went to take it, and showed it to him.

105. "a?a, maa-?aisii?ay lia kaxa.   maa-?aisi?ay axad-   a   isia i,
     oh   Rec-same   Asp iron   Rec-same   shaft   Lig that
     　 相同   　 鐵(箭頭) 相同   箭身   　 那

maa-?aisi?ay halupas, aawi lia."
same   long   Asp
相同   長   　

「哎呀！（和我的）相同：鐵頭相同、箭身相同，長度也相同。」

"Oh! It is the same! The arrowhead is the same, the arrowshaft is the same, the length is exactly the same!"

106. kaa-kan-ay daalian nia.
Red-eat-Fut lunch Asp
要吃 午餐
要吃午餐了。
They were eating lunch.

107. isia laiki, m\<a>aka-kawas-ay lia.
then thus AF-Prg-Red-talk-Fut Asp
那時 如此 談
那時他們要（更進一步）交談了。
Then they were talking to each other.

108. "imu ka, haima rubaŋ mamaləŋ suazi maamah? m-ara
you Conj how many young man younger sibling elder brother AF-take
你們 多少 年輕 男人 弟妹 兄 娶

tauxumak lia?"
Agt-house Asp
家後(妻)
「你們有多少兄弟姊妹？婚配了沒有？」
"How many brothers and sisters do you have? Are you married yet?"

109. "mayaw," isia lia. m\<a>aka-kawas-ay lia.
not yet he Asp AF-Prg-Red-talk-Fut Asp
還沒 他 談
「還沒有，」他答道。他們交談了。
"Not yet, " he said. They talked to each other.

110. "yaku ka, ma-purut, maxa-luak, kuah a saysay," rubaŋ mamaləŋ
I Conj Sta-stupid MAXA-poor none Lig anything young man
我 不能幹 變窮 沒 什麼 年輕 男

a maa-kuas.
Lig Rec-say
講
「我很笨拙、貧窮又一無所有。」男青年說。
"I am clumsy, poor, and have nothing." the young man said.

111. | kaw | isia | ki | ina | aba | ruban | mamais, | "kita?-i | na | isiw," | ki |
|-----|------|-----|-----|-----|-------|---------|----------|-----|--------|-----|
| till | then | Nom | mother | father | young | lady | look-Imp | | you | Nom |
| 到 | 那時 | 主 | 母 | 父 | 年輕 | 女 | 看 | | 你 | |

ruban	mamais.	"riak	say?	pauhinis-ən	sai?"
young	lady	good	Q	love-PF	Q
年輕	女	好	嗎	中意	嗎

然後那姑娘的父母對女兒說,「你看他,好嗎?中意嗎?」

Then, the parents of the young lady said to her, "You, look at him. Is it alright? Do you love him?"

112. | isia | laiki, | "m<a>a-baza. | imu | ki | ina | aba | ha. | haw | laiki | imu | ka |
|------|-------|-------------|-----|-----|-----|-----|-----|-----|-------|-----|-----|
| she | thus | AF-Prf-know | you | Nom | mother | father | | good | thus | you | Conj |
| 她 | 如此 | 不知 | 你們 | | 母 | 父 | | 好 | 如此 | 你們 | |

haw	i,	yaaku	ka	saila	la,"	ki	ruban	mamais	a	isia	maa-kuas	i.
good	I	Conj	no opinion		Asp	Nom	young	lady	Lig	that	Rec-talk	
好	我		沒意見				年輕	女		那	講	

那姑娘說,「我不知道。爸媽說好就好。我沒意見。」

"I don't know. If you, mother and father, think it alright, I have nothing to say," thus said the young girl.

113. | kaw | isia | ki | ruban | mamalən | a | isia | ka, | "aa | riak | u | ka, | maxa-luak |
|-----|------|-----|-------|---------|-----|------|-----|-----|------|-----|-----|-----------|
| till | then | Nom | young | man | Lig | that | Conj | ah | good | Conj | | MAXA-poor |
| 到 | 那時 | | 年輕 | 男 | | 那 | | | 好 | | | 變窮 |

ma-purut.	yaaku	yaaku	talima.	kuah	a	saisai."
Sta-stupid	I	I	alone	none	Lig	anything
不能幹	我	我	自己	沒		什麼

然後那男孩說,「即使我很窮、不能幹,除了自己什麼都沒有,也沒關係嗎?」

Then the young man said, "Is it alright even if I'm poor, clumsy, have nothing but myself?"

114. | kaw | isia | lia. | "haw | ka | ma-luhusu | ka | imu | ka | usa | ka, |
|-----|------|------|------|-----|-----------|-----|-----|-----|-----|-----|
| till | then | Asp | good | Conj | Sta-like that | Conj | you | Conj | go | Conj |
| 到 | 那時 | | 好 | | 那樣 | | 你們 | | 去 | |

pa-paxa-mamais-mamalən.	riak	say?	ma-hata-hatan	sai?"
Caus-PAXA-man-woman	good	Q	AF-Red-laugh	Q
使結為夫婦	好	嗎	高興	嗎

到那時,「你們既然如此,就結為夫婦吧!好嗎?高興嗎?」

And then, "Alright. If you are like that, go! We'll make you get married. Is it good? Are you happy?"

115. "ayo, ini mi-kita yaaku a ma-purut maxa-luak ka, haw laiki imu
     oh not AF-see I Lig Sta-stupid MAXA-poor Conj fine like this you
     沒 看 我 不能幹 變窮 好 如此 你們

ka, haw ka m<a>a-baza niam a hakə-hakəzəŋ," laiki rubaŋ
Conj fine Conj AF-Prf-know our Lig old men thus young
好 不知 我們 老人 如此 年輕

mamaləŋ a isia pabarət.
man Lig that answer
男 那 回答

「啊唷，你們不嫌棄我不能幹又窮。即使你們說好，可是不知我父母怎麼樣。」
男青年回答。
"Ayo! You don't see I'm clumsy and poor. Even if you are alright, in this way, I'm not sure about my parents," answered the young man.

116. "haa, haw. nimu a lama, nimu a maaka-hapət."
     good your Lig fate your Lig Rec-love
     好 你們的 命運 你們 相愛

「唉唷，好吧，這是你們的命運，你們相愛。」
"Alright, this is your fate. You love each other."

117. rubaŋ mamaləŋ a isia, haapət isia, haw hinis-ən.
     young man Lig that love her good mind-PF
     年輕 男 那 愛 她 好 心

那青年愛她，且他是快樂的。
That young man loved her, and he was happy.

118. rubaŋ mamais a isia, haapət isia, haw hinis-ən.
     young lady Lig that love him good mind-PF
     年輕 女 那 愛 他 好 心

那少女也有意於他，她是快樂的。
That young girl loved him, and she was happy.

119. isia lia, "haw ka ma-luhusu ka, kaxa-mamais-mamaləŋ laimu uhuni."
     that Asp fine Conj Sta-like this Conj KAXA-man-woman you now
     那樣 好 這樣 結為夫妻 你們 現在

既然如此，（女孩父母說，）「你們現在就結為夫妻吧！」
Thus, (her parents said,) "If it is good in this way, you get married today!"

120. "maa-baxa aku a rahan ina, maa-baxa rahan a aba," isia laiki.
Rec-give I Lig words mother Rec-give words Lig father he thus
給 我 話 母 給 話 父 他 如此
「要告訴我的父母，」他（男的）這樣說。
"I'll tell Mother, I'll tell Father," he said like this.

121. maa. uka ni saw a sən nia, "pa-pa-rəzərəz-ən nia, isia laiki."
other of people Lig said Asp Caus-PA-together-PF Asp that thus
其他 人 說 使在一起 那 如此
有些人說，「讓他們結婚。」
Some people said, "Let them get married."

122. kaw ahuan isia, dusa isia, tuuturu ahuan isia laiki m<a>aka-kawas-ay
then night that two that three night that thus AF-Prg-Red-talk-Fut
晚上 那 二 那 三 晚 那 如此 告訴彼此

lia.
Asp

然後第一晚，第二晚，第三晚，他們討論了。
The first night, the second night, the third night, they talked with each other.

123. m<a>aka-kawas-ay laiki ruban mamalən a isia i, "aa ta-usaʔ-ay na
AF-Prg-Red-talk-Fut thus young man Lig that erh we-go-Fut
要講 年輕 男 那 咱去

ha. mausay kaisay lia laiki naki a ina aba. "ta-usaʔ-ay na
will go how Asp thus my Lig mother father we-go-Fut
要去 怎麼樣 如此 我的 母 父 咱去

iu nahaniʔ-ay."
again come here-Fut
再 來
男青年對他們說，「我得要走了，我要去告訴我父母，看他們的意見如何。我會再回來的。」
The young man talked to them, "I'm leaving. I'll go to see how my parents are. I'll come here again."

124. kawki   ina   aba   a   yaasia   ka,   "mausay   ka,   haw.   m\<a\>a-lalən-ay
     then   mother father Lig they   Conj   will go   Conj   fine   AF-Prg-stay-Fut
              母   父   他們   要去   好   住

     hanisay   a   xinian,   aasi [= ka]   m\<a\>a-tawarək-ay   lia.   hii,   ini
     how many   Lig night   perhaps   AF-Prg-return-Fut   Asp   not
     多少   夜   也許   回來   不

     atu ma-lalən   adaŋ   ahuan,   dusa   ahuan.   haka   riak."
         AF-live   one   night   two   night   really good
         住   一   夜   二   夜   真   好

     她的父母說，「若你要走，沒關係。要住幾夜呢？也許很快。不必住一晚或二晚
     才好。」

     *Her parents said, "If you are leaving, alright. How many nights are you going to stay there?
     Perhaps you'll go and come. You can't come back soon. You'll have to stay a couple of nights, but
     it's alright."*

125. maa-ka-kawas   taxu-bilih.
     Rec-Red-talk   TAXU-return
     ·商量   回去
     商量要回去。
     They talked over about returning.

126. kawki   ina   aba   isia   ka,   "ay,   kaw   ma-luhusu   ka   taə-ʔədər.
     then   mother father that   Conj   oh   then   Sta-like   that Conj TAə-true
     然後   母   父   那個   這樣   說真的

     usa,   imu   ka   usa.   paa-rəzərət."
     go   you   Conj go   Caus-together
     去   你們   去   一起

     然後她父母說，「既然如此，好吧，你們一起去。」
     Her parents said, "If it's really like that, alright. Go! You (two) go together!"

127. haaka   ini   ma-sadial   a   maxa-kə-kəla.
     really   not   Sta-bad   Lig MAXA-Re d-think
     真的   沒   壞   想
     （若他們一起去）他們就不用擔憂。
     (If they went together,) they didn't have to worry.

128. m\<a\>a-kawas   a   isia   ki   maaxa-mamais-mamaləŋ-ay.
     AF-Prg-tell   that   MAAXA-man-woman-Fut
     說   那   結為夫婦
     他們討論要結婚的事。
     They talked over with each other about getting married.

Text 4. 看風水 *Practicing Geomancy*

Narrated by Pan Wan-ji (male, 87)
Recorded by Shigeru Tsuchida in 1969
Interpreted by Pan Jin-yu and translated by Paul Li in 1997.
潘萬吉（男，87歲）口述
土田滋記錄，埔里愛蘭，1969 年 11 月
潘金玉解說，李壬癸翻譯，1997 年

1. ta-duduʔ-aw minah rahan u maa-xaxiray.
   let's-talk-Fut again words Rec-joke
   咱講 再 話 談笑
   咱們再說笑談吧。
   Let's talk about a fun story again.

2. iki maxa-riak a saw la. m<a>a-ha-hadas di disiw i di laŋu lia.
   Nom MAXA-rich Lig man AF-Prg-Red-have fun at there at yard Asp
   富 人 遊玩 那裡 庭院
   有一個富人，他在庭院裡遊玩。
   A rich man was having fun there in the front yard.

3. lahadəŋ daran tasiaw lia i.
   gate road perhaps Asp
   大門 路 可能
   可能門外就是馬路。
   Perhaps the road was outside the gate.

4. laiki kii-kitaʔ-ay na saw a sən a takarat kii-kita daxə
   thus Red-see-Fut person Lig was said Lig geomancer Red-look ground
   如此 看 人 據說 風水師 看 地

   tasiaw lia. haui lia.
   perhaps Asp
   可能
   據說有位看風水的先生正好在附近觀看。
   It was said a geomancer was looking around.

5. "p<a>uzah di asay ki takarad- a isiw? saasay pai siw?"
   Prg-come at where Nom geomancer Lig you what Q you
   來 何處 風水師 你 什麼 你
   「你風水先生從哪裡來的？你在做什麼？」
   "Where are you from, geomancer? What are you doing?"

6. kawki   takarad- a   isia ka,   "yaaku ka   kii-kita   daxə,   kii-kita
   then   geomancer Lig that Conj   I   Conj Red-look   ground Red-look
            風水師   那   我   看   地理   看

   maatu-xuma,   ra-rubaŋ-ən saw   a   daxə,   ka   m<a>a-ha-hadas."
   build-house   Red-burry-PF person Lig ground Conj AF-Prg-Red-have fun
   蓋房子   埋   人   地理   遊玩

   風水先生說，「我在看地理、看蓋房子和埋葬地。我（到此地）遊玩。」
   Then that geomancer said, "I am a practicing geomancy, discerning the geography where to build a house or where to bury a (dead) person, and I'm just playing around."

7. "aay." kaw   ki   maxa-riak   a   saw   isia ka.
   yes   then Nom MAXA-rich   Lig person that Conj
                      富   人   那

   那個富人說，「喔！」。
   "Oh, I see," said the rich man.

8. isia ka sɛ̃   oŋ   sən, oŋ   gii sən   isia lia.
   that Conj family name Ong said Ong Gi   said that Asp
   那   （姓   王）據說   王   義   據說   那

   那個富人姓王，名義。
   He was Ong by family name, and was called Ong Gi.

9. maxa-riak   a   saw   u, uka   nu saw   a   sən.
   MAXA-rich   Lig person other   people Lig is said
   富有   人   其他   人   所說

   如人們所說，他很富有。
   Other people said that he was a rich man.

10. kaw isia ki   sɛ̃   oŋ   a   oŋ   gii a   isia laiki maxa-kə-kəlaʔ-ay.
    till   then Nom family name Ong Lig Ong Gi   Lig that thus MAXA-Red-think-Fut
    到 那時   姓   王   王   義   那   如此 想

    王義在考慮。
    Then that Ong Gi was thinking like this.

11. "p<a>uzah di   asay   a   takarat   pai siw?" laila i.
    Prg-come   at   where Lig geomancer you thus
    來   何處   風水師   Q   你   那樣

    「你風水先生從哪裡來的？」他那樣問。
    "Where are you from, geomancer?" he asked.

12. isia laiki, "yaaku ka p<a>uzah di miaadua awas a saw hayaku."
    that thus I Conj Prg-come at yonder ocean Lig person I
    那個 如此 我 來 那邊(海外) 海 人 我
    那個（風水先生）說，「我是在那邊海外的人。」
    He said, "I am a man from overseas."

13. yamisiw ki x<in>api tasiaw lia.
    they Nom Prf-hairbraided perhaps Asp
    他們 編髮 可能
    他們可能編髮。
    Maybe they had braided hair.

14. isia laiki, kaw isia laiki uŋ gii isia lia. maxa-riak a saw u,
    that thus then till then Ong Gi that Asp MAXA-rich Lig person
    那個 如此 到 那時 王 義 那 富有 人

    haapəd- u rakihan ali. haapəd- u ma-taru a taumalaʔ-ən, isia
    love child grandchild love Sta-big Lig officer-PF that
    愛 子 孫 愛 大 官 那個

    laiki haw lia.
    thus fine Asp
    如此 好
    那個王義有錢人，愛子孫，愛當大官，那樣就好。
    That Ung Gi was a rich man, who loved his descendants, and wanted them to become great officers.

15. asuʔ-un di naamisiw karum a xuma maaka-kawas-ay lia.
    carry-PF at their inside Lig house Rec-talk-Fut Asp
    帶 他們 裡 家 交談 了
    他帶風水先生到他家裡去談。
    He took the geomancer to their home to talk to each other.

16. isia laiki, "haw lia."
    he thus fine Asp
    他 如此 好 了
    他說，「好。」
    He said, "Good!"

17. kaw isia i lia, ma-laləŋ adaŋ a xinian dida lia a, ma-laləŋ laisia.
    till then Asp AF-live one Lig night there Asp AF-stay there
    到 那時 住 一 夜 那裡 住 那
    到那時，他留（風水先生）在他那裡住一晚。
    Then he stayed (the geomancer) overnight there.

18. kaw   duu-dusa   dali   pədəsax   a   isia   lia.   mausay   lia.
    till   second   day   light   Lig   that   Asp   will go   Asp
    到   第二   日   天亮   要去   了

    到第二天天亮了。要去了。

    On the second day it became light. He was leaving.

19. "maanu   alih   ki   nimu   a   dini   ra-rubaŋ-an   u   saw,"   tasiaw   lia.
    far   near Nom   your   Lig   here   Red-bury-LF   people   perhaps   Asp
    遠   近   你們   這兒 墓地   人   可能

    「你們這裡的墓地遠還是近？」他那樣問。

    "Is your graveyard far or near?" maybe he asked.

20. isia   laiki,   "maanu   maanu   nahada,   alih   alih   nahada."
    he   thus   far   far   exist   near   near   exist
    他   如此   遠   遠   有   近   近   有

    「遠的有，近的也有。」他如此說。

    He said, "Some are far, while the others are near."

21. "haw   ka   ma-luhusu   ka   tia   na   ta-kitaʔ-aw,"   isia   laiki   takarad- a
    fine   Conj   Sta-like this   Conj   go   let's-see-Fut   he   thus   geomancer   Lig
    好   如此   去   咱看   他   如此   風水師

    isia   i.
    that
    那

    「既然如此，好，走吧！咱們去看吧！」那風水先生說。

    "If that's the case, good! Let's go and see!" the geomancer said like this.

22. kaw   maxa-riak   a   saw   isia   i,   haimisiw   a   paray,   haimisiw   a   daxə,
    then   MAXA-rich   Lig   person   that   that much   Lig   money   that much   land
    富有   人   那   那麼多   錢   那麼多   地

    haapəd- u   rakihan   a   maxa-taumalaʔ-ən,   haapəd- ali   a
    love   child   Lig   become-officer-PF   love   grandchild   Lig
    愛   子   做官   愛   孫

    maxa-taumalaʔ-ən,   tasiaw   lia.
    become-officer-PF   maybe   Asp
    做官   可能

    大概那個富人有很多錢、很多地，他愛兒子做大官，愛孫子做大官。

    Maybe that rich man had much money, many lands, wanted his children to become great officers, his grandchildren to get great titles.

23. mayaw nahada u [sooi to si ane la hõ.] (in Taiwanese)[1]
    still exist all
    還沒 有   所以 都 是 安呢 吧?
    還有其他的。
    (But his offsprings) did not become big officers yet. [That's the case, isn't it?]

24. isia laiki, mausay lia piaalay lia mu-ririx u uka u a saw a sən
    he   thus will go Asp begin Asp AF-search other   person is said
    他   如此 要去   開始   找   別   人   據說

    [uka ni saw a sən] a ra-rubaŋ-an a binayu tasiaw lia i.
    other by people Lig said Lig Red-bury-LF Lig mountain maybe Asp
    別   人   據說   墓地(埋)   山   可能
    那時他們要去開始找,如人所說的可以埋藏的山。
    Perhaps then they were going to begin to look for a good graveyard in the mountain.

25. isia laiki, mi-kita lia la, haw i lia. mu-ririx u daxə lia.
    that thus AF-see Asp   fine Asp AF-search land Asp
    那個 如此 看   好   找   地   了
    那時他們看(地),也找到地了。
    Then they looked for land and found a piece of land.

26. kii-kitaʔ-ay dua, mata di asay a mi-kita, mata di daya rabaxan, tasiaw
    Red-see-Fut   there from at where Lig AF-see from at east south   maybe
    看   那邊 從   何處 Lig 看   從   東 南   可能

    lia i.
    Asp

    要看那邊,從那邊看,據說向東南。
    They were looking at the land, from where did they look at? Maybe from south-east.

27. "niima r<in>ubaŋ pai ni i mu-zizay" isia lia i.
    whose Prf-bury Q this Sta-old   he   Asp
    誰的 埋   這個 舊   他
    「這是誰的舊墓?」
    "Whose grave is this old one?" he said.

---

[1] Pazih equivalent for the Taiwanese expression is *kinaluhusuʔ-an*. Here after all Taiwanese expressions are indicated by [ ].

28. "imini ka, hii, ima nahada. nimu a akuŋ sai apu sai?
    this Conj who exist your Lig grandfather grandmother
    這 誰 有 你們 公 Q 祖母 Q

    ima a bul adu sən dini. aubil a dali ka, rakihan ali ka,
    who Lig bone put away said here later Lig day Conj child grandchild
    誰 骨 放 據說 這兒 後 日 子 孫

    m<a>a-rukad-ay nahada?-ay maaxa-taumala?-ən haa," lailai ki takarad-
    AF-Prg-go out-Fut exist-Fut become-officer-PF thus Nom geomancer
    出來 有 做官 如此 風水師

    a isia m<a>a-kuas i.
    Lig that AF-Prg-say
    那 講

是你們的祖父或祖母？據說誰的骨頭放在這兒，日後出來的子孫會當大官。」那個風水先生說。

"This one, who is (buried here)? Your grandfather? Or your grandmother? Whose bones are put away here? In later days there may be your descendants becoming great officers," said that geomancer.

29. kaw isia ki uŋ gi a isia a m<a>a-kuas i. "siũ tio." [= haw] hai
    till then Nom Ong Gi Lig that Lig AF-Prg-say fine
    到 那時 主 王 義 那 講 好

    maxa-kəla lia, hii.
    MAXA-think Asp
    想

然後王義要說，「好。」他想。

Then that Oŋ Gi thought, saying, "Good!"

30. "kuah a imisu a daxə aa, kau nahada imisiw a daxə, nahada,..."
    none Lig that Lig land till exist that Lig land exist
    沒 那 地 到 有 那 地 有

    imisiw a takarad- a mu-baza maa-kuas.
    that Lig geomancer Lig AF-know Rec-tell
    那 先生 知 講

「沒有那塊地。若有那塊地…」那個風水先生知道那樣講。

"There is no that land, then there is that land, and there is...," said that geomancer.

31. "aay, paray ka nahada. mausay haima?" ma-siup laiki nisia
    Oh money Conj exist will go how much AF-caress this way by him
    錢 有 要去 多少 撫摸 如此 他

maxa-kəla.
MAXA-think
想

「喔！（如果要）錢，（我）有。要多少才可以擺平呢？」（有錢人）撫（鬚）心裡想。

"Oh, (if he requires) money, (I) do have some. How much will it cost?" Thus he thought, caressing his beard.

32. kaw isia ki takarad- a isia m\<a>a-kuas i. isia laiki, "niima pai
till then Nom geomancer Lig that AF-Prg-say he thus whose Q
到 那時 主 風水師 那 講 他 如此 誰的

mini rubaŋ-ən saw ki daxə a imini?"
here buried-PF person Nom ground Lig here
這兒 埋 人 地 這兒

然後風水先生說，「這塊地是誰埋在這裡的？」

Then, that geomancer said, "whose was buried in this ground?"

33. "sasaiʔ-ən a gagam?" lailaiki, un gi a isia i.
what to do-PF Lig looking thus Ong Gi Lig that
如何,什麼 樣子 如此 王 義 那

「這樣子如何是好？」王義問道。

"How should it be done?" asked Oŋ Gi.

34. kaw ki takarad- a isia ka "kaluhuniʔi. nahada paray isiw. niima
till Nom geomancer Lig that Conj do like this exist money you whose
到 主 風水師 那 這樣 有 錢 你 誰的

pai mini, paturuʔ-i di adaŋ" ka, "mausay haima paray?" lailaiki.
Q this move-Imp at other place Conj will go how much money thus
這 使遷移 別處 要去 多少 錢 如此

風水先生如此說，「這樣吧，你有錢。誰的在這裡就叫他遷移至別處，看要多少錢。」

Then the geomancer said, "Do like this. You have got money. Whosever this grave may be, make them move to some other place." "How much will it cost?" asked the man.

35. takarad- a isia m\<a>a-kuas. "isia laiki, aa, haapət," tasiaw,
geomancer Lig that AF-Prg-say they thus oh love maybe
先生 那 講 他們 如此 愛 可能

風水先生說，「若你給他們這麼多錢，他們會接受的。」

The geomancer said, "If you give such an amount of money, they will accept it."

36. [nah tu] "nahada paray, maxa-luak a saw ka [kong tio] paray.
    　　　　　exist　money　MAXA-poor Lig person Conj mention　money
    　　　　　有　　錢　　變窮　　　　人　　　　　講著　　錢

    haw ha ta-paturuʔ-aw."
    fine　　let's move-Fut
    好　　咱還移

    「我有錢。窮人一談到錢就會答應還移。」
    "I have got money. For a poor man, money can make him move the grave!"

37. mausay laiki nisia nu saw a maxa-kəla.
    will go　thus　his　of　person Lig MAXA-think
    要去　　如此　他的　　人　　　想

    他那樣地想。
    That is what he thought.

38. [ikeesi] takarad- a m<a>a-kuas ki uŋ gii a isia, "paturuʔ-i ka
    　　　　　geomancer Lig AF-Prg-say Nom Ong Gi Lig that move-Imp Conj
    　　　　　風水師　　講　　　　王 義　那　　遷移

    mausay haima paray [paarahudun]" siiki maa-kuas.
    will go how much money　　　　　　　thus　Rec-tell
    要去　多少　　錢　　　　　　　　　這樣 講

    風水先生對王義這樣說,「遷移的話,不知要花多少錢。」
    The geomancer said to Ung Gi, "We don't know how much it will cost to make them move (the grave)."

39. haw lai lia. kaw isia lia. m<a>aka-kawas-ay lia, "niima pai mini?"
    fine　　Asp till　then Asp AF-Prg-Red-talk-Fut Asp whose Q this
    好　　　　到　那時　　交談　　　　　　　　　　誰的　　這個

    那就好,到那時,交談了了,「這個是誰的?」
    Good, They were talking to each other, "Whose grave is this?"

40. isia ki "niam," laila.
    that ours　　thus
    那　我們的　那樣

    那人那樣說,「是我們的。」
    "That is ours," he said.

41. "[sẽ　　　sã hũe] pai mu?"
    family name what　Q you
    [姓什麼]　　　　　你們
    「你們姓什麼?」
    "What is your family name?"

42. "sɛ̃   tan,"   laila.
    family name Tan   thus
    姓   陳   那樣
    「姓陳，」那樣回答。
    "It's Tan," he said.

43. aa,   ləkət   la.
    oh   just right   Asp
          恰巧,剛好
    剛好。
    It is just right.

44. takarad- a   isia ka   m<a>a-kuas   ka,   "imu   mu-ruban   dini   a
    geomancer Lig that Conj AF-Prg-say   Conj you   AF-bury   here   Lig
    風水師   那   講   你們   埋   此地

    daxə   ka,   aubin a   dali m<a>arukad-ay   taumalaʔ-ən,   naki a
    ground Conj later Lig   day   AF-Prg-come out-Fut   great officer-PF my   Lig
    地   後   日   出來   大官   我的

    ma-kuas.   yaku ka   p<in>auzah   di   masu-ruhun   a   saw.   pitərəd-i."
    AF-tell   I   Conj Prf-come   at   Mainland   Lig   person   remember-Imp
    講話   我   來   外地   人   記住
    那個風水先生說，「你們在此埋葬，將來會生出做大官的（子孫），這是我講的
    話。我是從外地來的。記住！」
    That geomancer told, "If you bury (the dead) in this ground, a great officer will come out (= be born),
    I would say. I am a man from the mainland. Remember it."

45. isia   lia   ka   m-ukusa   m<a>a-kuas   di   yamisiw-an   yasia ka   namisiw
    that   Asp   Conj AF-go   AF-Prg-say   at   they-Loc   they   Top   their
    那時   去   講   他們   他們   他們的

    m<a>a-kuas,   "imu   hapət   riak,   yamin   hapət   riak.   (sii)   kaluhusuʔi
    AF-Prg-say   you   want   good   we   want   good   do like this
    講   你們 要 好   我們 要 好   這樣

    m<a>a-kuas.
    AF-Prg-say
    講
    那時（地理先生）去對墳主人的地方說，教他們要那樣講才好，「你們要好，我
    們也要好。你要那樣講」
    He went to them to tell them, "You want a good thing, we also want a good thing. You should talk
    like this!" he said.

46. haw "yaku ka mausay lia," liaki takarat.
    fine I Conj will go Asp thus geomancer
    好 我 要去 了 如此 風水師

    「我要走了。」地理先生說。

    "I'll go now," thus the geomancer said.

47. taxu isia lia ka, turu a dali lia ka, mi-kiliw balas mausay
    till then Asp Conj three Lig day Asp Conj AF-cry worker will go
    到 那時 了 三 天 叫 工人 要去

    mu-daxan r<in>ubaŋ a isia.
    AF-dig out Prf-buried Lig that
    挖 埋 那

    到那時第三天，叫工人去挖掘那個埋葬的地方。

    After three days, he sent for workers to dig out the buried (corpse).

48. daa-daxan-ay lia ka, puzah adaŋ a rubaŋ mamais.
    Red-dig-Fut Asp Conj come one Lig young lady
    挖掘 來 一 年輕 女

    剛要挖掘時，來了一個年輕女子。

    When they were about to dig, one young girl came.

49. "saasay pai mu? daa-daxan-ay niam a aba r<in>ubaŋ dini pai mu?
    do what Q you Red-dig-Fut our Lig father Prf-bury here Q you
    做什麼 Q 你們 挖 我們 父 埋 此地 你們

    yaku ka ma-baza imu hapət dini riak a daxə. aubin a dali ka
    I Conj AF-know you love here good Lig land later Lig day Conj
    我 知 你們 愛 此地 好 地方 後 日

    m<a>a-rukad-ay riak a rakihan ali. iu yamin ka sasay-ən
    AF-Prg-go out-Fut good Lig child grandchild and we Conj what to do-PF
    出來 好 子 孫 且 我們 怎麼辦

    lia? imu ka hapət taumala?-ən, yamin ka hapət taumala?-ən.
    Asp you Conj love officer-PF we Conj love officer-PF
    你們 愛 做官 我們 愛 做官

ana	mu-daxan	ka	niam.	mausay	pidudu	taumalaʔ-ən	haxamin."
don't	AF-dig out	Conj	Ours	will go	tell	officer-PF	we
別	挖		我們的	去	告	官	我們

「你們在幹什麼？你們要挖我們父親在這裡的墳？我知到你們喜歡這塊好地方，將來會出生好子孫。那我們怎麼辦？你們愛做官，我們也愛做官。別挖我們的（墳地）。（不然）我們要去告官。」

"What are you doing? Here you are digging up the place where our father was buried. I know you love this nice place. In the future good descendants will be born. What shall we do? You want to become great officers, we also want to become great officers. Don't dig up ours! (Or else) we'll go and sue you at the court."

D. Pazih Texts Recorded by Erin Asai

淺井惠倫在烏牛欄採集 (1936)，發音人大概是潘登貴（年齡不詳）
李壬癸根據潘金玉修訂 (2000.11.5)

　　這三則原來由淺井惠倫 (1936) 所記錄的部分巴宰語料，前二則由李壬癸在
2000 年 11 月 5 日，根據潘金玉的口述修訂於愛蘭。第三則「射太陽」於 2001
年 9 月 10 日才由土田滋譯解出來。語料第一行粗體字是淺井的原記錄，第二行
則是李壬癸或土田滋修訂。

　　The following three Pazih texts were recorded by Erin Asai in 1936, his informant being
probably Pan Teng-kuei, and edited by Paul Li (Texts 1 and 2) and Shigeru Tsuchida (Text 3)
with the assistance of a Pazih native speaker, Pan Jin-yu, in November 2000 and September
2001 respectively. In each sentence the first line in boldface is the original transcription by
Asai, while the second line is the edited version by Li (Texts 1 and 2) or Tsuchida (text 3).

Text 1. 競爭 Competition

1. **iminika　　pijarai　madusa　　daxə　aubina　dari　pirulik　a　kakawas.**
   imini　ka　pialay　maa-dusa　　daxə,　aubin　a　dali　pirurik　a　ka-kawas.
   this　　first　AF/Rec-divide　land　later　day　violate　Red-word
   這　　　起初　分開　　　土地　後來　日　違背　　故事
   這個故事是說起初人們把土地分為兩半，但後來他們卻違背（當初的協定）。
   This is a story that, in the beginning the land was divided into two parts, but later on (the people)
   violated (the original agreement).

2. **pijarai　　　makarja,　　aubirjaka　　mataŋiz.**
   pialay　ka　maaka-riak,　aubin lia ka　maa-taŋis.
   first　　Rec-good　　later　　　Rec-hostile
   起初　　和好　　　後來　　互不和睦
   起初大家相安無事，後來卻不和睦。
   In the beginning they were friendly to each other, but later on they became hostile.

3. **zaxu　　rjaka　muttaxai　nitta　a　sau　　paze.**
   zaaxu　liaka　mu-tahay　nita　a　saw　pazih.
   aborigines　then　AF-kill　　our　　people　Pazih
   生番　　然後　殺　　　咱　　人　　巴宰
   然後生番殺害咱們巴宰人。
   Then the mountain aborigines killed our Pazih people.

4. znira   ka imini tia di azaŋ   malarəŋ
   "ini riak ka imini, tia di adaŋ   ma-laləŋ."
   not good   this go   other place AF-live
   不   好   這 去   別處   住
   「此處不好，就到別處去住吧！」（他們說）
   "This place is no good, go somewhere else to live!" (they said).

5. xao baba ha   sau.
   haw, baabah a saw.
   good many   people
   好   多   人
   好了，很多人了。
   Good! (We) got many people then.

6. aobil nahaza. hakəzuŋ mamais   makawas   ana   matururu.   tomaraji
   aubil nahada hakəzəŋ mamais ma-kawas, "ana matu-ruru! tumalaʔ-i
   later exist   old   woman   AF-say   don't MATU-move listen-Imp
   後來 有   老   婦   說   別   遷移   聽！
   naki   **kakawas—paobabazai.**   **paubabazaji**   **mitalam**
   naki   a   ka-kawas—pa-u-ba-bazaʔ-i.   pa-u-ba-bazaʔ-i   mi-talam,
   my   Red-word Caus-U-Red-know-Imp Caus-U-Red-know-Imp AF-race
   我的   話   學！   學！   跑
   rakirakihal sau   aubiladari. lirjakaita.
   raki-rakihan saw.   aubil a dali ri-riak a ita."
   Red-young   people later   day Red-good   we
   年輕   人   後來   日   好   咱
   後來有一個老婦說，「別搬遷了！聽我的話！學習賽跑，年輕人！將來對咱們好。」
   Later an old woman said, "Don't move (to another place)! Listen to me! Learn to race, young men! It will be good for us."

7. xəzəm a sau   mahara-ai   rakirakihan sau   paobabaza-ai   mitaram.
   xəzəm a saw   ma-xaraʔ-ay raki-rakihan saw   pa-u-ba-bazaʔ-ay mi-talam.
   estate   people AF-call-Fut   Red-young   people Caus-U-Red-know-Fut AF-race
   地產   人   叫   年輕   人   要學   跑
   地主叫年輕人要學習賽跑。
   The landlady told young men to learn to race.

8. **musiŋar banais. musiŋar kau muzaməz.**

mu-siŋar	banais,	mu-siŋar	kau[1]	mu-zamut.
AF-chase	name	AF-chase	until	AF-catch up
追趕	人名	追趕	到	追上

追趕 Banais 一直追到追上為止。

They chased after Banais until they caught up with him.

9. **maosa-ai marababarəd.**

m\<a>usaʔ-ay	marababarət.
AF-Prg-go-Fut	revenge?
要去	復仇?

他們要去復仇(?)。

They wanted to revenge(?).

10. **pijarai isija makarja ka-ini matururu daxə**

pialay	isia	maaka-riak	ka,	ini	matu-ruru	daxə.
since	that	Rec-good		not	MATU-move	land
從此	那	和好		不	還移	地

從此大家和睦相處,就不還移到別處。

They had been friendly to each other ever since, so that they did not move to any other place.

---

1 The form *kau* is a loan from Taiwanese 到 *kau* 'till, until'.

Text 2. 洪水 *Flood*

1. **tadudo   manu(h) raraparai rja   awas rja.**
   ta-dudu   maanu   mə-rərap   lia ki awas lia.
   let's-talk ancient AF-overflow Asp   sea   Asp
   說   遠古   溢出   了   海   了
   讓我講遠古海水溢出的故事。
   Let's talk about the ancient overflow of the sea.

2. **isija pərət a sau.   tuzwaka zinakai turwaka kinawas.**
   isia   pərəd a saw,   tuzuak a z<in>akay, tuzuak a k<in>awas.
   that   place people bad   Prf-behavior bad   Prf-word
   那   處   人   壞   行為   壞   話
   那地方的人言行敗壞。
   The people there were ill-behaved and spoke ill of others.

3. **maisa   diaki aba kaibabau.   maxa paudarai   udaru sinaxu.**
   ma-isat lia ki aba kai-babaw, maxa pa-udal-ay udal u sinaw.
   Sta-angry Asp God Sta-above then Caus-rain-Fut rain wash
   生氣   了   神   上   然後 使降下   雨   洗
   天神震怒，使天降下大雨洗劫大地。
   God was enraged and then caused it to rain hard to wash the earth.

4. **isija rja makatətənəbai   awas. binibini/tənətənəb rja.**
   Isia lia maxa təə-tənəb-ay   awas, bini-bini/tənətənəp lia.
   that then Red-inundate-Fut   sea   Red-full   Asp
   那   然後 淹水   海   滿滿   了
   然後海水淹起來，滿滿地（溢出陸地）。
   The sea was full, overflowed, and inundated all the lands.

5. **kaidua   haduwa   tipoza   rarju.**
   kai-dua hadua   tipuzu a rariw.
   stay-there there   top   mountain name
   在那邊   就在那邊 尖頂   山名
   （快要淹到）那邊 Rariw 山頂上了。
   (It was going to reach) there the top of Rariw Mountain.

6. **banakaisi   saboŋakaisi.   maxa-mausa-ai.   tiporu a rarju.**

bana	kaisi	sabuŋ	a	kaisi	maxa m-a-usaʔ-ay	tipuzu	a	rariw.
male name		female name			AF-Prg-go-Fut	top		mountain name
男名		女名			去	尖頂		山名

Bana Kaisi 和 Sabuŋ Kaisi 他們就要到山頂上去。

Bana Kaisi (man) and Sabung Kaisi (woman) were going to the top of Rariw.

7. **makamawa-kərai   tipozua   rarju.   babireh   raisja   tənəbtənəb a darom.**

maxa	pa-sakəl-ay	tipuzu	a	rariw,	babilih	laisia	tənə-tənəb-	a	dalum.
then	AF-arrive-Fut	top		name	look back	they	Red-inundate		water
然後	快抵達	尖頂		山名	回頭看	他們	淹		水

快要到達 Rariw 山頂時，他們回頭一看，水逐漸淹上來。

As they were arriving at the top of Rariw, they looked back and saw that the water was coming up.

8. **maxamaxato   kərai   tipuzua   rarju.**

maxa	ma-xatukul-ay	tipuzu	a	rariw.
then	AF-climb-Fut	top		mountain name
然後	一直爬上	尖頂		山名

於是他們一直向上爬到 Rariw 山頂。

Then they were climbing to the top of Rariw.

9. **maxamaxatokərai   itoko   babau.**

maxa	ma-xatukul-ay	di	ituk	babaw.
then	AF-climb-Fut		top	above
然後	要爬上		頂	上

他們爬到山頂上。

Then they climbed to the very top.

10. **tənəbtənəb   darom   maxamaxato   kərai   ŋazus   batakan.**

tənə-tənəp	dalum	maxa	ma-xatukul-ay	ŋadus	patakan.
Red-inundate	water		AF-climb-Fut	top	bamboo
淹	水		要爬上	尖端	竹

水逐漸淹上來，要升高到竹子的末端了。

The water was inundating and reaching the top of bamboos.

11. **asai   ka   imini   paurihadai   rja.**

asay	ka	imini	p<a>urihad-ay	lia.
why		this	Prg-die-Fut	Asp
為什麼		這	死	了

為什麼這樣？（我們）快要死了嗎？

Why is it so (bad)? (Are we) going to die?

12. maxara   raŋadai. sinusana   kaduxu   makasesehaŋai   udaru   sinixu.

ma-xara	laŋad-ay	sinusana	kaduxu	maka-si-sihaŋ-ay	udal	sinixu.
AF-call	name-Fut	chant	incantation	MAKA-Red-stop-Fut	rain	big
叫	名字	用	咒語	停	雨	大?

他們念咒語要大雨停。

They chanted incantations to stop the heavy rain.

13. maxahopiai   darəm awas.

maxa	hupi-ay	ki	dalum	awas.
then	recede-Fut	Nom	water	sea
然後	退		水	海

因此海水退了。

So the water of the sea was receding.

14. makakakitaan   tipuzu a   binaju.

maxa	ka-kitaʔ-ən	tipuzu	a	binayu.
then	Red-look-PF	top	Lig	mountain
然後	看	尖頂		山

快要看得見各山頂了。

Then the tops of mountains showed up.

15. maka kikizihai   tipuz   a rarju.

maxa	kii-kizih-ay	tipuzu	a	rariw.
then	Red-come down-Fut	top		mountain name
然後	在下來	尖頂		山名

他們就要從高山頂上下來。

They descended from the top of Rariw Mountain.

16. maxamasakərai   ruburubu a daxə.

maxa	ma-sakəl-ay	ruburubu	a	daxə.
then	AF-arrive-Fut	below		land
然後	到達	下面		地

他們要到達下面的陸地上。

They were arriving at the land down below.

17. aza   maxaruwaru abasaysuazi.

haza	maxa-ruaru	abasan	suazi.
exist	produce-sad	elder sibling	younger sibling
有	傷心	兄姊	弟妹

他們兄妹（姊弟）很傷心。

They siblings were sad.

18. makakikitaai   ajam darupit.

maxa ki-kitaʔ-ay   ayam darupit.

then Red-see-Fut   bird black bulbul

然後 看   鳥   紅嘴黑鵯

他們看得到紅嘴黑鵯了。

Then they saw a black bulbul (bird sp., *hypsipetes madagascariensis*).

19. asai   paimisu   maxakaiarixai   mikita.

"asay pai misiw? maxa kayalih-ay mi-kita.

what Q that   then near-Fut   AF-see

什麼   那   然後 靠近   看

「那是什麼？」然後他們靠近去看。

"What is it there?" Then they went close to look at it.

20. kitakita siaun   rja pijaxun   maixih.

kita-kita siaən lia piaxun

Red-look carefully Asp millet   bundle

一直看 好,仔細 了 小米   一束

仔細地看是一束小米。

They looked at it carefully, and it was a bundle of millet.

21. raru   isija   xoma   rikiburu.

raru   isia   xuma   rikibul.

maybe that home   granary

大概   那個 家   穀倉

那大概是人家的穀倉（在他們找到小米的地方）。

That was probably the barn of a house (where they found the millet).

22. rikiburai dini   maxamara-ai   paridaxai.

rikibul aidini. maxa m-araʔ-ay pa-ridax-ay.

granary here   then AF-take-Fut Caus-sun-Fut

穀倉   這裡   然後 拿   曬

穀倉在這裡了。他們拿（小米）去曬。

Here was a granary. Then they took the millet to dry in the sun.

23. nahada piaxun   kwaxaruzuŋ.

nahada piaxun, kuah a luzuŋ.

exist   millet   none   mortar

有   小米   沒   臼

有小米，卻沒有臼。

There was millet, but no mortar.

24. madurjarjah   raijasija.
matu-ria-riax   lai   yasia.
AF-Red-seek   Asp   they
一直找   了   他們
他們到處找。
They looked around.

25. maxakikitaai   haosamakasadit.
maxa   kii-kitaʔ-ay   haw   sa-maka-sadit.
then   Red-see-Fut   good   SA-MAKA-brick
然後   看   好   黏板岩(原意指"可用來舖的磚")
然後他們找到了黏板岩。
Then they found a slate.

26. makasusubuai   piaxun   u   mairih.
maxa   su-suruʔ-ay   piaxun   u   ma-irix.
then   Red-pound-Fut   millet   Sta-smooth
然後   搗   小米   滑
用來搗小米很平滑。
Then they pounded millet and it was smooth.

27. naxada   rikipijaxun   kwah   burajan.
nahada   lia   ki   piaxun,   kuah   bulayan.
exist   Asp   millet   none   pan
有   了   小米   沒   鍋
有了小米,卻沒有鍋子。
Now that they had millet, but there was no pan.

28. madukarikarijah.   maxakikitaai   rati ka   burajan.
matu-kariakariax,   maxa   kii-kitaʔ-ay   ratik   a   bulayan.
look around   then   Red-see-Fut   broken   pan
到處找   然後   看   破   鍋
他們到處找,然後找到了一個破鍋子。
They looked around and then found a broken pan.

29. maxabaurjakai   madukoh   batu.
maxa   b<a>uriak-ay   mu-dukuh   batu.
then   Prg-make-Fut   AF-prop up   stone
然後   要製作   舉起來   石
他們把石頭支撐起來(做灶)。
They propped up stones (to make a stove).

30. **sasaiinirja kwah hapui.**
"sasay-ən lia kuah hapuy?"
what to do-PF Asp none fire
怎麼辦 了 沒有 火
「沒有火,怎麼辦?」（他們自己問道）
"What shall we do without fire?" (they asked themselves)

31. **maxaduduruai ajam a kasju. usa su manuh babau kawas.**
maxa du-dulu?-ay ayam a kidis, "usa siw maanu babaw kawas
then Red-send-Fut bird big black drongo go you far above sky
然後 推派 鳥 大卷尾(烏秋) 去 你 遠 上 天

arai hapui.
ara-i hapuy."
take-Imp fire
拿 火
然後他們推派一隻大卷尾鳥,「你到遠處天上去取火!」
Then they sent a big black drongo (bird) to get it, "You go far away to the sky above to get fire!"

32. **mukusa raisja mara kuira. maasa kərairja. putjuk rjaki hapui.**
m-ukusa lai sia m-ara kuila, m<a>a-sakəl-ay putiuk lia ki hapuy.
AF-go Asp it AF-take although AF-Prg-arrive-Fut extinguish Asp fire
去 了 牠 拿 雖然 快到達 熄 了 火
雖然牠去取了（火回來）,但快到達時火卻熄滅了。
Although it went to get fire, as it was arriving, the fire extinguished.

33. **makamadukarikarja.**
maxa madukariakariax lia.
then look around Asp
然後 找 了
他們到處找。
They looked around.

34. **maxakikitaai xaxawas pauzut.**
maxa ki-kita?-ay xaxawas p<a>uzut.
then Red-see-Fut vine drill
然後 看 肉藤 鑽子
他們看到了肉藤和鑽子（生火的材料）。
Then they saw a vine and a drill (i.e., materials to make a fire).

35. azam   a   maxaxatan   jasija   kausa.
azəm   a   ma-ha-hatan   yasia   kausa.
suddenly   AF-Red-laugh   they   two
突然   高興,笑   他們   兩人
他們倆忽然高興地笑起來。
All of a sudden they two bacame very happy and laughed.

36. makaxataxatan   jasija   kausa.
maka-hata-hatan   yasia   kausa.
MAKA-Red-happy   they   two
很高興   他們   兩人
他們兩人真的很高興。
Both of them were really very happy.

37. maxamararamai   piaxunu   mairih.
maxa   ma-ra-ramay   piaxun   ma-irix.
then   AF-Red-cook   millet   Sta-smooth
然後   煮   小米   滑
他們煮滑潤的小米。
They cooked the well pounded millet.

38. piarai   isija   rja   maxa-raramaxai   ruburubu   daxə.
pialay   isia   lia   maxa raa-rarum-ay   ruburubu   daxə.
since   that   then   Red-increase-Fut   below   ground
從此   那   然後   要增加(人)   下面   地
從那時起,他們想要增加人口。
From then on, they would like to increase human population.

39. sasaiənirja   kuwah   a   sausau.
"sasay-ən   lia   kuah   a   sawsaw?"   maxa-hinis-ay   yasia   kausa.
what to do-PF   Asp   none   people   MAXA-mind-Fut   they   two
怎麼辦   了   沒有   人們   心煩   他們   兩人
「沒有什麼人,怎麼辦呢?」他們兩人很煩惱。
"What shall we do without many people?" those two people were worried.

40. maxaxirəd dai   jasja   kausa.
maxa   xirəd-ay   yasia   kausa.
then   unite-Fut   they   two
然後   結婚   他們   兩人
於是他們兩人結婚了。
Then those two people got married.

41. maxaparisanai   rakkihan   mamarəŋ.

mɑxɑ	parisan-ay	rakihan	mamaləŋ.
then	give birth-Fut	baby	boy
然後	要生子	孩子	男

他們生了個男孩。

Then they had a baby boy.

42. pialai   isia rja   maxa naxadaai   aubil   a bazuah.

pialay	isia	lia,	maxa	nahadaʔ-ay	aubil	a	bazuah.
since	that	Asp	then	exist-Fut	succeeding		generation
從此	那	了	才	有	後續		同一代

從那時起，就有後代的人了。

From then on, they had the succeeding generation

43. maxa raraŋadai   sinusana   kaduxu.

ma-xara	la-laŋad-ay	sinusana	kaduxu.
AF-call	Red-name-Fut	use?	incantation
取名	名字	用?	咒語

他們念咒語來取名字。

They named their babies by chanting incantations.

44. adaŋ a rarəd   usa   paxaiisiasu arausu   rabaxan.

adaŋ	a	rarus	usa	paxaisiasu	arausu	rabaxan
one		group	go	become	Hoanya	south
一		群	去	變成	北投蕃	南投蕃

有一群人去變成北投蕃跟南投蕃（洪雅人）。

A group of people went to become Hoanya people.

45. maxa   makawasai.

maxa	makawas-ay.
then	talk-Fut
然後	要說話

然後他們要說話（念咒語）了。

Then they would talk (by chanting incantations).

46. adaŋa   rarəd   usa   paxaisiasju budor.

adaŋ	a	rarus	usa	paxaisiasiu	budur.
one		group	go	become	Papora village name
一		群	去	變成	大肚蕃

有一群人到大肚社（巴布拉）去成為巴布拉人。

A group of people went to the village of Budur to become Papora people.

47. **maxamakawasai   minah.**
    maxa makawas-ay   minah.
    then   talk-Fut   again
    然後 要說話   再
    要再說話（念咒語）。
    They would talk (by chanting incantations) again.

48. **usapaxai   siasju   balua.**
    usa paxaisiasiw   balua.
    go   become   Taokas village name
    去   變成   房里,水尾,日南,雙寮
    變成道卡斯族的人。
    They went to the village of Balua (Taokas) and became Taokas people.

49. **maramakawasai   mina.**
    maxa makawas-ay   minah.
    then   talk-Fut   again
    然後 要說話   再
    要再說話（念咒語）。
    They would talk (by chanting incantations) again.

50. **usapaxaisiasju   tarawil.**
    usa paxaisiasiw   talawil.
    go   become   village name
    去   變成   蜈蚣崙
    變成蜈蚣崙的人。
    They went to the village of Talawil (Pazih) and became Pazih people.

51. **maxamakawasai   minah**
    maxa makawas-ay   minah.
    then   talk-Fut   again
    然後 要說話   再
    要再說話（念咒語）。
    Then they would talk (by chanting incantations) again.

52. **usapaxai   siasju   aruh   aoran**
    usa paxaisiasiw   arux   auran.
    go   become   village name village name
    去   變成   岸裡社   烏牛欄
    變成岸裡社和烏牛欄的人。
    They went to the villages of Arux (Pazih) and Auran (Pazih) and became Pazih people.

53. maxamakawasai　　minah

maxa　makawas-ay　　minah.
then　talk-Fut　　　again
然後　要說話　　　　再
要再說話（念咒語）。
Then they would talk (by chanting incantations) again.

54. usapaxai　siasju　narusai

usa　paxaisiasiw　　lalusay.
go　become　　　village name
去　變成　　　　　阿里史
變成阿里史的人。
They went to the village of Lalusay (Pazih) and became Pazih people.

Text 3. 射太陽 *Shooting the Sun*

1. **tadudo aumina makuai nibara**
   ta-dudu-aw   minah   makuay   nibara.
   let's-tell-Fut   again   personal name
   將講   再   人名
   （我）再講有關 Makuay Nibara 的故事。
   (I)'ll tell you about Makuay Nibara again.

2. **mausa hajaku. muririx binaju.**
   ma-usaʔ-ay   aku   mu-ririx   binayu.
   AF-go-Fut   I   AF-check-traps mountain
   去   我   巡查陷阱   山
   我去山裡巡察陷阱。
   "I'll go to the mountains to check traps," (he said.)

3. **makamjatautaunai rauhiro puzadiriŋ.**
   maxa ??   rawil u buzux adəŋ.
   then ??[2]   bow[3] and arrow ready
   準備   弓 和 箭   已預備好的,齊備的
   （他）準備好弓和箭。
   Then (he) prepared for a bow and arrows.

4. **makamasakrai rjaka pasura.**
   maxa[4] ma-sakəl-ay riak a ??[5].
   then   AF-arrive-Fut good   place(??)
   然後   將到   好   地方
   （他）到達一個好地方。
   Then (he) arrived at a good place.

---

[2] Glossed by Asai as 準備スル (prepare).

[3] Glossed by Asai as 銃 (gun).

[4] *maka-* or *maxa-* which occurs very often in this text could not be a prefix, but a type of conjunction such as 'and then'.

[5] Glossed by Asai as 良キ處 (good place).

5. **makabaurjakai**   **parau[6]**   **paxirihan[7].**

maxa	bauriak-ay	pazay	pa-kizih-ən
then	make-Fut	glutinous rice	Caus-put down-PF
然後	將做	糯米	放下

（他）做湯圓並放下。

(He) made glutinous rice dumpling (and) put it down.

6. **maxamaitokuai.**   **makuainibara.**   **maxakikitaai.**   **rohotomuris.**

maxa	m-a-ituku-ay	makuai	nibara	maxa-ki-kita-ay	ruhut-u-muris[8].
then	AF-Prg-sit-Fut	personal name		MAXA-Red-see-Fut	antelope
然後	將坐	人 名		看到	羚羊

Makuai Nibara 坐下並看著一隻山羊下來。

Makuai Nibara was sitting and looked at an antelope.

7. **maxararakadai**   **makuonibara,**   **raka**   **dinirja rohoto muris.**

maxa	la-lakad-ay	makuai	nibara,	lakad-ən	lia	ruhut-u-muris.
then	Red-shoot-Fut	personal name		shot-PF	Asp	antelope
然後	射	人 名		射中	了	羚羊

Makuai Nibara 射箭，山羊被射中了。

Makuai Nibara was shooting, and the antelope was shot.

8. **maxamaraai**   **rja maxatata xaijai.**

maxa	m-araʔ-ay	lia	maxa	ta-tahay-ay	lia.
then	AF-catch-AF	Asp	then	Red-kill-Fut	Asp
然後	捉	了	然後	殺	了

他捉了牠並殺了牠（羚羊）。

He took it and killed it.

---

[6] Glossed by Asai as ダンゴ (dumpling).

[7] Glossed by Asai as ヲ見ル (look at).

[8] *muris* 'goat' and *ruhut-* 'to come down', and the whole phrase *ruhut-u-muris* most likely means 'goat crawling on the cliffs, i.e. antelope'.

9. **makamaaxupudaxai   xoma   kiniburan.**

maxa	xaaxu-pudah-ay	xuma	kinixidan[9]
then	return-Fut	home	nearby
然後	回	家	附近

他回到家的附近。

He returned nearby his home.

10. **maxakikitaai   mamais   nisia.   kita   sian   rja.**

maxa	ki-kita-ay	mamais	nisia.	kita	siaən	lia.
then	Red-look-Fut	wife	his	look	carefully	Asp
然後	看	妻子	他的	看	仔細地	了

他的妻子仔細地看了。

His wife looked carefully.

11. **kuah   pasipu.   kuahai   isija   pasipu.**

kuah	paasipu.	kuah-ay	isia	paasipu.
none	pancreas.	not have-Fut	that	pancreas.
沒有	胰臟	沒有	牠	胰臟

沒有胰臟。牠（羚羊）沒有胰臟。

There was no pancreas. That (antelope) had no pancreas.

12. **makaduduruai   adam   a kuai.**

maxa	du-duluʔ-ay	adam-a-kuay	rakihan.
then	Red-send on errand-Fut	personal name	child
然後	派遣	人名	兒子

（她）派她的兒子 Adam-a-Kuay 去辦事。

(She) sent (her) son Adam-a-Kuay on an errand.

13. **kaidida(h)xadoa   usakitai.   kita   siaun   rja. kaizaudər[10].**

"kai-dida	hauha	usa	kita-i."	kita	siaən	lia.	kai-za	ədər.
be-over there	certain	go	look-Imp	look	carefully	Asp.	be-there	really
在那裡	確定	去	看	看	仔細地	了	在那	真的

「應該還在那裡。去找一找（胰臟）！」他仔細地找，果真在那裡。

"It must be over there. Go and look for it!" He looked carefully, and it was there.

---

[9] *k<in>ixid-an* 'nearby' or *t<in>aubur-an*?? Cf. *taubur* 'men's house'.

[10] Glossed by Asai 'exist'.

14. **maka   matabirixai   adam a kuai.**
    maxa   ma-tabilih-ay   adam-a-kuay.
    then   return-Fut   personal name
    然後   回去   人名
    然後 Adam-a-Kuay 回去。
    Then Adam-a-Kuay went back.

15. **maxamasakərai   xuma   kiniburan.**
    maxa xa-sakəl-ay   xuma   kinixidan
    then   Red-arrive-Fut   home   nearby
    然後   抵達   家   附近
    他到家的附近了。
    He arrived nearby his home.

16. **talu-lau   axarəkət   di   rja.**
    taruraw   axa-rəkət   di   isia.
    eaves[11]   just-right   at   that
    屋簷   剛好   在   那
    他剛到屋簷（？）
    He just arrived there at the eaves(?).

17. **ridax   saljusau.   adama kowai.   taxau   rarai**
    ridax   ??   adam-a-kuay   taxaw   ?
    sun   hot,strong[12]   personal name   reach
    太陽   人名   到
    炙熱的太陽直射到 Adam-a-Kuay....
    The hot sun reached Adam a Kuay.

18. **maxaxaxəlmən   karau   raisija.**
    maxa ka-kəxət-ən   karaw   laisia
    then   cut off   leg   like-that
    然後   切斷   腿   像那樣
    他的腿像那樣被切斷了。
    His leg was cut off like that.

---

[11] Glossed by Asai as 口一下 (corridor).

[12] Glossed as '熱, strong'.

19. **iniraisija   makuainibara.**
    ini   laisia   makuai   nibara.
    not   like-that[13]   personal   name
    沒   像那樣   人   名
    Makuai Nibara（想），不應該這樣。
    It should not be like that, Makuai Nibara (thought).

20. **asai   paisu   masoxari   naki   rakihan.**
    "asay   pai   siw?   ma-suhari   naki   rakihan."
    what   Q   you   AF-ensnare   my   child
    什麼   你   陷害   我的   子
    「你做了什麼？（你）害了我兒子。」
    "What did you do? (You) did harm to my son."

21. **mausa-ai   hajaku.   mupana   ridah.**
    m-a-usaʔ-ay   hayaku   mu-pana   ridax.
    AF-Prg-go-Fut   I   AF-shoot   sun
    去   我   射   太陽
    「我要去射太陽。」
    "I'll go to shoot the sun."

22. **maxamasoa-ai   babisibisji.   arim   haimini.   kadoh   aimini.   arim**
    maxa   m-asuʔ-ay   ba-bisi-bisi,   arim   haimini,   kaduh   haimini,
    then   AF-bring-Fut   Red-Red-seeds,   peach   this,   plum   this,
    然後   帶   各種種子   桃子   這個   李子   這個

    saŋas   banai.
    saŋas,   banay.
    ume-plum,   pomelo
    梅子   柚子
    他帶了許多種子，有桃子、李子、梅子和柚子。
    He was bringing various kinds of seeds: this peach, this plum, ume-plum, and pomelo.

---

[13] Glossed ソレハイケナイ (that is no good; that should not be).

23. **makamausaai   sja makuanibara.**
    maxa   m-a-usaʔ-ay   isia   makuai nibara.
    然後   AF-Prg-go-Fut   that   personal name
    然後   要去   那   人名
    Makuai Nibura 要去了。
    Then Makuay-Nibura was going.

24. **makamaxasoai   wazu takəruban.**
    maxa   m-asuʔ-ay   wazu   takərəban.
    then   AF-bring-Fut   dog   dog's name
    然後   帶   狗   狗名
    他帶了一隻名叫 Takərəban 的狗。
    He took with him the dog Takərəban.

25. **maxa masakərai   tatəŋabaŋ.**
    maxa   ma-sakəl-ay   ta-təŋab-an   ridax.
    then   AF-arrive-Fut   place-sunrise   sun
    然後   到達   日出處   日
    他終於到達了日出處。
    Then he arrived at the place where the sun came out.

26. **aru   ka   naisu   raraqadai   aku.**
    alu   ka   na   isiw   laa-lakad-ay   aku.
    come   thou   Red-shoot-Fut   I
    來   你   射   我
    「你出來吧！我要射你。」
    "Come! Thou! I'll shoot thee."

27. **rukadurirja.   rakadjurai   sija.**
    rukad-ən   lia.   lakad-ən lia   sia.
    come out-PF   Asp   shot-PF   Asp   he
    升   了   射   了   他
    太陽出來，被他射中了。
    It came out, and was shot by him.

28. **suma   dadua. inikitaan   daran.**
    səm a   dadua.   ini kita-an   daran.
    dark LIN   all   not see-LF   road
    暗   全部   沒 看   路
    到處都是黑暗一片。看不到路。
    It was all dark. The roads were not visible.

29. **makamatabixai   makuai nibara.**
maka-ma-tabilih-ay   makuai nibara
MAKA-AF-return-Fut   personal name
返回   人名
Makuai Nibara 要回家了。
Makuai Nibara was going home.

30. **sassai inirja   inikitaan   daran.**
"sasay-ən   lia? ini kita-an   daran."
what to do-PF   Asp not seen   road
怎麼辦   了   沒   看   路
「我該怎麼辦？我看不到路。」
"What shall I do? I can't see the road."

31. **wazu takərəban masu   daran.**
wazu takərəban m-asu   daran
dog   dog's name AF-bring   road
狗   狗名   帶   路
由 Takərəban 這隻狗帶路。
The dog Takərəban was leading him on the way.

32. **makamasakərai   puŋubabanai.**
maxa ma-sakəl-ay   puŋu ba-banay.
then AF-arrive-Fut trunk pomelos
然後 將到達   樹幹   柚子
他們即將到達柚子的樹幹。
They would arrive at the trunk of pomelos.

33. **zaqaimina   rai sija.   maxamasakərai.**
zakay minah   lai sia,   maxa ma-sakəl-ay
walk   again   Asp he   then AF-arrive-Fut
走   再   了   他   然後   將到達
他繼續走了，就到達（那裡）了。
He walked again and would arrive there.

34. **xamaxam rai sija. saŋasaimini.**
xamaxam lai sia,   saŋas haimini.
grope   Asp he   梅   this
暗中摸索 了   他   plum   這個
他在暗中摸索了，到梅子樹處。
He groped in the dark and touched the ume-plum tree.

35. **zaqai mina makamasakrai xamaxam rai sija kadoh haimini.**

zakay	minah	maxa	ma-sakəl-ay	xamaxam	lai	sia,	kaduh	haimini
walk	again	then	AF-arrive-Fut	grope	Asp	he	plum	this
走	再	然後	將到	暗中摸索	了	他	李子	這個

他又繼續在黑暗中摸索前進，到李子樹處。

He walked again, and arrived by groping in the dark. This was the plum tree.

36. **zaqaimina makamasakrai xamaxam rai sija. arim haimini.**

zakay	minah	maxa	ma-sakəl-ay	xamaxam	lai	sia	arim	haimini
walk	again	then	AF-arrive-Fut	grope	Asp	he	peach	this
走	再	然後	將到	暗中摸索	了	他	桃	這個

他又繼續在黑暗中摸索前進，將到桃子樹處。

He walked again, and arrived by groping in the dark. This was the peach tree.

37. **zaqai mina maxamasakrai xamaxam rai sija xoma haimini.**

zakay	minah	maxa	ma-sakel-ay	xamaxam	lai	sia,	xuma	haimini
walk	again	then	arrive-Fut	grope	Asp	he	house	this
走	再	然後	將到	暗中摸索	了	他	家	這個

他又繼續在黑暗中摸索前進，將到他家了。

He walked again, and arrived by groping in the dark. This was (his) house.

E. Pazih Text Recorded by Ino

下面的巴宰語料，伊能嘉矩大概在 1897 年在埔里採集，由李壬癸根據巴宰發音人潘榮章和潘金玉加以修訂，愛蘭，1997 年 2 月。第一行粗體字是伊能的記音，第二行是李壬癸的修訂。本語料內容和體例都跟其他語料不同。本語料伊能分為十一節。日文翻譯是根據伊能的原記錄，而中、英文翻譯是李壬癸所做。

The following Pazih text was recorded by Ino in Puli, in 1897 (?), edited by Paul Li, with assistance of Pazih speakers, Pan Rong-Jang and Pan Jin-yu in February 1997. The Japanese translation for each sentence was given by Ino. The first line in boldface is the original transcription by Ino, while the second line is as edited by Li. This text is different in nature from all the others, so the format is also somewhat different. It is divided into eleven sections, as Ino did in his manuscripts. The Japanese translation was given by Ino, while the Chinese and English translations were by Paul Li.

第一節

1. **kaidini ka, nahaza muhalid u, rakehal a rima a sau,**
   kaidini ka, nahaza mu-xalid- u rakihal a rima a saw.
   here Top exist AF-hold Obl child Lig hand Lig person
   這裡 有 牽 小孩 手 人
   此に小兒の手を曳きて行く人がある。
   這裡有一個人牽著小孩的手。
   There is a person holding a child's hand.

2. **rakehal u isia ka, paiyatudu wazu,**
   rakihal u isia ka, p<a>yatudu wazu.
   child that Top Prg-point dog
   小孩 那個 指 狗
   其の小兒は犬を指さして居る。
   那個小孩指著狗。
   The child is pointing at a dog.

3. **wazu ka, mikita u babao kahhui a ayamu, ka marawa,**
   wazu ka, mi-kita u babaw kahuy a ayam, ka ma-lawa.
   dog AF-see Obl above tree Lig bird Conj AF-bark
   狗 看 上 樹 鳥 吠
   犬は木の上の鳥を見て吠えて居る。
   狗看到樹上的鳥在吠。
   The dog looking at a bird on the tree is barking.

第二節

1. **rakehal   u, imine   ka baoryak binayu,   iu   ralbun   ki   ituk   babao,**
   rakihal   u imini   ka, bauriak binayu   iu   aləb-ən   di   ituk   babaw.
   child   this   make   mountain   and   close-PF   Loc   top   above
   小孩   這個   做   山   且   圍起來   頂   上
   小兒が山をつくり（其上に池を鑿つた）。
   這個小孩堆山並在上面圍起（池子）來。
   This child was building a hill and made a pond on top of it.

2. **paokusa-an   u dalum laike   lubongu ka,   maha darudaru   lea,**
   paukusaʔ-an   u dalum lai ki   rubuŋ ka,   maxa-darudaru   lia.
   pour-LF   water   Asp Nom   pond   Conj   become-waterfall   Asp
   倒入   水   了   池   變成瀑布   了
   池に水を入れしに瀧が出来た。
   把水倒入池子，變成瀑布。
   He poured water into the pond and it became a waterfall.

3. **dalum   darudaru   ka,   murahot   maha rahong   di   ruburubu   binayu**
   dalum   darudaru   ka,   mu-rahut   maxa-raxuŋ   di   ruburubu   binayu.
   water   waterfall   Top   AF-flow   become-river   Loc   below   mountain
   水   瀑布   流   變成河川   下   山
   瀧の水は麓に流れて川となつた。
   瀑布的水流到山腳下變成河川。
   The water of the waterfall flowed below the mountain to become a stream.

4. **pusongud-an   ki   rahung,**
   pu-suŋud-an   ki   raxuŋ.
   build-bridge-LF   river
   架橋   河川
   川に橋がかかつてある。
   河上架著橋。
   A bridge was made over the stream.

第三節

1. **karu turao a baoryak u alis a rakehal, baoryak u daorik ka kalu**
   kalu turaw a bauriak u alis a rakihan, bauriak u daurik ka kalu
   use ear of make rabit child make eye use
   用 茅穗 做 兔 小孩 做 眼睛 用

   kadoh a,
   kaduh a.
   plum
   李子
   小兒はカヤの穂で兔をつくり目は李でこしらへた。
   小孩用穀子的空殼做兔子，眼睛則用李子做。
   The child made a rabbit with a dried ear of miscanthus and its eyes with plum.

2. **kitai huhul naike rahal ka sangira na,**
   kita-i huhul lai ki rahal ka saŋira na.
   look-Imp carefully Asp Nom mouth and ear
   看 仔細地 嘴巴 和 耳朵
   あの口と耳とを能く見よ。
   仔細地看那嘴巴和耳朵！
   Look at the mouth and ears carefully!

3. **sangira ka halupas, rahal ka mahatulu a buiz,**
   saŋira ka halupas, rahal ka maxa-turu a buiz.
   ear long mouth become-three split apart
   耳朵 長 嘴巴 變三 裂開
   耳は長く口は三つに裂けて居る。
   耳朵很長，嘴巴裂為三片。
   The ears are long, and the mouth is hare-lipped.

4. **paikulul a alis ka mauduh,**
   paikulul a alis ka ma-idəh.
   leap Lig rabit Top Sta-fast
   跳 兔子 快
   兔の，はねるのは早くある。
   兔子跳得很快。
   The rabbit leaps fast.

第四節

1. **tutūngap   a   lizaha   ki ohoni,**
tə-təŋab- a   rizax   ki uhuni.
Red-rise   sun   now
上升   太陽   現在
今日がのぼるところである。
現在太陽正要昇起。
The sun is rising now.

2. **mutungap   a   lizaha   liaka,   pudusah   a   ilas   ka   marupai marupai,**
mə-təŋap a   rizax   lia ka   pədəsax   a   ilas   ka   ma-lupay ma-lupay.
AF-rise   sun   Asp Nom   light   moon   Sta-dim   Sta-dim
昇起   太陽   了   光   月   暗淡   暗淡
日が登れば月の光はだんだん薄くなり。
太陽昇起，月光漸漸暗淡下去。
The sun is rising, and the moonlight is waning.

3. **pudusah   pudusah   aike   wazan   u   rahong,   babātobatu   ka**
pədəsax   pədəsax   lai ki   wazan   u   raxuŋ,   ba-batu-batu   ka
bright   bright   Asp Nom   middle Obl river   Red-Red-stone
明亮   明亮   了   中   河川   石頭等等

kita-an   huhul   lea,
kita?-an   huhul   lia.
see-LF   clearly   Asp
看見   仔細
川の中は次第にあかるくなりて、石などがよく見ゆるやうになる。
河川中漸漸明亮，可以看清石頭等。
It becomes brighter and brighter in the stream, in which the stones become clear.

第五節

1. **kalu daorik a mikita, kalu rahal a makawas, kalu sangera a**
   kalu daurik a mi-kita, kalu rahal a ma-kawas, kalu saŋira a
   use eye Lig AF-see use mouth Lig AF-speak use ear Lig
   用 眼睛 看見 用 嘴巴 說 用 耳朵

   tumala,
   tumala.
   hear
   聽
   目にて見，口にて言ひ，耳にて聞く。
   用眼睛看，用嘴巴說，用耳朵聽。
   (We) see with eyes, talk with a mouth, and hear with ears.

2. **daorik u sangera ka dusa, rahal ka adadumud,**
   daurik u saŋira ka dusa, rahal ka adadumut.
   eye and ear Top two mouth Top only one
   眼睛 和 耳朵 二個 嘴巴 只有一個
   目と耳とは二つありて，口は只一つである。
   眼睛和耳朵各有兩個，嘴巴只有一個。
   There are two eyes and ears, while there is only one mouth.

3. **mahaki tumala mikita ka pakadahon, makawas ka pakatatengun,**
   mahaki tumala mi-kita ka paka-dahu, ma-kawas ka paka-tatiŋ-ən.
   seem hear AF-see Caus-much AF-speak Caus-little-PF
   似乎 聽 見 使多 說話 使少
   夫れ故見聞くことを多くして話を少くせよ。
   似乎聽得多、看得多，卻說得少。
   Therefore (we) hear and see a lot, but to talk only a little.

164

第六節

1. **rakehal u mamais imine ka, azang-a-sasonan   azang-a-sasonan   a**
   rakihal   u mamais   imini ka adaŋ a   sasunan, adaŋ a   sasunan a
   child   girl   this   one Lig morning one Lig morning Lig
   小孩   女   這個   每一   早上   每一   早上

   mudukul   maha-hatulai   a   barabo,
   mə-dəkəl   maxa-hatəl-ay   a   barabu.
   AF-pick   become-hundred-Fut   snail
   拾撿   接近一百   田螺
   此小兒は每朝タニシを百ばかり拾ふ。
   這女孩每天早上撿近一百個田螺。
   This girl picks up about a hundred snails every morning.

2. **plyalai ohone, isiza dali maluhoso a mudukul   liaka,   maha-sahanai**
   pialay uhuni, isiza dali maluhusu a   mə-dəkəl lia ka, maxa-sahanay
   begin   now   ten   day   in that way AF-pick   lia ka, become-thousand-Fut
   開始   現在   十   天   如此   拾撿   接近一千

   lia'a,
   liaʔa.
   Asp
   了
   これから十日つづけて拾ふならば千ばかりになるだらう。
   以後接著十天撿的話，就會撿近一千個了。
   If she keeps picking for ten days from now on, there will be nearly a thousand snails.

3. **talukun a barabo, ka ryaka   kakanun,**
   talək-ən a barabu ka riak a ka-kan-ən.
   cook-PF   snail   Top good   Red-eat-PF
   煮   田螺   很好   吃
   たにしは煮て食すればうまくある。
   煮的田螺很好吃。
   Cooked snails are good to eat.

第七節

1. **dadang   a   rabahan-dale   ki   ohoni,**
   daadaŋ   a   rabaxan   dali   ki   uhuni.
   warm   summer   day   Nom   now
   暖   夏   日子   現在
   今は暖かな春の日である。
   現在是溫暖的夏天
   It is warm summer now.

2. **rakehal   ka   maso   wazu,   mahadas   di   binayu,**
   rakihal   ka   m-asu   wazu,   ma-hadas   di   binayu.
   child   AF-bring   dog   AF-travel   mountain
   小孩   帶   狗   旅遊   山上
   小兒は犬をつれて山に遊んで居る。
   小孩帶著狗在山上玩。
   The child takes along with him a dog and is playing in the mountain.

3. **ruborubo   binayu   ka   nahaza   rahong,   de   barubarud   rahong   isia**
   rubu-rubu   binayu   ka   nahaza   raxuŋ,   di   barə-barət   raxuŋ   isia
   Red-below   mountain   exist   river   Red-beside   river   that
   下   山   有   河流   旁邊   河流   那

   ka,   daho   a   umama   ka   karid,
   ka,   dahu   a   umamah   ka   karit.
   many   rice field   and   swidden field
   很多的   稻田   和   旱田
   山の下に川があり其の川の兩側に多くの田と畑とがある。
   山下有河流，河的兩旁有許多稻田和旱田。
   There is a stream below the mountain, and there are many rice paddies and swidden fields on both sides of the stream.

4. **kaizizaka   babaha   sao   a   marunguhu,**
   kaiziza   ka   baabah   a   saw   a   ma-ruŋuh.
   there   many   person   AF-turn the soil over
   在那邊   許多   人   翻土
   かしこにあまたの人が土をすきかへして居る。
   在那邊有許多人在挖地。
   Many people are turning the soil over there.

第八節

1.

ahowan	a	dare	inapa	a	hahehahe-mai	a	paranaha	ka	paizaho
ahuan	a	dali	in-apa	a	hahihahimai	a	paranah	ka	p\<a>izaux
evening		day	Prf-carry		cargo?		boat		Prg-go down
傍晚		日	裝載		貨物?		船		下去

u	rahong,
u	raxuŋ.
	river
	河川

夕暮に荷を積んだ舟が川を下り行く。

傍晚載貨的船順流而下。

In the evening the boat carrying cargo is going down the stream.

2.

uka	de	myadoa	binayu	a	daran	ka	tātarao	noang	a	rakehal,
uka	di	miadua	binayu	a	daran	ka	taa-taraw	nuaŋ	a	rakihal.
other		that yonder	mountain		road	Conj	Red-chase	carabao		child
其他		那邊	山		路		趕	牛		小孩

又あちらの山路を小兒が牛を逐ふて行く。

還有，那邊的山路小孩趕牛而去。

And, a child is chasing a carabao on the mountain path over there.

3.

noang	lia	ka	ini	kapajie	ki	sūsumai	panate	a	muhalid	u
nuaŋ	lia	ka	ini	ka-apa-ən	ki	səə-səm-ay	panati	a	mu-xalid	u
carabao		Nom	not	KA-carry-PF		Red-dark-Fut	slowly		AF-pull	Obl
牛		主	不	揹		暗的	慢慢地		拉著	

paripari,
paripari.
cart
車

牛は暗くなるにかまはず、ゆるゆる車をひきて行く。[1]

牛快拖不動了，天色暗了，就拉著車走捷徑。

The load is too heavy for the carabao, and as it is getting dark, it pulls the cart slowly.

---

[1] According to Ino's original notes, it reads: Despite the darkness, the carabao pulls (away) the cart slowly.

第九節

1. **rakehal u mamalung kaidi kinihizan u lubongu babao bato a**
rakihal a mamaləŋ kaidi kinixidan u rubuŋ babaw batu a
child man stay beside pond above stone
小孩 男 在 旁邊 池 上 石

   ma-tahapes,
   ma-taxapis.
   AF-fish
   釣魚
   男の兒は池のはたの石の上にて魚を釣りて居る。
   男孩在池旁的石頭上釣魚。
   A boy is fishing on the rock by a pond.

2. **ryaka mupuzaha babazoai siatu a rakehal u mamais lia,**
liaka mu-puzah a ba-bazuʔ-ay siatu a rakihal u mamais lia.
then AF-come Red-wash-Fut clothes child girl Asp
然後 來 洗 衣 小孩 女
そこへ女の兒がきものを洗ひに來た。
那時女孩來洗衣服。
Then a girl came to wash clothes.

3. **ike rakehal u mamalung lyaka, babao bato denika ryak a**
iki rakihal u mamaləŋ liaka, "babaw batu dini ka riak a
that child man then above stone here Top good
那 小孩 男 然後 上 石 這裡 好

   babazu an aonisu lailaka, mukusa di myadoa
   ba-bazuʔ-an, auni siw," laila ka, m-ukusa di miadua
   Red-wash clothes-LF for you in that way AF-go that yonder
   洗衣 給 你 那樣 去 那邊

   kinihezan lia,
   kinixidan lia.
   beside
   岸邊
   男の兒はこの石の上は洗ひものをするによいからあげましやう[sic]と言ひてむか
   ふの岸へいつた。
   那個男孩説,「這石頭上面可以洗衣服,讓你洗。」他就到對岸去了。
   The boy said, "It is good to wash clothes on the rock here. This place is for you." Then he went to the other side (of the stream).

第十節

1. **rakehal   rabuhu   ka   ibaun   niki   ina,**
   rakihal   rabəx   ka   iba-ən   niki   ina.
   child   baby   hold-PF   Gen   mother
   小孩   嬰   抱著   屬   母
   小さな小兒は母にだかれて居る。
   嬰兒被母親抱著。
   The baby is carried by the mother in her arms.

2. **nimiso   a   mamaha,   pauzaha   langu   a   mangasa,   babaha   u   kiaraun**
   nimisiw   a   mamah   p<a>uzah   laŋu   a   ma-ŋasa,   ba-baxa   u   kiaarən
   his   elder brother   Prg-come   courtyard   AF-arrive   Red-give   pretty
   他的   哥哥   正在來   庭外   到達   給   漂亮的

   a   arimu,
   a   arim.
       peach
       桃子
   彼れの兄は歸つて來てうつくしき桃をくれた。
   他的哥哥正從外面進來,給他漂亮的桃子。
   His elder brother came back and gave him pretty peaches.

3. **iki   inaduan   u   arimu   a   karaha   ka   niki   aba   a   tinu'un,**
   iki   in-adu-an   u   arim   a   kalaha   ka   niki   aba   a   t<in>uʔun.
   that   Prf-contain-LF   peach   basket   Gen   father   Prf-make
   那   放   桃子   籃子   父親   做
   あの桃を入れた籠は父の こしらへた(も)のである。
   放那桃子的籃子是父親做的。
   The basket containing the peaches was made by Father.

4. **abasan-soaji   yamini   ka   hanisai   a   kawas,**
   abasan   suazi   yamini   ka   hanisay   a   kawas?
   elder sibling   younger sibling   these   how many   age
   兄姉   弟妹   這些   多少   歲
   この兄弟は幾歲であるか?
   這對兄弟(或兄妹)幾歲?
   How old are these brothers?

5. | mamaha | ka | hasub | a | kawas, | soaji | ka | turu | a | kawas, |
mamah	ka	xasəb-	a	kawas,	suazi	ka	turu	a	kawas.
elder brother	Top	five		year	younger brother	Top	three		year
兄		五		歲	弟		三		歲

兄は五歳で弟は三歳である。

哥哥五歳，弟弟三歳。

The elder is five years old, and the younger is three.

第十一節

1. **myadoa** **karid** **ka** **kizuhu a** **sau,** **myadine** **a** **wazan** **u**
   miadua karit ka kizəx a saw, miadini a wazan u
   that yonder swidden field Top stand person here center
   那邊 旱田 站著 人 這邊 中

   omaomaha **ka** **pahoruma,**
   umamah ka paxuruma.
   rice field Top plant
   稻田 種植

   あちらの畑には人が立ち、こちらの田の中には苗をうゑて居る。
   那邊的旱田站著人，這邊的稻田在插秧。
   People are standing in the swidden field over there, while (the others) are planting rice in the rice paddy over here.

2. **baruz** **daran** **ka** **padalak a** **hapui,** **sau** **ka** **mai dalam ki daran**
   baraz a daran ka padalak a hapuy, saw ka m<a>italam di daran
   side road Top burn fire person Top AF-Prg-run road
   旁 路 燃燒 火 人 在跑 路

   u **disu,**
   u disiw.
   there
   那裡

   路のはたに火が燃え人がその路を走る。
   路旁燒著火，人在那條路跑。
   A fire is burning on the side of the road, while people are running on the road.

3. **manu a** **babao** **binayu** **kikita-an a** **ilas,** **kialehe** **a** **rahong** **ka**
   maanu a babaw binayu ki-kita?-an a ilas, kialih a raxuŋ ka
   far above mountain Red-see-LF moon near river
   遠 上 山 看見 月 近 河川

   maokusa **a** **paranaha,**
   m-a-ukusa a paranah.
   AF-Prg-go boat
   去 船

   遠き山の上に月が見え近き川を舟が行く。
   遠處山上看到月亮，近溪邊有人要到船那邊去。
   Far above the mountain we can see the moon, nearby the stream people are going on the boat.

Pazih Texts and Songs

Part Two: Pazih Songs 巴宰歌謠

A. Pazih Songs in Auran 愛蘭的巴宰歌謠

愛蘭潘金玉女士（87 歲），於 2001 年 6 月 3 日，在埔里鎮愛蘭里獨唱童謠四首、祭典歌 ayan 四首和聖詩二首，由李壬癸錄音、記音、翻譯。

The following four children's songs and four ritual songs *ayan* were sung by Pan Jin-yu (female, 87) on June 3, 2001 in Auran, Puli, and recorded, transcribed and translated by Paul Li.

Children's Songs 童謠

Song 1. tautaukua 螞蟻王 *Leader of Ants*

1. tautaukua   pakupakusia.
leader   subordinate
首領   屬下

Leader and subordinates

2. alu, ta-kan-i   niam a sumay
come let's-eat-Imp we   rice
來   咱吃   我們   飯

iu punu luxut!
and head deer
和 頭 鹿
來，咱們吃我們的飯和鹿頭吧！
Come, let's eat our rice and the head of a deer!

3. alu, ta-kan-i   sumay iu
come let's-eat-Imp rice   and
來   咱吃   飯   和

punu luxut!
head deer
頭 鹿
來，咱們吃飯和鹿頭吧！
Come, let's eat rice and the head of a deer!

Song 2. punəŋ 蟬 *Cicadas*

1. lailailai   lai piaw.
cry of cicadas
蟬叫聲
蟬在叫。
Cries of cicadas.

2. piaw sauri, sauri   batu.
find   place   place   egg
找   地方   在那地方   蛋
蟬到樹上找地方下卵。
(The cicadas) look for places to lay their eggs.

3. batu rakihan, raki yauzu.
egg   child   baby come out to act
卵   子   子   出來活動
卵孵子，小蟬出來活動。
The eggs hatch, and the baby cicadas come out to act.

4. tuntun   amayuk.
flap wings fly
振翅   飛
振翼而飛。
They flap their wings and fly.

Song 3. badi alu 同伴來 *Friends, Come*

1. badi, alu, ta-kitaʔ-i away.
   friend come let's-look-Imp moon
   同伴 來 咱看吧 月亮
   同伴，來，咱們看月亮吧！
   Friends, come, let's look at the moon!

Song 4. tulala, rapiaw, ayam 欣賞花、蝴蝶、鳥之歌 *Flowers, Butterflies, and Birds*

1. ita, ita dadua
   we we all
   咱 咱 大家
   咱們，咱們大家！
   We, we, all

第一版	第二版
ta-kitaʔ-i tulala	ta-kizib-i tulala!
let's-look-Imp flower	let's-pluck-Imp flower
咱看 花	咱摘 花
咱們看花吧！	咱們摘花吧！
Let's look at the flowers!	*Let's pluck the flowers!*
lubahiŋ iu risilaw.	ta-zubuʔ-aw di punu.
red and white	let's wear-Fut head
紅 和 白	咱-插-將 頭
紅色和白色。	咱們要插在頭上。
Red and white.	*Let's wear them on the head!*
ay, kiaarən tulala.	ay, kiaarən haisiw ʔi.
oh beautiful flower	oh beautiful you
啊 美 花	啊 美 你
啊，花很美麗！	啊，你很美麗！
Ay, beautiful flowers!	*Ay, you are so beautiful!*

2. ita, ita dadua.   ta-kitaʔ-i rapiaw na!
   we we all   let's-look-Imp butterfly
   咱 咱 大家   咱看 蝴蝶
   咱們，咱們大家！   咱們看蝴蝶吧！
   We, we, all   *Let's look at the butterflies!*

tabarak   iu   risilaw.
yellow   and   white
黃   和   白
黃色和白色。
Yellow and white.

ay,   kiaarən   rapiaw   na!
Ay   beautiful   butterfly
啊   美   蝴蝶
啊！美麗的蝴蝶！
Ay, beautiful butterflies!

3. ita,   ita   dadua.
we   we   all
咱   咱   大家
咱們，咱們大家！
We, we, all

ta-kitaʔ-i   ayam   na!
let's-look-Imp   bird
咱看   鳥
咱們看鳥吧！
Let's look at the birds!

kaidi   babaw   di   kahuy.
at   above   Loc   tree
在   上面   樹
牠在樹上。
They are on the trees.

ay,   kiaarən   ayam   na!
beautiful   bird
啊   美   鳥
啊！美麗的鳥兒！
Ay, beautiful birds!

Editor's note: This children's song is sung with Pazih words but with Japanese melody. Pan Jin-yu said she had learned it from a missionary named *tata pholat* 'Aunt Pholat' at a Sunday School when she was twelve or thirteen years old.

說明： 這是一首童謠，使用日本曲調，但用巴宰歌詞。潘金玉年小時（約十二、三歲）上主日學，傳教士所教（稱她為 tata pholat）。

B. Ritual Songs in Auran 愛蘭的祭典歌

Song 1. 大水氾濫後分居 *Separation after the Big Flood*

The words of the following three ritual songs were based on a Japanese written document but revised by Pan Rung-jang, narrated by Pan Jin-yu, and transcribed and translated by Paul Li, in Auran, Puli, June 9, 1998. They were sung by Pan Jin-yu and recorded by Paul Li on Jan.6, 1999, and then video-taped on June 3, 2001.

這三首傳統歌謠都是潘榮章根據日治時期的記錄所改寫的歌，再由潘金玉念詞，李壬癸記音，1998 年 6 月 9 日於埔里鎮愛蘭里。日治時期伊能嘉矩曾記錄過大水氾濫之歌，潘榮章就根據它改寫歌詞。潘金玉唱，1999 年 1 月 6 日李壬癸錄音，2001 年 6 月 3 日重新錄影及錄音。

1. ayan nu[1] ayan, ayan nu laita.
                        we
   根源   咱們
   咱們唱根源的歌。
   Let's sing ayan, the song of our origin.

2. ayan nu ayan ta-dudu iu maanu.
                  Let's-talk and far
   根源   咱講   及 遠
   咱們談到根源，那是很久遠以前。
   Talking about our origin, it's ages in the past.

3. d<a>uduw-ay lia ha ka, uba pini, ada pini.
   Prg-talk-Fut   Asp   Top female surname female surname
   將講   女名 父名 女名 父名
   要講 Uba Pini 和 Ada Pini 兩姊妹。
   We have to trace back to (two sisters), Uba Pini and Ada Pini.

4. maxa maa-kitaʔ-ay tabanan ma-taru.
   then Rec-meet-Fut   name   Sta-big
   然後 將相見   男名   大
   然後要和長輩 Tabanan 相見。
   Then they would meet with the elder Tabanan.

---

[1] The function of *nu* in this sentence is not clear. The initial *n* could be due to the liaison of the preceding form *ayan*. If so, then the vowel *u* 'and' conjoins two *ayans*.

5. maxa maa-kawas-ay, "mausay pai mu ?"
   then Rec-talk-Fut will go Q you
   然後 交談 去 你們
   他們交談。（他問，）「你們要到哪裡去？」
   Then they talked to each other, "Where are you going?"

6. tabanan ma-taru maxa m<a>a-kawas-ay.
   name Sta-big then AF-Prg-tell-Fut
   男名 大 然後 交談
   她們要告訴長輩 Tabanan。
   They would tell the elder Tabanan.

7. abasan suadi, "mausay haiyami.
   elder sister youner sister will go we
   姊 妹 去 我們
   姊妹兩人說，「我們要去
   The two sisters said, "We are going

8. mausay maxa-pazih, pazih si ki daya."
   will go become-Pazih Pazih Nom east, above
   去 變成巴宰 巴宰 東,上方
   要去當巴宰人，巴宰在東方。」
   Going to become Pazih people, the Pazih in the east."

重複 1-8 Repeat 1-8

9. tə-təŋap nu rizax, tə-təŋap nu rizax.
   Red-rise sun Red-rise sun
   出來,上升 太陽 出來,上升 太陽
   太陽在升上來，太陽在升上來。
   The sun was rising; the sun was rising.

10. manaw amisan ka, manaw rabaxan.
    toward north toward south
    向 北 向 南
    向北再向南。
    To the north and then to the south.

11. daudauduway iu tau mamauway.
    male name and male name
    男名 和 男名
    Daudauduway 和 Tau mamauway。
    Daudauduway and Tau mamauway.

12. maxa ma-sakəl-ay tabanan ma-taru.
    then AF-arrive-Fut male name Sta-big
    然後 到達   男名   大
    他們到達長輩 Tabanan 的地方。
    Then they arrived at the place of the elder Tabanan.

13. maxa pabarət   ki   laihayu   haw   riak.
    then reply to each other Nom personal name good good
    然後 相應答   人名(?)   好   好
    Laihayu 他們互相問好。
    They said 'hello' to each other.

14. "mausay haiyami maxa daxə saraumaw.
    will go we   then place place name
    去   我們   然後 地方 地名
    「我們要到 Saraumaw（今梨山?）那地方去。
    "We are going to Saraumaw Mountain.

15. ana   maxa-ruaru, tabanan   ma-taru."
    don't produce-tears male name Sta-big
    別   傷心   男名   大
    別傷心，Tabanan 長輩。」
    Don't be sad, the elder Tabanan."

16. inihaw isia   maxa p<a>u-suŋud-ay.
    good   there then Prg-build-bridge-Fut
    好   那裡   然後 要鋪橋
    在那裡似乎正要鋪橋。
    Then they were building a bridge.

17. suŋut   ma-bidabit i tatu maumauwan.
    bridge AF-wobble   name of an old man
    橋   搖晃   老人名
    老人 Tatu Maumauwan 在橋上搖晃。
    The old man, Tatu Maumauwan, was staggering on the bridge.

18. tatu maumauwan   ka, pisurixit di   suŋut.
    name of an old man   slip off   Loc bridge
    老人名   滑倒   在   橋
    Tatu Maumauwan 在橋上滑倒了。
    Tatu Maumauwan slipped off on the bridge.

19. tatu maumauwan ka, tatu maumauwan.
    name of an old man name of an old man
    老人名 老人名
    老人 Tatu Maumauwan 就是 Tatu Maumauwan。
    The old man Tatu Maumauwan was Tatu Maumauwan.

20. usa lai siw, mausay yaku. mausay lai yaku.
    go Asp you will go I will go Asp I
    去 了 你 去 我 要去 了 我
    你去了，我也要去。我要去了。
    If you go, I'll go also. I'll go also.

21. nahada luxut ka, luxud- u nuaŋ.
    exist deer deer ox
    有 鹿 鹿 牛(公鹿)
    有鹿是公鹿。
    There was a deer, and it was a male deer.

22. tatu maumauwan mausay maxa-daxu.
    name of an old man will go become-savage
    老人名 要去 當生番
    老人 Tatu Maumauwan 他要到山地去當生番。
    The old man named Tatu Maumauwan would go to become a savage.

23. ana maxa-ruaru, tabanan ma-taru.
    don't produce-tears personal name Sta-big
    別 傷心 人名 大
    別傷心，Tabanan 長輩。
    Don't be sad, the elder Tabanan.

24. aubin a dali ka, maa-ʔisa-ʔisakup.
    later day Rec-Red-get together
    後 日 在一起
    日後一直在一起。
    (We'll) get together later on.

25. hauha ka iu naki, mu-dudu ma-mərək.
    sure and my AF-talk AF-unable
    確定 及 我的 講話 不會
    我的話確定只有這些，我不擅言辭。
    Certainly all these are what I have to say, and I am not expressive.

26. ayan nu ayan, ayan ni laita.
                                    we
　　根源　　　　　　　　咱們
　　咱們唱根源的歌。
　　Let's sing ayan, the song of our origin.

27. ayan nu ayan, saysay yawira.
                    what   end
　　根源　　　　　　什麼　結束
　　根源歌到此什麼都結束了。
　　This is the end of the song of ayan.

Song 2a. mazuah 走標（完整版）*Racing* (full version)

1. ayan nu ayan, ayan ni laita.
 Gen we
 根源 咱們
 根源，咱們唱根源。
 Let's sing ayan, the song of our origin.

2. hauha ka imisu dali iu uhuni.
 sure that day and now
 確定 那 日 和 現在
 確定是那時候的今天。
 It is certain that it is the present time on that day.

3. laila ki isia ma-dudu ki apuan.
 in that way Nom he AF-talk Nom elderly people
 那樣 他 講 長輩
 長輩他那樣講話。
 The elderly said so.

4. tumala ki apuan k<in>awas ka kasibat.
 listen Nom elderly people Prf-word instruction
 聽 長輩 話 教誨
 聽長輩教誨的話。
 (We should) listen to the instructions of the elderly.

5. uhuni iu dali ka ma-taru iu razəm.
 now and day Top Sta-big and New Year
 現今 和 日 大 和 新年
 今天是大新年。
 Today is the New Year's day.

6. abasan u suadi maaka-hata-hatan.
 elder sibling and younger sibling Rec-Red-happy
 兄姊 和 弟妹 高興
 兄弟姊妹都很高興。
 Brothers and sisters are all happy.

7. ita, ita dadua ka maaka-ria-riak.
 we we all Top Rec-Red-nice
 咱 咱 大家 和好!
 咱們大家都要和好！
 Let's all be nice to each other!

8. rətən a taukua ka, laila ki mu-kawas.
   village chief in that way Nom AF-talk
   村 頭目 那樣 講
   村中的頭目那樣講話了。
   The head of the village said so.

9. "uhuni iu dali ka, ma-taru iu razəm."
   now day Sta-big New Year
   現在 日 大 新年
   「今天是大新年。」
   "Today is the great New Year's day."

10. laila ka isia, laila ka imisu.
    in that way that in that way he, that
    那樣 那 那樣 他,那
    他那樣（講）。
    That's what he said.

11. nahani ki taubarət maamaaləŋ ma-gizəm.
    come neighbor young men Sta-strong
    來 隔壁 男青年們 強壯
    鄰村的強壯青年來了。
    The strong young men came from the neighboring villages.

12. nahani mi-talam, mi-talam barəbar.
    come AF-race AF-race flag
    來 跑 跑 旗
    他們來賽跑奪旗。
    They came to race for the flag.

13. imu, imu maamaaləŋ ka, ma-gizəm dadua.
    you you young men Top Sta-strong all
    你們 你們 男青年們 強 都
    你們男青年都很強壯。
    "You young men are all strong.

14. yagira ki ima ka, ana suan taubarət.
    Bravo! who don't lose neighbor
    加油 誰 別 輸 鄰
    誰都要加油,別輸給鄰村的人。
    Whoever participates in the race should work hard, and not to lose to the neighboring villagers."

182

15. mu-puzah lia ki taubarət maamaaləŋ.
　　AF-come　Asp　Nom　neighbor　young men
　　來　　　了　鄰　　男青年們
　　鄰村的少年都來了。
　　The neighboring young men all came.

16. p<in>a-siatu　maamaaləŋ　purarilak　dadua.
　　wear-Prg-clothes　young men　glitter　all
　　穿衣　　　　　　男青年們　穿閃閃發光　都
　　少年們都穿著閃亮的衣服。
　　The young men all wore clothes in bright color.

17. taubarət　maamaaləŋ　ka,　ma-gizəm　maamaaləŋ.
　　neighbor　young men　Top　Sta-strong　young men
　　鄰　　　男青年們　　　　強　　　男青年
　　鄰村的少年很強壯。
　　The neighboring young men were all strong.

18. nita　rətən　maamaaləŋ　ka,　purarilak　lubahiŋ.
　　our　village　young men　Top　glitter　red
　　咱　村　　男青年們　　　穿閃亮　紅
　　咱們村的少年穿閃亮的紅衣。
　　The young men in our village wore clothes in bright red color.

19. taubarət　maamaaləŋ　pasakən　dadua.
　　neighbor　young men　arrive　all
　　鄰　　　男青年們　　到達　都
　　鄰村的少年都到齊了。
　　The neighboring young men all arrived.

20. m-itun　di　babaw　lia　taukua　m<a>a-kawas.
　　AF-rise　above　Asp　chief　AF-Prg-tell
　　起來　　上　了　長官　在講
　　長官起來在上面講話了。
　　The chief rose and was talking from above.

21. laila　　ka,　"uhuni　m<a>i-talam　barəbar.
　　in that way　Top　now　AF-Prg-run　flag
　　那樣　　　現在　將跑　　旗
　　他那樣說，「現在要賽跑奪旗。
　　He said, "Now you'll be racing for the flag.

22. taubarət maamaaləŋ,   nita rətən   maamaaləŋ,
    neighbor   young men   our   village   young men
    鄰   男青年   咱   村   男青年們
    鄰村的少年和咱們村的少年，
    The young men from the neighboring village and our village.

23. ma-gizəm dadua, ma-gizəm   maamaaləŋ."
    Sta-strong all   Sta-strong young men
    壯   都   強   男青年們
    大家都很強壯，少年們都強壯。」
    They are all strong, and the young men are strong."

24. laila   ka, "uhuni ka, ma-zuah di dini.
    in that way Top   now   Top   AF-race   here
    那樣   現在   走標   這裡
    （主持人）那樣說，「現在從這裡走標（賽跑）。
    (The chief) said, "Now you start racing from here.

25. m<a>i-talam   di daran ka, mata   di daya.
    AF-Prg-run   road   toward   east
    將跑   路   向   東
    要跑的路線是向東。
    You'll run on the road to the east.

26. pasakən daya ka, mata   di amisan.
    arrive   east   toward   north
    到達   東   向   北
    到了東方再轉向北。
    After you arrive at the east, then turn to the north.

27. mata   di taubarət ka, balua   ni   rətən.
    toward   neighbor   village name Gen village
    向   鄰   日南   的   村
    再向鄰近的 Balua 村。
    Then you go to the neighboring village of Balua.

28. imu, imu   maamaaləŋ ma-baza k<in>awas?"
    you   you   young men   AF-know Prf-word
    你們 你們 男青年們   知   話
    你們少年聽懂話了嗎？」
    You, you young men, do you understand my words (= do you follow me)?"

29. laila   ka   pikadun,   laila   ka   m\<a\>i-talam.
    so   set out   Asp   AF-Prg-run
    那樣   出發   了   跑
    就那樣出發了，在賽跑了。
    So they set out, and they were racing.

30. pikadun   dadua   ma-gizəm   maamaaləŋ.
    set out   all   Sta-strong   young men
    出發   全體   強壯   男青年們
    全體強壯的少年都出發了。
    All the strong young men set out.

31. baabah   saw   ka   mu-kawas,   "ima   ki   ma-gizəm?"
    many   people   AF-talk   who   Nom   Sta-strong
    多   人   說   誰   強
    很多人問，「誰最強？」
    Many people asked, "Who is the strongest?"

32. "ta-kitaʔ-i   ima   ka,   mi-talam   ma-ula   lia."
    let's-look-Imp   who   AF-run   AF-lead   Asp
    咱看   誰   跑   先   了
    「咱們看誰跑得最快！」
    "Let's see who is the fastest runner."

33. apu,   apu   ka,   pa-duən   lia,   duən,   duən,   ma-hatan.
    old woman   old woman   Top   play-gong   Asp   gong   gong   AF-laugh
    婆   婆   敲鑼   了   鑼   鑼   笑
    老婆婆敲鑼了，鑼聲笑聲。
    The old woman played the gong, the sounds of the gong, and they were laughing.

34. hauha   ki   pasakən.   "ima   ki   m-ula   lia?
    sure   Nom   arrive   who   Nom   AF-first   Asp
    確定   到達   誰   先   了
    要確定到達終點。「看誰領先了？
    Make sure that they reach the terminal. "Who is leading?

35. p\<in\>a-siatu   lubahiŋ   nita,   nita   maamaaləŋ.
    Prg-wear-clothes   red   we   we   young men
    穿衣   紅   咱   咱   男青年
    穿紅衣的是咱們的男青年。
    The ones in red are our young men.

36. takita   ima   ki   ma-gizəm   iu   m-ula.
     let's look   who   Nom   Sta-strong   and   AF-lead
     咱看   誰   強   和   先
     咱們看誰最強壯和領先。
     Let's see who is the strongest and leading.

37. haiha   ki   asilu,   haiha   ki   damuri.
     seem   Nom   personal name   seem   Nom   personal name
     似乎   人名   似乎   人名
     似乎是 Asilu 和 Damuri（領先）。
     It seems to be Asilu and Damuri (who are leading).

38. m-ula   pasakən   ka,   nita,   nita   maamaaləŋ."
     AF-lead   arrive   our   our   young men
     先   到達   咱的   咱的   男青年們
     領先到達的是咱們的少年。」
     The ones who led and arrived first are our young men.

39. taukua   iu   baabah   saw,   ma-hatan   iu   hatan.
     chief   and   many   people   AF-laugh   and   laugh
     長官   和   多   人   笑   和   笑
     長官和許多人笑了又笑。
     The chief and many people laughed and laughed.

40. m-itun   lia   ki   taukua   ka   mu-kawas   iu   ma-taru.
     AF-stand up   Asp   Nom   chief   AF-talk   and   Sta-big
     站   了   長官   說   和   大
     長官站了起來大聲說。
     The chief stood up and said in a loud voice,

41. uhuni   iu   razəm   ka,   mi-talam   barəbar.
     now   and   New Year's day   AF-run   flag
     現在   又   過年   跑   旗
     現在過年賽跑奪旗。
     "Today is the New Year's day and you raced for the flag."

42. suan   lia   ki   taubarət,   ma-sika-sikat.
     lose   Asp   Nom   neighbor   Sta-Red-shy
     輸   了   鄰   很難為情
     鄰村的少年輸了，很不好意思。
     The neighboring villagers lost, and they were embarassed.

43. taukua ka mu-dudu lia, "ta-ʔaraway-i lai nita!"
   chief AF-talk Asp let's-sing and dance-Imp Asp we
   長官 講 了 咱牽田 了 咱
   長官說了，「咱們牽田唱歌跳舞吧！」
   The chief said, "Let's sing and dance."

44. baabah saw ka, ma-hatan; hauha ka, imisu.
   many people AF-laugh sure that
   多 人 笑 確定 那
   很多人笑，那是確定的。
   Many people laughed, and that was certain.

45. hauha ka iu naki mu-dudu ma-mərək.
   sure and my AF-talk AF-unable
   確定 又 我的 講話 不會
   我的話確定只有這些，我不擅言辭。
   That's all what I have to say, and I don't know how to say it appropriately.

46. ayan nu ayan, saysay yawira.
   everything end
   根源 根源 每件 結束
   根源歌到此結束。
   The song of ayan ends here.

Song 2b. mazuah 走標（短版）*Racing* (short version)

1. ayan nu ayan ayan nu laita.
                               we
  根源   咱們
  根源，咱們唱根源。
  Let's sing ayan, the song of our origin.

2. hauha ka imisu dali iu uhuni.
  sure   that   day and now
  確定   那   日 和   現在
  確定是那時候的今天。
  It is certain that it is the present time on that day.

3. laila   ka isia mu-dudu ki apuan.
  in that way Top he AF-talk Nom elder people
  那樣   他 講   長輩
  長輩他那樣講話。
  The elderly said so.

4. mu-kawas ki apuan, tumala siana.
  AF-talk   Nom elderly people listen obey
  講   長輩   聽   遵從
  長輩講的話，要聽從。
  (We should) listen to the instructions of the elderly.

5. uhuni dali ka, nita, nita iu razəm.
  now   day Top our   our and New Year
  現今 日   咱的 咱的 和 新年
  今天是咱們的新年。
  Today is our New Year's day.

6. isit adaŋ iu ilas isit xasəp iu dali.
  ten one   month ten five   day
  十 一   月 十 五   日
  今天是十一月十五日。
  Today is December 15.

7. abasan   suadi   ka maa-ʔisakəp di dini.
  elder sibling younger sibling Top Rec-get together Loc here
  兄姊   弟妹   相聚在一起   這裡
  兄弟姊妹一起在這裡聚會。
  Brothers and sisters gather together here.

8. rətən a taukua ka laila ki mu-kawas.
   village   chief   in that way   AF-talk
   村   頭目   那樣   講
   村中的頭目那樣講話了。
   The head of the village said so.

9. "uhuni dali ka ma-taru iu razəm."
   now   day   Sta-big   New Year's day
   現在   日   大   新年
   「今天是大新年。」
   "Today is the great New Year's day."

10. nahani ki taubarət maamaalən ma-gizəm.
   come   neighbor young men Sta-strong
   來   隔壁   男青年們   強壯
   鄰村的強壯青年來了。
   The strong young men came from the neighboring villages.

11. nahani mi-talam, mi-talam barəbar.
   come   AF-race   AF-race flag
   來   跑   跑   旗
   他們來賽跑奪旗。
   They came to race for the flag.

12. "imu, imu maamaalən ka ma-gizəm dadua.
   you you young men   Sta-strong all
   你們 你們 男青年們   強   都
   你們男青年都很強壯。
   "You young men are all strong.

13. taubarət maamaalən, nita, nita maamaalən,
   neighbor young men   our   our young men
   鄰   男青年們   咱   咱 男青年們
   鄰村的少年，（跟）咱們村的少年，
   The young men from the neighboring village, (and) the young men in our village,

14. ma-gizəm dadua, ma-gizəm dadua.
   Sta-strong all   Sta-strong all
   強壯   全體   強   都
   全體都很強壯。
   They are all strong.

15. laila   ka,   "uhuni ka   ma-zuah di dini."
    in that way   now   AF-race   here
    那樣   現在   走標   這裡
    （主持人）那樣說，「現在從這裡走標（賽跑）。」
    (The chief) said, "Now you start racing from here.

16. pikadun   dadua   ma-gizəm   maamaaləŋ.
    set out   all   Sta-strong   young men
    出發   全體   強壯   男青年們
    全體強壯的少年都出發了。
    All the strong young men set out.

17. hauha ki pasakən.   "ima   ki m-ula   lia?
    sure   arrive   who   AF-first Asp
    確定   到達   誰   先   了
    要確定到達終點。「看誰領先了？
    Make sure that they reach the terminal. "Who is leading?

18. p<in>a-siatu   lubahiŋ   nita nita maamaaləŋ.
    Prf-wear-clothes   red   our   our   young men
    穿衣   紅   咱   咱   男青年們
    穿紅衣的是咱們的男青年。
    The ones in red are our young men.

19. haiha ki asilu,   haiha ki damuri.
    seem   personal name   seem   personal name
    似乎   人名   似乎   人名
    似乎是 Asilu 和 Damuri（領先）。
    It seems to be Asilu and Damuri (who are leading).

20. baabah saw   ma-hatan iu hatan.
    many   people   AF-laugh   and laugh
    多   人   笑   和   笑
    許多人笑了又笑。
    Many people laughed and laughed.

21. apu,   apu   p<a>a-duən, duən,   duən,   duən,   ma-hatan
    old woman old woman play-Prg-gong gong   gong   gong   AF-laugh
    老婆婆   老婆婆   在敲銅鑼   敲鑼   敲鑼   敲鑼   笑
    老婆婆在敲鑼，敲著，敲著，敲著，笑了。
    The old woman was playing the gong, the sounds of the gong, and they laughed.

22. baabah   saw   m-itun   lia,   ma-hatan   iu   hatan.
    many   people   AF-rise   Asp   AF-laugh   and   laugh
    多   人   站   了   笑   和   笑
    許多人站著，笑了又笑。
    Many people stood up and they laughed and laughed.

23. hauha   ka   iu   naki   mu-dudu   ma-mərək.
    sure   I   AF-talk   AF-unable
    確定   我   講話   不會
    我的話確定只有這些，我不擅言辭。
    That's all what I have to say, and I don't know how to say it appropriately.

24. ayan   nu   ayan,   saysay   yawira.
                          everything   end
    根源   每件   結束
    根源歌到此全部結束。
    The song of ayan ends here.

Song 3. razəm 新年請客 *Entertaining Guests during the New Year*

The words of this New Year's song were written by Pan Rung-jang, narrated by Pan Jin-yu, and transcribed and translated by Paul Li in Auran, Puli, June 9, 1998. Recorded on Jan. 6, 1999. Video-taped and recorded on June 3, 2001.

潘榮章作詞，潘金玉念詞，李壬癸記音、翻譯，1998 年 6 月 9 日於埔里鎮愛蘭里。潘金玉唱，1999 年 1 月 6 日錄音。2001 年 6 月 3 日重新錄音和錄影。

Let it be noted that there is a code-switching of Taiwanese (Southern Min) sentences and Pazih sentences in the following. But there is no mixture of languages in the same sentence. Sentences 2-5 and 12-23 are in Taiwanese, while Sentences 1, 6-11, and 24-34 are in Pazih.

請注意這首歌詞有語言轉換的現象，就是台灣閩南語跟巴宰語之間的轉換。每一句都是單純的台語或巴宰語。第 2-5, 12-23 句都是台語，而第 1, 6-11, 24-34 句都是巴宰語。

1. ayan nu ayan, ayan ni laita.
                              Gen we
   根源   咱們
   咱們唱根源的歌。
   Let's sing ayan, the song of our origin

2. kamsia siongte ci tua e untian.
   thank God most great benevolence
   感謝 上帝 至 大 恩典
   感謝上帝至大的恩典。
   Thank God for His great benevolence.

3. tit tio' inchua cit ni iu cit ni.
   get lead one year and one year
   得 著 引領 一 年 又 一 年
   得到引領一年又一年。
   He leads us year after year.

4. guan tann singsit kamsia cu tua-un.
   we now honest thank God great benevolence
   阮 今 誠實 感謝 主 大 恩
   阮今誠實感謝主大恩。
   We are really grateful to God's benevolence.

5. hɔ   guan thiann cu   na   tua iu   na   chim.
   let us   love   God more big and more deep
   乎   阮   疼   主   愈   大   又   愈   深
   乎阮疼主愈大又愈深。
   We love God even more and deeper.

6. dali iu   uhuni ka, ma-taru   iu dali.
   day   now Sta-big   day
   日   現在   大   日子
   今天是大日子。
   Today is a great day.

7. abasan   u   suadi   maa-ʔisa-ʔisakup.
   elder sibling   and younger sibling Rec-Red-get together
   兄姊   和   弟妹   一起
   兄弟姊妹聚在一起。
   Brothers and sisters are gathering together.

8. hauha   ka   isia,   laila   ka   imisu.
   sure   then   in that way   that
   確定   那時   那樣   那
   確定是在那個時候。
   It is certain that it is at that time.

9. mu-kawas ki   apuan,   riak ki   kaakawas.
   AF-talk   Nom elder people good Nom word
   講,說   前輩   好   話
   前輩說話,他們所說的都是吉利的話。
   Elderly people say only nice words.

10. mu-tudu   ki   apuan,   tumala ka   siana.
    AF-instruct Nom elderly people listen Conj obey
    教誨   前輩   聽   且   遵從
    前輩教誨,聽了要遵從。
    When elderly people give instructions, we should listen.

11. uhuni u   dali ka   raa-razaw   iu   razəm.
    now   day   Red-celebrate   New Year
    今   天   正在過   新年
    今天正在過新年。
    Today we are celebrating the New Year's day.

12. guan   tann   taike   chut   siann   lai   gimsi.
    we   now   all   speak out   come recite poetry
    阮   今   大家   出   聲   來   吟詩
    現在咱們大家出聲來吟詩。
    Now let's all chant and recite poetry.

13. kamsia   sioŋte   chua   guan   kue   sinni.
    thank   God   lead   us   celebrate New Year
    感謝   上帝   帶   阮   過   新年
    感謝上帝，帶領咱們過新年。
    Thank God for leading us to celebrate the New Year.

14. sekan   zit-ci   na   cui   it-tit   lau.
    world   day   like water keep   flow
    世間   日子   若   水   一直   流
    人世間過日子像水一般地流個不停。
    The days pass by just like the flowing of water.

15. guan   tio   hiong   cing   kin   kiann   bo   yanti.
    we   must   toward front haste   walk   without   delay
    阮   著   向   前   緊   行   無   延遲
    咱們要一直向前走，不延遲。
    We have to move forward without hesitation.

16. sinchun   banmi   khi   ku   lɔŋ   wann   sin.
    New Year   everything   throw away   old   all   change   new
    新春   萬物   去   舊   攏   換   新
    過年萬物除舊佈新。
    During the New Year all the old change to the new.

17. kiu   cu   ya   wann   guan   sim   ciann   cue   sin.
    ask   God   also   change   our   mind   become   as   new
    求   主   也   換   阮   心   成   作   新
    祈求上帝也將咱們的心情換新。
    Ask God to change the state of our mind also and renovate it.

18. cit   tai   kue   liau   cit   tai   iu   cai   lai.
    one   generation   after Asp   one   generation   and   again   come
    一   代   過   了   一   代   又   再   來
    一代過了，另一代又來了。
    Generation after generation.

19. citbakni ku   ciann cue lau tua lang.
    blink   long become as   old big person
    一目睨   久   成   作   老   大   人
    眨眼之間，人已變老了。
    People get old in just a blinking of the eyes.

20. guan e   zitci zu   cinn zu   cui   lau.
    our   Gen day   like arrow like water flow
    阮   的   日子   如   箭   如   水   流
    咱們的光陰似箭如流水。
    Our time passes by like an arrow and water flowing.

21. zit zit ti   i   kho cu   kiankɔ sin.
    day day devote effort rely God strong faith
    日   日   致   意   靠   主   堅固   信
    每天致意，依靠主有信心。
    We devote our efforts everyday, rely on God, and have faith in God.

22. guan kiann tinn   lɔ   kin   kiann bu   yanti.
    we   walk   heaven road haste walk   without delay
    阮   行   天   路   緊   行   無   延遲
    咱們走天路，快走不延遲。
    We walk to the heaven in a haste without delay.

23. hiong   cing   phau cau   tit   kau   cu   sin   pinn.
    toward front run   walk till arrive God body side
    向   前   跑   走   直   到   主   身   邊
    向前直行，到主身邊。
    Run forward all the way until we get close to God's side.

24. ita, ita dadua maa-ʔisakəp   di   dini.
    we   we   all   Rec-get together   Loc here
    咱   咱   大家   一起   此地
    咱們大家聚在這裡。
    We are all gathering together here.

25. kaidi   taukua ni   xuma, paka-tahayak taukua.
    here   chief   Gen home   Caus-weary   chief
    在此地 頭目   的   家   感謝   頭目
    在頭目的家，感謝頭目。
    Here at the chief's house, and thanks to the chief.

26. taukua iu   apuan   ka, ma-hatan   mu-kawas.
    chief   and old woman   Top AF-laugh   AF-talk
    頭目   和   老太婆   笑   說
    頭目和他老婆笑著說。
    The chief and his old wife said smilingly,

27. "uhuni   iu   dali ka, nita, nita iu razəm."
    now   day Top we   we   New Year
    現   日   咱   咱   新年
    「今天是咱們的新年。」
    "Today is our New Year's day."

28. mu-kawas   ki   apuan,   "kuaŋ   saysay, ma-sikat.
    AF-talk   Nom old woman none   what   Sta-embarassed
    說   老太婆   沒   什麼   不好意思
    老太婆（頭目夫人）說，「沒什麼，不好意思。
    The old woman said, "We have little to entertain the guests. We are embarrassed.

29. nahada   iu   dadua   p<a>uzah   di binayu.
    exist   all   Prg-come   mountain
    有   都,全部   來   山
    有從山上來的各種東西。
    There are various dishes from the mountains.

30. nahada   ki   saysay   p<a>uzah   ni   iu   raxuŋ.
    exist   all sorts of things Prg-come   Gen   stream
    有   各色各樣   來   溪
    有從溪中來的各種東西。
    The other dishes are from the streams.

31. ma-ŋazəp   ki   saysay   b<in>axa   ni   iu babaw."
    Sta-leftover   all sorts of things Prf-give   Gen   God
    剩   各物   給,賞賜   天上
    各種東西都有剩餘，是上天所賜的。」
    There is more than enough in each dish, as bestowed by God."

32. uhuni dali ka, paka-tahayak   taukua.
    now   day   Caus-weary   chief
    現在   日   感謝   頭目
    今天謝謝頭目。
    Let's thank the chief today.

33. hauha ka iu naki mu-dudu ma-mərək.
    sure   my   AF-talk   AF-unable
    確定   我的 講話   不會
    我的話確定只有這些，我不擅言辭。
    That's all what I have to say, and I don't know how to say it appropriately.

34. ayan nu ayan, saysay   yawira.
                      everything end
    根源   根源 每件   結束
    根源歌到此全部結束。
    The song of ayan ends here.

Song 4. 新居落成 *Inauguration of a New House*

The words for the inauguaration of a new house were written by Pan Jin-yu, with *ayan* melody, on Oct.5, 1995, transcribed and translated by Paul Li.

慶祝新居落成典禮的歌詞是潘金玉於 1995 年 10 月 5 日所作，也用 ayan 曲調，李壬癸記音、翻譯。

1. ayan nu ayan ayan nu laita.　　ayan nu ayan ayan nu laita.
　　　　　　　　　　　　　　our　　　　　　　　　　　　　　　　　our
   根源　　　根源 根源　　　咱們　　　根源　　　根源 根源　　　咱們
   根源，咱們唱根源。　　　　　　　　　根源，咱們唱根源。
   Let's sing ayan, the song of our origin.　　*Let's sing ayan, the song of our origin*

2. hauha ka imisu dali u uhuni.
   sure　　　　he　　day　now
   確定　　　　他　　天　　今
   他說確定在今天。
   He was certain that it was today.

3. laila　　　ka isia laila　　ka mu-dudu.
   in that way　　then　in that way　　AF-talk
   那樣　　　　　那時　那樣　　　　講
   那時講的就是那樣。
   That was what he said.

4. makahatan u hatan abasan u suazi.
   happy　　　　　laugh　elder sibling and younger sibling
   高興　　　　　　笑　　兄姊　　　　和　弟妹
   兄弟姊妹都很高興，也都笑了。
   Brothers and sisters were all happy and laughed.

5. maa-ʔisa-u-ʔisakup　　imu ita dadua.
   Rec-Red-get together　　you　we　all
   在一起　　　　　　　　　你們　咱　全體
   你們、我們咱們全體在一起。
   You and we are gathering together.

6. laila　　　ka isia mu-dudu ka iu rahan.
   in that way　　then　AF-talk　　and word
   那樣　　　　　那時　講　　　　和　話
   那時長輩所講的話就是那樣。
   That is what the elderly people said at that time.

7. p\<a\>uzah u apuan   rutud-aw   iu nita.
   Prg-come   elder people   pass down-PF   we
   來自   長輩   傳承,繼承   咱

   長輩傳下來的咱們要繼承。
   We should inherit the traditions passed down by the older generation.

8. ana   u paxaziŋ   apuan   nu iu rahan.
   don't Caus-miss   elder people   word
   別   丟失   長輩   話

   長輩的話別丟失了。
   Don't miss their words.

9. laila   ka mu-tudu   laila   ka mu-kawas.
   in that way   AF-instruction in that way   AF-talk
   那樣   教訓   那樣   講,說

   教訓我們的話就是那樣。
   That's their instruction.

10. hauha ka imisu laila   ka isia.
    sure   that   in that way   then
    確定   那個   那樣   那時

    確定是在那個時候。
    It is certain that it was at that time.

11. uhuni iu dali ka ma-taru   iu dali.
    now   day   Sta-big, good   day
    今   日   大,好   日

    今天是吉日。
    Today is a great day.

12. ita ka   mu-sumat tumala mu-sumat.
    we   Top AF-pray   listen AF-prayer
    咱   信主,祈禱 聽   祈禱,禱告

    咱們信基督的人禱告，也相信（聽信）禱告。
    We Christians pray and listen to prayers.

13. abababaw laila ka mu-rapun   yami lai.
    God   AF-protect, take care of us   Asp
    上帝   就   保護,照顧   我們 了

    上帝就會保護我們了。
    God takes care of us.

14. yami mu-sumat ka mu-baxa riak xumak.
    we AF-pray AF-give good house
    我們 祈禱 賞賜 好 房屋
    我們祈禱，上帝就賞賜好房子（給我們）。
    When we pray, God will give us a good house.

15. laila ka isia riak a pa-laləŋ-an.
    in that way that good PA-live-LF
    那樣 那 好 住
    那就好居住。
    It is comfortable to live in.

16. dali iu dali ka raa-rapun dadua.
    day day Red-protect, take care all
    日 日 保護,照顧 全體
    天天保護大家。
    God takes care of us everyday.

17. nahada dadua b<in>axa di babaw.
    exist all benevolence God
    有 全部 賞賜 上天
    什麼都有，都是上天賞賜的。
    We have all that we need, as given by God.

18. ana paxarihan abababaw b<in>axa.
    don't forget God benevolence
    別 忘記 上帝 賞賜
    別忘記上帝的賞賜。
    Don't you forget about the benevolence of God.

19. hauha ka iu naki mu-dudu ma-mərək.
    sure my AF-talk AF-unable
    確定 我的 講話 不會
    我的話確定只有這些，我不擅言辭。
    That's all what I have to say, and I don't know how to say it appropriately.

20. ayan nu ayan saysay yawira.
    everything end
    根源 根源 每件 結束
    唉焉到此全部結束。
    The song of ayan ends here.

C. Kaxabu Songs 四庄歌謠

Song 1. 四庄的傳統生活 *Kaxabu Traditional Life*

Sung and interpreted by Pan Ying-jiau (female, 75) at Niumian, Puli, on June 3, 2001
Recorded, transcribed and translated by Paul Li, video-taped by Jian Shih-lang and Lu Yi-jun
潘英嬌（女，75歲）唱及解說 (2001.6.3)
李壬癸錄音、記詞及翻譯，簡史朗、呂憶君錄影，地點：埔里鎮牛眠里

1. ʔuhuza yami ma-laləŋ dini.
before we AF-live here
從前 我們 住 這裡
從前我們住這裡
We live here in the past

paxuumaʔ mulasiʔ iu dadas.
plant rice plant and sweet potato
種 稻 又 地瓜
種稻和地瓜
planting rice and sweet potatoes

paxuuma xaidang iu baunay.
plant bean and peanut
種 豆 又 花生
種豆與花生
planting beans and peanuts

paxuuma kaziuk iu tupazay.
plant convolvulus and lettuce
種 空心菜 又 萬苣
種空心菜與萬苣
planting water convolvulus and lettuce.

2. mu-kusa binayuʔ mu-kumux luxut.
AF-go mountain AF-catch deer
去 山 捕 鹿
去山上捕鹿
(We) went to the mountains to catch deer

binayuʔ bauzak, binayuʔ balan,
mountain pig mountain cat
山 豬 山 貓
山豬，山貓，
wild pigs and mountain-cat,

binayuʔ muris, binayuʔ walis,
mountain deer mountain fox
山 羊 山 狐狸
山羊，山狐狸，
mountain goats and foxes,

binayuʔ patauʔ, iu maket.
mountain chicken and pygmy deer
山 雞 和 羌
山雞和羌
bamboo partridges and muntjac/pygmy deer

m-ukusaʔ axuŋ mu-kumux ʔalaw.
AF-go stream AF-catch fish
去 溪 捕 魚
去溪裡捕魚
(We) went to the streams to catch fish

mu-kumux upian iu tulaʔ.
AF-catch slippery fish and eel
捕 鯰魚 和 鰻
捉鯰魚和鰻
to catch slippery fish and eel

ʔatapi, buzing, ʔalaw-siaw.
loach goby fish name fish name
石貼仔 苦甘仔 石斑魚
石貼仔，苦甘仔，石斑
all kinds of fishes

kuzung iu tarituk.
shrimp and spiral shell
蝦 和 螺絲
蝦和螺絲
shrimps and spiral shells.

Song 2. 飲酒歌 *Let's Drink*

Sung and intrepreted by Pan Hsiu-mei (female), Puli, Jan.21, 1988
Transcribed and translated by Paul Li
潘秀梅 (1988.1.21) 唱
李壬癸記音、翻譯

1. ta-daux-i[1]　　?inusat,　　?ita,　　?ita　dadua?.
   let's-drink-Imp　wine　　　we　　　we　　all
   咱們喝　　　　酒　　　　咱　　咱　　全體
   咱們喝酒吧！咱們大家。
   Let's drink, all of us!

2. ?ita,　　?ita　dadua?,　　?abasan　　　suazi?[2].
   we　　　we　　all　　　　elder siblings　younger siblings
   咱　　咱　　全體　　　兄姊　　　　弟妹
   咱們大家，兄弟姊妹們。
   All of us, brothers and sisters.

---

[1] ta daux-i ‘咱們喝吧！’，mu-daux ‘喝（主事焦點）’，daux-i ‘喝！（受事焦點，命令式）’。

[2] ?abasan ‘兄姊’，suazi? ‘弟妹’，南島語一般只依年齡而分，不分性別。巴宰語另有 mamah ‘兄’，?iah ‘姊，姨’，?atan ‘嫂’，minu? ‘弟媳’等同輩親屬稱謂。

Song 3. 祭祖歌 ayan 1[1] *Ritual Song for Ancestors 1—Our Origin*

The words of both ritual songs of *ayan* in Kaxabu were written by Pan Jun-nai (male, 83), sung by Pan Hsiu-mei on Jan.21, 1988 and by Pan Ying-jiau on June 3, 2001, and transcribed and translated by Paul Li.

以下這兩首祭祖歌都是潘郡乃（男，83 歲）作詞，潘秀梅 (1988.1.21)、潘英嬌 (2001.6.3) 主唱，李壬癸記音、翻譯。

起首 The beginning:

Ɂayan[2] nu Ɂayan, Ɂayan nu laitaɁ.
                                     we
根源   根源   根源   咱們
咱們唱根源的歌。
Let's sing the ritual song of our origin.

ta-tuduɁ-i[3] Ɂapu[4] a nuki[5] ɁuhuzaɁ.
let's-talk-Imp ancestor Lig   ancient time
談   祖先   連   古時
談起從前的祖先。
Let's talk about ancient ancestors.

Ɂabuk sən ki laŋat.
name is said Nom name
人名   據說 主 名字
他的名字叫做阿木。
It is said he was named Abuk.

ɁisiaɁ ki p<in>ialay[6].
he Nom Prf-start
他   起首
起首的是他。
He was the beginner.

---

[1] 除了曲首的序段和曲尾的尾聲外，有五段。

[2] Ɂayan 或作Ɂaiyan '根源，起源' 是曲名。

[3] ta-duduɁ-i '咱們說吧！' ＜ dudu-, d-a-uduɁ-ay '將要說' 。

[4] Ɂapu '祖母，老（人）' 。

[5] nuki 可能是 nu 與 ki 的組合。

[6] p-in-ialay ＜ pialay '起首' 。

1. "ʔinai, ʔabai, mausay na yakuʔ."
     mother father   leave   I
     媽   爸   離去   我
   「爸爸,媽媽,我要走了。」
   "Dad, Mom, I'm leaving," he said.

   m-asuʔ lawin ʔiu buzux.
   AF-bring bow   and arrow
   帶   弓 和   箭
   （他）帶著弓箭。
   He took a bow and arrows with him.

   mausay dəəhən binayuʔ.
   go   dark   mountain
   去   陰暗   山
   到深山去。
   He was going to the dark (interior) mountains.

2. pikadun kaxu kawazawat daan.
   set out arrive half   road
   起程   到   半   路
   走到半路。
   He set out and went half of his way.

   m-idahin lia[7] ki ʔabuk.
   AF-afraid Asp   name
   怕   了   人名
   阿木害怕了。
   Abuk was afraid.

   ma-ŋəsən humhum mu-ŋazip.
   Sta-afraid animal AF-bite
   怕   猛獸   咬
   怕被猛獸咬。
   He was afraid of being bitten by wild animals.

---

[7] lia 完成貌。

ma-izux   m-ukusa   bayuʔ   ʔawas.
AF-go down   AF-go   side   sea
下山   去   邊   海
下山到海邊。
So he went to the beach.

3. yayi-yayix   lia   ʔisiaʔ.
    check   Asp   he
    查看   了   他
    他仔細查看了。
    He looked around carefully.

    mi-kita   ʔapu   lauluʔ   m<a>aru-batuʔ[8].
    AF-see   old   turtle   Prg-lay-egg
    看   老   龜   在生蛋
    看見一隻大龜正在生蛋。
    He saw a mother turtle laying eggs.

    ma-hata-hatan   lia   ki   ʔabuk.
    Sta-Red-happy   Asp   name
    很高興   了   人名
    阿木很高興。
    Abuk was very happy.

    mə-dəkən   batuʔ   lauluʔ.
    AF-pick   egg   turtle
    揀   蛋   龜
    （他）揀龜蛋。
    He was picking up turtle eggs.

4. mayaw   maru-batuʔ   ya[9]   ʔazang.
    not yet   lay-egg   one
    還沒   生蛋   一個
    有一個蛋還沒生下來。
    One egg was not laid yet.

---

[8] m<a>alu-batuʔ '正在生蛋' < batuʔ '蛋'。

[9] a, ya, wa '連結詞'，（描寫菲律賓語通稱為 ligature），這三種形式出現的語境不同，因此它們是同位語。此句 ya 似當'主語標記'而非'連結詞'。

mu-haday　　ima?　mu-zuzu?　lia.
AF-reach out　hand　AF-take out
伸　　　　　手　　掏
（他）伸手去掏。
He raised his hand to take out the egg.

hapit　　　lia　laulu?,　mə-kəmət[10]　?aaləp.
frightened　Asp　turtle　AF-shrink　　door
嚇　　　了　龜　　收縮　　　　門
海龜嚇了一跳，閉起陰戶。
The turtle was frightened and shrank its vagina.

mu-baza?　dali[11]　lia　ki　?abuk.
AF-know　　day　　Asp　　name
知　　　天　　了　　人名
阿木醒了過來。
Abuk came back to himself.

5. kai-bayu?　?awas,　kuang　saw-saw[12].
at shore　sea　none　person
在　邊　　海　　沒有　　人
在海邊，四下無人。
There was nobody at the seashore.

mi-kita?　kai-bayu?　lənət　　　　　hapuy.
AF-see　at shore　half-burnt firewood　fire
看　　　在 海邊　　餘燼　　　　火
在海邊（他）看見火的餘燼。
He saw a half-burned firewood fire at the beach.

---

[10] mə-kəmət‘收縮（主事焦點）’，kəməd-ən‘（受事焦點）’。這段敘述阿木的手被挾住在大龜的陰戶裡，人隨著大龜飄洋過海。

[11] m(a)-baza dali‘知道一天’，意思是指‘清醒過來’的時候。

[12] saw-saw‘眾多的人’＜ saw‘人’。

piitun   mu-lamut[13]   iax   saw.
go upstream   AF-search carefully   look for   person
溯溪而上   細查   找   人
溯溪而上仔細找人。
He traced back the stream to look for people.

mi-kita busubus, mu-tukah   hinis.
AF-look   smoke   AF-happy   mind
看   煙   開   心
看見炊煙，（他）心就開朗了。
When he saw smoke, his mind opened (he felt greatly relieved).

尾聲 The end：

ʔayan   laita, saysay   lailaʔ?
         we   everything   in that way
根源   咱們 每件
咱們唱根源的歌，到此全部結束。
This is the ritual song of our origin. Everything was like that.

---

[13] mu-lamut '仔細察看，學到，像（主事焦點）'，lamud-ən（受事焦點）。

Song 4. 祭祖歌 ayan 2 *Ritual Song for Ancestors 2—Christianization*

1. ʔayan nu ʔayan, ʔayan nu laitaʔ.

                                                we

   根源   根源   咱們

   咱們唱根源的歌。

   Let's sing the ritual song of our origin.

   ta-duduʔ-i ʔapu a nuki ʔuhuzaʔ.

   let's-talk-Imp ancestor   ancient

   談   祖先   古時

   咱們談從前的祖先。

   Let's talk about our ancestors.

   kapaus ki laŋat, ʔisiaʔ ki m-in-ulaʔ[1].

   name   name   he   AF-Prf-lead

   人名   名字   他   發源

   他的名字叫加保斯，由他起源。

   His name is Kapaus, who was the first (to adopt Christianity).

   mu-lutut[2] musumat[3] maa-iak a ta-tuduʔ.

   AF-get   AF-observe good   Lig Ca-instruction

   得到   敬奉   好   連   教訓

   得以敬奉良好的教訓。

   (We Kaxabu people) got good instructions.

2. ʔini ʔəŋəs sa kapaus, mu-puzah mu-tukut[4].

   not grudge   name   AF-come   AF-spread

   不 吝惜   人名   來   傳播

   加保斯並不吝惜，而來傳播。

   Kapaus spared no effort in spreading the Gospels.

---

[1] m-in-ula '起源' < mula

[2] mu-lutut '得到'，lu-lutud-ay '將會得到' < lutud-。

[3] mu-sumat '敬奉（主事焦點）'，sumad-en（受事焦點）< sumad-。

[4] m-tukut '播種，傳播' < tukut。t-in-ukut lia '已傳播了'。

hauyayakən lia ʔitaʔ mu-kalawaʔ iu lamaʔ[5].
fortunate Asp we AF-receive luck
幸運　　　了　咱們　承受　　　福氣
咱們幸運地承受了福氣。
We are fortunate to receive God's blessing.

tanip-ən[6] samian a ʔabaʔ ʔitaʔ ka daduaʔ.
save-PF God father we all
庇蔭　　神　　　父　　咱們　　全體
咱們大家受到上帝的恩典。
We are all bestowed on.

ʔini samian mu-tanip, ʔalasay mu-suax[7].
not God save almost throw away
不　神　　拯救　　差一點　丟棄
若不是神拯救，（咱們）差一點被遺棄。
We were almost abandoned without God.

3. lama-lamaʔ yu[8] nitaʔ[9] haki maa-səkəlaʔ.
Red-luck we so Rec-meet
幸運　　　　咱們　因此　相遇
咱們很幸運才能遇見（上帝）。
We are lucky so that we have come across God.

ʔazang a hatən a kawas sapan-ən iu nitaʔ[10].
one hundred year receive-PF we
一　　　百　　週年　接　　咱們
咱們迎接了一百週年。
We celebrate the 100th anniversary.

---

[5] mu-kalawaʔ yu lamaʔ 承受福氣，yu 是賓格標記，lamaʔ '福氣' 其重疊形式為 lama-lamaʔ '很多福氣'，比較下文第三段第一句。

[6] tanip-ən '庇蔭，拯救（受事焦點）'，mu-tanip '拯救（主事焦點）'，見下句。

[7] mu-suax '丟棄，遺棄（主事焦點）'，suax-en '（受事焦點）'。

[8] yu 語法功能不明。

[9] ni-ta '咱們的（屬格）'。

[10] 這句是受事焦點的句型，主題是 ʔazaŋ a hatən a kawas，謂語是 sapan-ən iu ni-ta。

dali? ?ilas kai baisia? kaidi sa-sumat-an.
day month at place name at Ins-pray-Loc
天 月 在 地名 在 教堂
每日每月都在牛眠山上教堂。
We go to church every day and month in Baisia?.

pa-pa-luzuax[11] ki nami? kaxu? hanisay saxan.
Caus-PA-transmit we till how many thousand
使傳承 我們 到 數 千
我們要傳承數千年。
We want to transmit (Christianity) for hundreds of years.

?ayan nu ?ayan laita, saysay laila?.
we everything in that way
根源 根源 咱們 任何東西
咱們唱根源的歌,一切都是那樣。
This is the ritual song of our origin. Everything goes that way.

---

11 pa-pa-luzuax '使傳承' ＜luzuax；ma-luzuax(主事焦點),luzuax-ən(受事焦點);pa-
'使役'。

Song 5. 祭祖歌 Ayan 3 父子對唱 Dialogue between Father and Son

This ritual song of *ayan* was sung and interpreted by Lin A-shuang (female, 88) in Niumian, Puli, on Jan.15, 1988 and again on Sept.3, 1998 at the age of 98, transcribed and translated by Paul Li. She said she learned it when she was in her 30s.

林阿雙唱及解說 (1988.1.15)，李壬癸錄音、記詞及翻譯

地點：埔里鎮牛眠里

1. ʔayan   nu,   ʔayan   nu,   ʔayan   nu,   ʔayan   u.

    根源   根源   根源   根源

    咱們唱根源的歌。

    Let's sing the ritual song of our origin.

2. ʔimu   (ka)   daduaʔ i,   ʔabasan,   ʔabasan   suaziʔ   ka   kaidiniʔ
   you   all   elder   elder   younger   stay here
   你們   全部   兄姊   兄姊   弟妹   在這裡

    ma-hata-hatan.
    AF-Red-happy
    高興

    你們兄弟姊妹們在裡都很高興。

    You brothers and sisters are happy here.

3. ka   ʔaluʔ-i,   ka   ʔaluʔ tasan,   ta-daux-i   ʔinusat.
   come-Imp   come   ?   let's-drink-Imp wine
   來   來   咱們喝   酒

    來！來！咱們喝酒吧！

    Come! Come! Let's drink!

4. ʔabaʔi, ʔabasan   suaziʔ   ka   kaidini   ma-hata-hatan.
   Dad   elder   younger   stay here   AF-Red-happy
   父   兄姊   弟妹   在此   快樂

    爸爸，兄弟姊妹們在裡都很快樂。

    Father, brothers and sisters are happy here.

5. ka   ʔaluʔ-i   ka   ta-daux-i   ʔinusat.
   come-Imp   let's-drink-Imp   wine
   來吧   咱們喝   酒

    咱們喝酒吧！

    Come! Let's drink!

子唱 The son sings：

6. "ʔabaʔi ka mausay lia -kuʔ mataru rətən mu-tahan paray.
   Dad　　　　 will go Asp I　　 Sta-big village AF-make money
   爸　　　　　 要走　了 我　　 大　　 部落　 賺　　 錢

爸爸，我要走了，到城市去賺錢。
Father, I'm going to a city to make money.

7. nahazaʔ ka (paray) nahani mu-baxaʔ ka ʔisiw i ka ʔabaʔ i.
   have　　　　 money　 come AF-give　　 you　　 Dad
   有　　　　　 錢　　 回來 給　　　　 你　　 爸

有錢就會拿回來給你，爸爸。
When I come with some money, I'll return and give it to you, Dad.

8. ʔana maxakəkəla yakuʔ.
   don't miss　　　 me
   別　 想念　　　 我

請別想念我！
Don't miss me!

9. ʔisiw ka yak, dusa rakihan mamaləŋ.
   you　 fine two child　 male
   你　 好　 二　 孩　　 男

你好，兩個男孩。
You are fine with two sons.

10. ka ʔana maxakəkəla yakuʔ.
    　　 don't miss　　　 me
    　　 別　 想念　　　 我

別想念我！
Don't miss me!

11. naki a ʔina　 ka ʔini mi-kita yaku ka kuah rəsək.
    my　 mother　 not AF-look me　　 not with respect
    我的 母親　　 不 看　 我　　 沒 看得起

我的母親【繼母】看不起我。
My [step] mother looks down upon me.

12. ka sasay-ən ma-laləŋ ka xumaʔ i ka ʔabaʔ i?
    how-PF　 AF-stay　 home　　 Dad
    如何　 住　　 家　　 爸

我怎麼還能住家裡呢，爸爸？
How can I stay at home, Dad?

13. ka　mausay　ʔada　rətən.
　　will go　　other　village
　　要去　　　別　　部落
　　我要到別的部落去。
　　I'm going to another village.

14. nahaniʔ　ka　mu-baxaʔ　ka　ʔisiw　a　ʔabaʔ.
　　come　　　AF-give　　you　　　Dad
　　回來　　　給　　　　你　　　爸
　　（賺錢）回來給你，爸爸。
　　I'll come back to give you (some money).

15. mausay　disiw　dapidapiʔ.
　　will go　there　cliffs
　　要去　　那裡　懸崖
　　到懸崖那裡。
　　I'm going to the cliffs there.

16. nahazaʔ　dalum　kakanən　ka　yak　lia.
　　have　　water　eat　　　　　　fine　Asp
　　有　　　水　　吃　　　　　好　　了
　　有水可以喝就好了。
　　If there is water to drink, that will be fine.

17. ka　ʔabaʔ,　ʔana　maxakəkəla　ka　yakuʔ　iŋ.
　　Dad　　　don't　miss　　　　　　　me　　Asp
　　爸　　　別　　想念　　　　　　　我
　　爸爸，別想念我。
　　Dad, don't miss me!

18. ʔisiw　ka　yak　dusaʔ　ka　ra-rakihan　ka　mamaləŋ."
　　you　　　good　two　　　Red-child　　male
　　你　　　好　　二　　　孩子　　　　　男
　　你好在還有兩個孩子！」
　　You (still) have two sons."

父唱 The father sings：

19. "rakihan　ʔi.　ʔədər　mausay　lia　siw?
　　son　　　　really　will go　Asp　you
　　孩子　　　真　　要走　　了　　你
　　「兒子，你真的要走了嗎？
　　"Are you really leaving, son?

20. ka   ʔini maxakəkəla ʔabaʔʔ
      not   miss   Dad
      不   想念   爸
    （你）不想念爸爸嗎？
    Don't you miss Dad?

21. rakihan   ʔi,   yakuʔ   ka   saziah.
     son   I   Top bad
     孩子   我   不好
    兒子，是我不好。
    It's my fault, son.

22. ʔana m-ara   nisiw a ʔinaʔ   ka   ʔini ma-luhusu ka   rakihan   iŋ."
    don't AF-marry your   mother   not Sta-like that   son
    若非 娶   你的   母親   不   如此   孩子
    我若沒娶你繼母，孩子，就不會這樣了。」
    If I had not married your (step) mother, it wouldn't have been like that, son."

tautaukua (螞蟻王)

記音 a＝實音 f

♩ = 80

潘金玉 唱(2001/6/3)
李壬癸 錄音/記音(2001/6)
溫秋菊 記譜(2002/6)

tau - tau - kua　　pa - ku - pa - ku - sia.

a - lu,　ta - ka - ni　pu - nu lu - xut.

tau - tau - kua　　pa - ku - pa - ku - sia.

a - lu,　ta - ka - ni　su - may iu　pu - nu lu - xut.

蟬

記音 a = 實音 f

♩ = 84

潘金玉 唱(2001/6/3)
李壬癸 錄音／記音(2001/6)
溫秋菊 記譜(2002/6)

lai - lai - lai　　lai - pia - w.

pia - w sau - ri　　sau - ri ba - tu.

ba - tu ra - ki - han,　　ra - ki yau - zu.

tun - tun am - a - yuk.

216

同伴來看月亮

實音記譜

♩ = 80

潘金玉 唱(2001/6/3)
李壬癸 錄音／記音(2001/6)
溫秋菊 記譜(2002/6)

ba - di,　　a - lu,　　ta - ki - ta - 'i　a - way.

欣賞花、蝴蝶、鳥之歌

記音 g = 實音 f

♩ = 80

潘金玉 唱(2001/6/3)
李壬癸 錄音／記音
溫秋菊 記譜(2002/6)

(1) i - ta, i - ta　da - du - a!　　ta - ki - ta - 'i　tu - la - la!

lu - ba - hing iu　ri - si - law.　　a - y, kiaa - ren　tu - la - la.

(2) ita, ita dadua, ta-kita'i rapiaw na! tabarak iu risilaw. ay, kiaaren rapiaw na!

(3) ita, ita dadua, ta-kita'i ayam na! kaidi babaw di kahuy. ay, kiaaren ayam na!

大水氾濫後分居
Separation after the Big Flood

潘榮章　改寫自日治時期記錄
潘金玉　念詞／唱(1998,1999,2001)
李壬癸　記音(1998,1999,2001)
溫秋菊　記譜(2002)

♩ = 76~80

記音 g = 實音 e～c

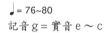

1.a - yan nu a - yan a - yannu la - i - ta

2.a - yan nu a - yan a - yannu la - i - ta ①

①（自第３節起至第２４節曲調同上，單節數曲調同第一行，偶數節同第二行。在反覆
　　歌唱中，音高有逐漸下降趨勢，在第１３節開始稍微提高，但仍低於 g，直到最後一
　　節，才大致回到原來起唱的音高。此外，唱者依自己的習慣將第２節歌詞改變，也就
　　是不用編詞者的歌詞，而重覆第１節歌詞，但大意相同。）

25.hau ka iu na - ki mu - tu - du ma - me - rek

25.hau ka iu na - ki mu - tu - du ma - me - rek ②

26.a - yan nu a - yan say - say ya - wi - ra

rit.

26.a - yan nu a - yan say - say ya - wi - ra ③

②③演唱者依經驗知道結尾的習慣性唱法是反覆同一節特定的詞，亦即第２６節歌詞
　　以呼應方式反覆一次；如此一來第２５節歌詞為保持習慣性的上下句呼應唱法，
　　也必須反覆一次歌詞。從整曲的形式而言，第２５節詞也是進入尾聲前慣用的，
　　因此，這個反覆成為合理的改變。

ayan (走標)
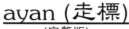
(完整版)

潘榮章 編作(1998)
潘金玉 領唱(1996)
愛蘭松年團契和腔
李壬癸 記音(1998)
溫秋菊 錄音記譜(1996)

記音 g ＝ 實音 e

♩ = 80

(第3～第45節歌詞皆套用上述曲調；單數節配合前兩行，
偶數節配合後兩行。曲調配合歌詞之不同會稍有變化。)

ayan (走標)
(短版)

記音 g = 實音 e
♩ = 78

潘榮章 編作(1998)
潘金玉 領唱(1999)
李壬癸 記音
溫秋菊 錄音記譜(1999)

(領)

(1) a - yan nu a - yan, a - yan nu la - i - ta.

(和)

a - yan nu a - yan, a - yan nu la - i - ta.

(領)

(2) hau - ha ka i - mi - su da - li iu u - hu - ni.

(和)

hau - ha ka i - mi - su da - li iu u - hu - ni.

(第3～第22節歌詞皆套用上述曲調；單數節配合前兩行，
偶數節配合後兩行。曲調配合歌詞之不同會稍有變化。)

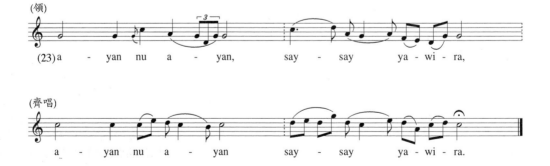

(領)

(23) a - yan nu a - yan, say - say ya - wi - ra,

(齊唱)

a - yan nu a - yan say - say ya - wi - ra.

ayan(新年請客)

潘榮章 編作(1994)
潘金玉 領唱(1996)
愛蘭教會松年團契和腔
李壬癸 記音
溫秋菊 錄音記譜(1996)

記音 g＝實音 e

♩ = 80

(領)
(1) a - yan nu a - yan　　a - yan nu la - i - ta
(2) 感　謝　上　帝　　至　大　的　恩　典，

(和)
(1) a - yan nu a - yan　　a - yan la - i - ta
(2) 感　謝　上　帝　　至　大　的　恩　典。

(第3～第5節曲調同上；略)

(領)
(6) da - li iu u - hu - ni ka ma - ta - ru iu da li
(8) hau - ha ka i - si - a lai - la ka i - mi - su

(和)
da - li iu u - hu - ni　ma - ta - ru iu da - li
hau - ha ka i - si - a lai - la ka i - mi - su

(領)
(7) a - ba - san u su - a - zi maa - 'i - isa - 'i - sa - kup
(9) mu - ka - was ki a - pu - an riak ki kaa - ka - was

(和)
a - ba - san su - a - zi maa - 'i - sa - 'i - sa - kup
mu - ka - was ki a - pu - an riak ki kaa - ka - was

(第10～第33節使用同上曲調；略)

(齊唱)
(34) a - yan nu a - yan say say ya - wi - ra

221

ayan(新居落成(一))

記音 g = 實音 e

♩ = 80

潘金玉 詞 (1995/10/5)
潘金玉 唱 (2001/6/3)
李壬癸 錄音 / 記音
溫秋菊 記譜 (2002/6)

(1) a - yan nu a - yan a - yan nu

a - yan nu la - i - ta

ma - u' sa - i ka i - mi - su

da - li u u - hu - ni.

(2) laila ka isia, laila ka mududu. makahatan u hatan, abasan u suazi.

(3). maa'isau'isakup, imu ita dadua. laila ka isia mududu ka iu rahan.

222

ayan(新居落成(二))

記音 g＝實音 e

♩ = 80

潘金玉 詞(1995/10)
李壬癸 重錄／記音(2001/6/3)
溫秋菊 記譜(2002/6)

(1) a - yan nu a - yan a - yan nu la - i - ta

hau - ha ka i - mi - su, da - li u u - hu - ni,

lai - la ka i - si - a, lai - la ka mu - du - du

ma - ka - ha - tan u ha - tan a - ba - san su - a - zi.

(2) maa 'isau 'isakup imu ita dadua. laila ka isia mudadu ka iu rahan.
pauzah u apuan rutudaw iu nita. ana u paxazing apuan nu iu rahan.

(3) laila ka mutudu laila ka mukawas. hauha ka imisu laila ka isia.
uhuni iu dali, ka mataru iu dali. ita ka musumat tumala musumat.

(4) abababaw laila ka murapun yami lai. yami musumat ka mubaxa riak xumak.
laila ka isia riak a palalengan. dali iu dali ka raarapun dadua.

(5) nahada dadua binaxa di babaw. ana paxarihan abababaw binaxa.
hauha ka iu naki mududu mamerek. ayan nu ayan saysay yawira.

Kaxabu Songs

四庄歌集
飲酒歌

潘郡乃　作詞
潘秀梅　主唱
林清財　錄音採譜
李壬癸　記詞

記音 c = 實音 d

♩ = 104

ta‑dau xi　'i　‑　i　‑　nu　‑　sat

'i ‑ta 'i ‑　ta　‑　a　da　‑　du　‑　a'

'i ‑ ta 'i ‑ ta da‑du‑a'　'a‑ba‑san　sua　‑　zi'

(1)　　　　　　　　　　　(2)

Ayan (1)

潘郡乃　作詞
潘秀梅　主唱
林清財　錄音採譜
李壬癸　記詞

演唱順序：序段
　　　　　中段　　5遍歌詞　旋律同
　　　　　尾聲

Ayan (2)

潘郡乃　作歌
潘秀梅　主唱
林清財　錄音採譜
李壬癸　記詞

記音 d = 實音 b

♩ = 88

'a - yan nu 'a-i-yan　'a - yan nu la-i-ta-a'

ta-du-du-'i 'a-pu-wa　na ki 'u-hu-za'

ka-paus sen ki la-ngat　'i - sia ki mi-nu-la-a'

mu-lu-tu-t mu-su-mat　maa-ya-ka ta-tu-du'

'a-yan 'ai-yan lai-i-ta　sai-sai-la-i-la'

'aiyan (父子對唱)

林阿雙　唱(1995)
溫秋菊　錄音記音整理記譜(1998)
李壬癸　錄音記詞(1990)

Appendix 1. Three Ritual Songs of *Ayan* Recorded by the Japanese 岸裡大社番歌— 野村氏所採

The following three ritual songs of *ayan* were earlier recorded by some Japanese (perhaps Nomura) and found in Ogawa's files. The words of the songs were translated into classical Japanese and annotated by Ogawa or Ino. These songs were published with translation in Japanese by Sato (1934). The original manuscripts by Nomura were then interpreted by Pan Jin-yu on September 1-2, 2002, edited and translated into Chinese and English by Paul Li. Notice that the song in B1 (pp.176-79) is nearly the same as the second song below, and that the first and third songs have not been recorded ever since. Compare the first song below with D Text 2 recorded by Asai.

一、大水氾濫之歌 *The Song of the Great Flood*

1. **ai-yan   nu   ai-yan   dau-doai   lai-tah.**
   ayan   nu   ayan   d<a>uduʔay laita
                              Prf-talk-Fut we
   根源   根源   講故事   咱們
   韻母也，吾要論
   在祭歌中咱們要講咱們的根源。
   In the song of ayan, *we shall talk about (our origin).*

2. **tap-ba-nan   nu   mat-taro   sap-bung   nya   kai-sih**
   tabanan   u   ma-taru   sabuŋ   a   kaisi
   male name   Obl Sta-big   female name   surname
   男名   大   女名   父名
   タバナン長者，サボンカイシ（人名，長者之妹）。
   長者 Tabanan 和他妹妹 Sabuŋ a Kaisi。
   The elder Tabanan and (his sister) Sabuŋ a Kaisi.

3. **ma-hah   ki kid deh-haih   tuppu du a   lal-liuh**
   maxa   kii-kidih-ay   tipuzu   a   rariw.
   then   Red-go down-Fut   top   mountain name
   然後   下來   山峰   山名
   則要落來，高峰アラリウ（山名）
   從山峰下來。
   They were going down from the top of Mount Rariw.

233

4. **mahah   ma sak ku laih di   nguji ngut da   bokgijih**
maxa   maa-sakəl-ay   di   ŋuziŋud-a   bugizi.
then   arrive-Fut   tip   place name
然後   到達   尾端   地名
是以要到在山尾ボギジ（地名）。
快要到達 Bugizi 山尾。
They were arriving at the tip of Mount Bugizi.

5. **ma-hah-pau sungut daih su-ngut du ma bi da-bit**
maxa p<a>u-suŋud-ay   suŋud-u   ma-bidabit
then Prg-build-bridge-Fut bridge   AF-wobble
然後 要舖橋   橋   搖晃
則將造橋，橋曰美好。
那時正要舖橋，而橋搖晃。
They were constructing a bridge, but the bridge wobbled.

6. **di   ma rabahan rahong ini lau isiah, tabanan mataro   sabong nga**
di   mia rabaxan raxuŋ inihaw isia   tabanan ma-taru   sabuŋ   a
Loc   south   river good   then   name   Sta-big   name
南   溪   好   那時   人名   大   名
kaisih.
kaisi
surname
父名
在溪南，敢是伊タバナン長者，サボンカイシ（人名）（沙望皆是）。
到溪南長者 Tabanan 和 Sabuŋ a Kaisi 之處。
To the south of the river were the elder Tabanan and Sabuŋ a Kaisi.

7. **mahah   tau malaai   hommau   a tutut**
maxa   t<a>umala?-ay humaw   a tutut.
then   Prg-hear-Fut   bird name sound
那時   聽   鳥名   聲音
則聽得鳥之聲。
正聽到鳥鳴聲。
Then they heard of the sound of a bird called humaw.

234

8. **at-da maha roaro, tabanan mataro**
ana   maxaruaru,   tabanan   ma-taru.
don't   sad   name   Sta-big
別   傷心   男名   大
又有悶心タバナン長者。
Tabanan，別傷心！
Don't be sad, Elder Tabanan.

9. **kah   mahah   ma sakkul-lai mau-jut-a kat-jau-wan.**
ka   maxa   ma-sakəl-ay   mazəd-a   kazauwan.
then   AF-arrive-Fut   narrow   name
然後   將到
則要到山腰ナルカザワントイウ地二。
快要到 Kazawan 山腰了。
(They) were arriving at the narrow passage of Mount Kazauwan.

10. **mahah   masakul-lai di bun-nu-bun-na tau-man**
maxa   ma-sakəl-ay di bunubun   a   tauman.
          AF-arrive-Fut   mountain name
          將到   山股   山名
則能到山股タウマン。
快要到 Tauman 山股。
(They) were arriving at half way up Mount Tauman.

11. **mit-da-lun di ribunan**
midalum   di ribunan.
get water   place name
取水?   地名
擔水在リブナン。
在 Ribunan 提水。
(They) got water at Ribunan.

12. **mahah   kikitta-ai   ap-boah   likkah   yu   i   ub-bach a lik-kah**
maxa   kii-kitaʔ-ay   abua   lika   iu   uba   lika.
then   Red-see-Fut   female name name   and   female name   name
然後   看   女名   和   女名
所以見得アボアリカ—(阿抹利甲)與ウバアリッカ—(烏肉利甲)。
然後要見 Abua Lika 和 Uba Lika。
Then they were to see Abua Lika and Uba Lika.

13. **ya sia kau-sah a-ba-san-na soa-jih**
yasia kausa abasan a suazi.
they two elder younger
他們 二人 姊 妹
彼二人姊妹。
她們兩人是姊妹。
Those two were sisters.

14. **mahah ma kakau wasai, rahallu hauliah**
maxa maaka-kawas-ay rahal u haw lia.
then Rec-speak-Fut word good Asp
然後 說 話 好 了
則說出好言語。
然後她們互相說好話。
Then they were saying nice words to each other.

15. **atda mahah roaro tabanna mataro**
ana maxaruaru, tabanna ma-taru.
don't sad name Sta-big
別 傷心 人名 大
又有悶心タバナン長者。
別傷心，Tabanan 長者！
Don't be sad, Elder Tabanan.

16. **i-ni lau is siya, tabanna ma-ta-ro**
iniraw isia tabanan ma-taru
that name Sta-big
那個 人名 大
敢是此人乃是長者。
那是 Tabanan 長者。
That is the elder Tabanan (?)

17. **kah ma-hah pau sung-ngut-dai, di mia mi-san nu ra-hong**
ka maxa p<a>u-suŋud-ay di mia amisan u raxuŋ.
then Prg-build-bridge-Fut there north Obl river
然後 造橋 那裡 北 溪
則由此要造橋在西北勢。
他們要在溪北造橋。
Then they were to construct a bridge to the north of the river.

236

18. **sung-ngut du   mabit-da-bit.**
    suŋud-u   ma-bidabit.
    bridge   AF-wobble
    橋   搖晃
    橋曰美章。
    橋搖晃。
    The bridge wobbled.

19. **ma-hah   ma-sa-kul-lai   di bai-yu   au-was.**
    maxa   maa-sakəl-ay   di baiyu   awas.
    then   arrive-Fut   side   sea
    然後   到   水邊   海
    則能到于海邊
    他們到達海邊。
    Then they were arriving at the seaside.

20. **kah   mahah ki-kit-ta-ai,   ai-yam-mu   pa-sukkuwan lak-gu lak-gu   dar-ru-pit**
    ka   maxa   kii-kitaʔ-ay   ayam u   paasukan   lagulagu   darupit.
           then   Red-see-Fut   bird   story   small   bird sp.
           然後   看   鳥   故事   小   鳥名
    所以見得鳥的古事，細細隻鳥（雀ヨリモ小ナル鳥二）。
    然後他們要去看 darupit 鳥講故事。
    Then they were to see the bird called darupit telling a story.

21. **dar-ri   bap-bu bap-bu-kah,   bu bun-nat au-was**
    dali   babu-babukah   bunat   awas.
    day   Red-scratch   sand   ocean
    日   抓   沙   海
    鳥以足爪爬沙乃是海沙。
    有一天鳥在扒海沙。
    On a certain day (the bird) kept scratching the sea sand.

22. **ma-hah   u ki-kit-ta-ai,   kin-nu-hoh   rik-ki-bul**
    maxa   u kii-kitaʔ-ay   k<in>uhuh   rikibul.
    then   Red-see-Fut   barn
    然後   看   做的   穀倉
    所以見得粟倉。
    然後他們看到穀倉。
    Then they were to see an erected(?) barn.

23. **ma-hah   kikit-ta-ai,   pia-hun   ma-ri-his.**
maxa   kii-kita?-ay   piaxun   marihis.
then   Red-see-Fut   millet
然後   看   小米
所以見得黍。
看到小米。
Then they were to see millet.

24. **i-ni lau   is-sia,   tap-ban-nu   mat-taro.**
iniraw   isia   tabanan   ma-taru.
    that   name   Sta-big
那個   男名   大
敢是此個タバナン長者。
那就是長者 Tabanan。
That is the elder Tabanan.

25. **ma-hah   u   matu-hu-mak-kai,   hum-mak   par-ril.**
maxa   u   ma-tu-xumak-ay,   xumak   paril.
then   AF-build-house-Fut   house   kitchen
然後   蓋房子   房子   廚房
則要築室、厝與廚房。
然後要蓋房子和廚房。
Then they were to build a house and kitchen.

26. **ma-hah   na hat-da-ai,   pia-hun   ma-ri-his   di   rub-bu-rub-bu   a   kau-was**
maxa   nahada?-ay   piaxun   marihis   di   ruburubu   kawas.
then   have-Fut   millet   ?   below   sky
然後   有   小米   下   天
由是則有黍在地下。
於是地上他們有小米。
Then they would have millet (on earth) under the sky.

27. **as-su un   nu   uhuni,   au-bil-la   bat-doach**
asu?-un   nu   uhuni,   aubil a   bazuah.
bring-PF   now   later   generation
帶   現在   後   同一代的人
則傳至後世。
代代相傳。
It was passed down to the next generation.

28. ai-yia-nu   ai-yan, sai-sai ya-wi-lan.
   ayan   nu   ayan   saysay   yawira
   根源   根源   所有   結束
   語至此可以也
   根源歌到此全部結束。
   The ritual song of ayan ends here.

全體意譯（黃秀敏譯）：

　　我現在在此講述故事。有名叫 Tabanan 的長者和其妹 Sabuŋ a Kaisi。從高峰下來，來到山尾稱為 Bugizi 的地方，在那裡造橋，命名為美好。在溪南，兩人又聽到鳥叫而悲喜交集。於是去到山腰稱為 Kazauwan 的地方，而且又到山股稱為 Tauman 的地方。其後因擔水在 Ribunan 的地方，會見 Abua Lika 和 Uba Lika，這一對姊妹，彼此交談，不禁歡喜。在此意想不到的地方遇到別人，而又悲從中來。長者又在溪北造橋，命名為美章。可以將常到海邊，在此看到小鳥扒海沙，那裡面有小米倉，同時也看到有黍，於是在此建築房屋，設置房間，並在下面儲存黍，從此以後，黍便在地下，傳至後世。而且故事便如此傳述下來。

二、汜濫後人民分居之歌 *The Song of Living Separately after the Flood*

1. **aiyan nu aiyan, ta du dwau manoh.**
ayan nu ayan, ta-dudu-aw maanu.
               Let's-talk far
根源 咱講 遠
（起唱之語），請論古事。
咱們談到根源，那是很久遠以前。
In the song of ayan, we shall talk about far back in the past.

2. **dauduwai liahah, ubach-pini adapini.**
d<a>uduw-ay lia ha, uba pini, ada pini.
Prg-talk-Fut Asp female name surname female name surname
將講 女名 父名 女名 父名
要論之也，鳥肉比耳阿踏比耳。
要講 Uba Pini 和 Ada Pini 兩姊妹。
We shall trace back to (two sisters), Uba Pini and Ada Pini.

3. **paitul rahong, abasan soadi.**
p<a>itul raxuŋ abasan suadi.
Prg-go up river elder younger
往上 溪 姊 妹
從溪而上兄弟。
姊妹溯溪而上。
The sisters were going up the river.

4. **maha makitaai, tap-banan mataro**
maxa maa-kita?-ay tabanan ma-taru.
then Rec-meet-Fut name Sta-big
然後 將相見 男名 大
是以見得夕バナン長者。
然後要和長輩 Tabanan 相見。
Then they would meet with the elder Tabanan.

5. **maha makauwasai, mausai paimoh**
maxa maa-kawas-ay, "mausay pai mu?"
then Rec-talk-Fut will go Q you
然後 交談 去 你們
故相問情(?)從何去乎？
他們交談。（他問，）「你們要到哪裡去？」
Then they were to talk to each other. He asked, "Where will you go?"

6. **lahai tap-banna mataro, mahah makauwasai.**
   lahay tabanan ma-taru maxa m<a>a-kawas-ay.
       name Sta-big then AF-Prg-tell-Fut
       男名 大 然後 交談

   長者如此問，固有說曰。

   Tabanan 長者問了，所以他們要回答。

   The elder asked them, so they were to reply.

7. **abasan soadi, mausai haiyamih**
   abasan suadi, "mausay haiyami.
    elder sister youner sister will go we
    姉 妹 去 我們

   兄第二人，我等要往我所

   姊妹兩人說，「我們要去⋯

   The sisters said, "We shall go...

8. **mausai mahapajech, pajech u sik-ki daiya.**
   mausay maxa-pazih, pazih u si ki daya."
   will go become-Pazih Pazih   Nom east, above
   去 變成巴宰 巴宰   東,上方

   乃是要為蕃人，蕃乃是東蕃也。

   （我們）要去東方當巴宰人。」

   (We) shall go to the east to become Pazih people."

9. **tatung ngap-ban nu lij-jach.**
   tə-təŋab-an u rizax.
   Red-rise-Loc Obl sun
   出來,上升 的 太陽

   在日出之所也。

   就是日出的地方。

   It is where the sun rises.

10. **manau amisan, manau rapbahan.**
    manaw amisan, manaw rabaxan.
    toward north toward south
    向 北 向 南

    向北向南。

    向北再向南。

    Toward the north, and then toward the south.

11. **haudauduwai,   tatu   maumauwan   tau   maumauwan.**
    haw   d<a>uduw-ay   tatu   maumauwan   tau   maumauwan.
    Prg-talk-Fut   male name   male name
    　　說　　　　　男名　　　　　　男名
    再論甲乙二人。
    他們要說 Tatu Maumauwan 和 Tau Maumauwan 的故事。
    They were to talk about Tatu Maumauwan and Tau Maumauwan.

12. **maha   masik-kulaih   tap-banna   mataro.**
    maxa   masi-kəla   tabanan   ma-taru.
    then   move-meet   name   Sta-big
    然後　　去見　　　　　男名　　　大
    則相遇長者之所。
    然後他們要去見長輩 Tabanan。
    Then they would meet with the elder Tabanan.

13. **mahah   pabaruddai,   rahal-lu   hauliak.**
    maxa   pabarəd-ay   rahal u   hau-riak.
    then   reply-Fut   word   very fine
    然後　　相應答　　　話　　很好
    則有答好言語。
    然後他們會互相問好。
    Then they would say "Very fine" to each other.

14. **mausai   haiyami,   mahadahah,   dahoh   saraumoh.**
    "mausay   haiyami   maxa-daxə   daxu   saraumaw.
    will go   we   become-savage savage place name
    去　　　我們　　變成生番　　　生番　　地名
    我等要去我所，乃是為生番，是生番沙漏毛 (サラウモ一蕃號也)。
    「我們要到 Saraumaw（今梨山？）那地方去變生番。
    "We shall go and become savages like those living in Saraumaw.

15. **ada   mahah   roaro,   tap-banna   mat-taro.**
    ana   maxa-ruaru,   tabanan   ma-taru."
    don't produce-tears   name   Sta-big
    別　　傷心　　　　　男名　　　大
    聞得憂悶者乃是長者。
    別傷心，Tabanan 長輩。」
    Don't be sad, elder Tabanan."

16. **inilau   issia,   mahah pau   sug-ngut-dai.**
    iniraw   isia   maxa   p<a>u-suŋud-ay.
             there   then   Prg-build-bridge-Fut
             那裡   然後   要鋪橋
    敢是如此則要造橋。
    在那裡似乎正要鋪橋。
    Then they were constructing a bridge.

17. **sug-ngut du ma bit-da-bit, i tat-tu maumauwan.**
    suŋud-u   ma-bidabit   i tatu   maumauwan.
    bridge   AF-wobble   male name
    橋   搖晃   男名
    橋號マビダビ，乃是タトウマウマウワン。
    Tatu Maumauwan 在橋上搖晃。
    Tatu Maumauwan was staggering on the bridge.

18. **taumaumauwan, pis-su lik-khit di   sug-ngut.**
    tau maumauwan pisurixit   di   suŋut.
    male name   slip off   Loc bridge
    男名   滑下去   在   橋
    投茅茅灣滑落于橋下。
    Tau Maumauwan 在橋上滑下去了。
    Tau Maumauwan slipped off from the bridge.

19. **alulaisiah,   tattu maumauwan.**
    "alu" lai sia tatu   maumauwan.
    come Asp he   male name
    來   他 男名
    喚其上來者乃是タトウマウマウワン（人名）
    Tatu Maumauwan 叫他道，「上來吧！」
    Tatu Maumauwan said, "Come on!"

20. **us-sa laisu,   mausaih-yakuh**
    "usa   lai siw. mausay yaku
    go   Asp you   will go I
    去   了   你   去   我
    答曰：汝自回去，我要去。
    （Tau Maumauwan 答說，）「你先去。我也要離去了。
    "You go ahead. I'm leaving

21. **mahah luk-khut, luk-khut-tu noang.**

maxa-luxut,	luxud-u	nuaŋ."
become-deer	deer	ox
變鹿	鹿	牛

變為鹿，乃是麕鹿也。

變成鹿，是麕鹿。」

to become a deer, a pygmy deer."

22. **tatu maumauwan, mahah mausai mahah dakho.**

tatu maumauwan	maxa	mausay	maxa-daxu.
male name	then	will go	become-savage
男名	於是	要去	當生番

不得已自去為生蕃也。

於是 Tatu Maumauwan 變成生番了。

Tatu Maumauwan then became a savage.

23. **aiyan nu aiyan, saisaiya wilan.**

ayan	nu	ayan	saysay	yawira.
			everything	end
			全部	結束

息唱，論至此可以也。

根源歌到此全部結束。

The song of ayan ends here.

全體意譯（黃秀敏譯）：

　　來講故事。有名叫 Uba Pini（鳥肉比耳）和 Ada Pini（阿踏比耳）的兩兄弟，沿溪上來，與 Tabanan（踏萬）長者相遇了。長者問曰，「要到哪兒去啊？」兩人回答曰，「我們要去我們的地方當蕃人。」蕃人即東蕃，在日出的地方，往北再往南。（在這裡中斷）

　　另外，有名叫 Tatu Maumauwan（踏蛛茅茅灣）和 Tau Maumauwan（投茅茅灣）的兩人，在 Tabanan 的地方相遇，彼此交談。我們要去我們的地方當生蕃。據說蕃即 Saraumaw（沙漏毛）蕃。長者聽到此非常傷心（傷心必須各自分居），於是造橋，命名為美好。兩人要度過此橋時，Tau Maumauwan 滑落於橋下，Tatu Maumauwan 在橋上呼喚他，他對 Tatu Maumauwan 說，「你自己回去吧！我離去將變成鹿。」據說鹿即麕鹿。Tatu Maumauwan 不得已離開成為生蕃。又若講故事的話，大概如此。

三、開基之歌 *The Song of Our Origin*

1. **aiyan nu aiyan, dauduwai laitah.**
ayan	nu	ayan	d\<a>uduw-ay	laita.
			Prg-talk-Fut	we
根源		根源	講	咱們

   要論古代
   要講咱們的根源。
   In the song of ayan, we shall talk about (our origin).

2. **apu-tia maha tadupurai, rubuhrubuh a kauwas.**
apu	tia,	maxa	tadupuray	ruburubu	kawas.
old lady	female name	then		below	sky
阿婆	女名	然後	視察	下	天

   祖知仔是以視察地下
   阿婆 Tia 視察天下的大地。
   The old woman Tia inspected (the earth) below the sky.

3. **kitah kitah siaun, durrusippi lapilach.**
kita-kita	siaən	dulut	sipilapilax.
Red-look	carefully	extreme	barren, with scabies
看	小心	盡頭	貧瘠

   看的是空虛。
   她仔細地視察著，發現大地是貧瘠如疥癬一般。
   She looked carefully to the extremes and it was all barren as if it had scabies.

4. **mahah dudulluwai, apu magiauwas matah lak-kang kauwas,**
maxa	duu-duruŋ-ay	apu	magiauwas	mata	lakaŋ	kawas,
then	Red-fall-Fut	old lady	female name	from	space	sky
然後	掉落	阿婆	女名	從	縫隙	天空

   papai rullung.
papa-i-ruruŋ.
ride-cloud
乘雲

   則差遣祖馬堯日由天隙坐雲降下。
   於是 Magiauwas 阿婆就乘雲從天空的縫隙下來地面。
   Then the old woman Magiauwas was coming down through the space of the sky by riding the clouds.

5. mahah   kikiddehhai,   rubburubbuh a   kauwas.
maxa   kii-kidih-ay   ruburubu   a   kawas.
           Red-descend-Fut   below   sky
           降下   下   天
故隨降下地面。
她降落到地面。
Then she descended to the earth.

6. kaduhu   hauliak,   ni   apu-tiya.
kaduxu   hauriak   ni   apu   tia.
incantation   very good   old lady   name
唸咒   很好   阿婆   女名
好法術祖知仔所賜的。
阿婆 Tia 唸咒。
The old woman Tia chanted incantations and it came out well.

7. maudadang   daiya,   mahah   kaulah ngat-dai.
m<a>udadaŋ   daya,   maxa   k<a>ulaŋad-ay.
Prg-get warm   east   then   Prg-name-Fut
變暖   東   然後   命名
黎明在東故要號名。
東方漸漸泛白，然後她要命名了。
The day was dawning in the east, and then she was to name it.

8. adamadang   yi   daiya   mahah   kaulangngat-dai.
adamadaŋ   di   daya,   maxa   k<a>ulaŋad-ay.
name   east   then   Prg-name-Fut
人名   東   然後   命名
（人名）在東故要號名。
Adamadaŋ 在東方，因此他要以此命名。
Adamadaŋ was in the east, and then she was to name it.

9. dahah-mat-dang   yi   daiya,   mahakaulangatdai.
dahamadaŋ   di   daya,   maxa   k<a>ulaŋad-ay.
name   east   then   Prg-name-Fut
人名   東   然後   命名
（人名）在東故要號名。
Dahamadaŋ 在東方，所以要以此命名。
Dahamadaŋ was in the east, and then she was to name it.

10. **silapbang yi daiya, mahakaulangngatdai.**
    silabaŋ   di daya,   maxa k<a>ulaŋad-ay.
    name   east   then Prg-name-Fut
    人名   東   然後 命名
    是蚋望在東故號名。
    Silabaŋ 在東方，所以以此命名。
    Silabaŋ was in the east, and then she was to name it.

11. **silapbang yi rahot, mahakaulangngatdai.**
    silabaŋ   di rahut,   maxa k<a>ulaŋad-ay.
    name   west   then Prg-name-Fut
    人名   西   然後 命名
    （別人也）在西故要號名。
    （另一個）Silabaŋ 在西方，故以此命名。
    (Another) silabaŋ was in the west, and then she was to name it.

12. **papak hahraruma-aih, mahahkaulangngatdai.**
    pa-paka-rarumaʔ-ay,   maxa k<a>ulaŋad-ay.
    Caus-bamboo-Fut   then Prg-name-Fut
    竹   然後 命名
    使彼作竹桂竹故要號名。
    使它成為桂竹，以此命名。
    It was made to be a bamboo sp., and then she was to name it.

13. **burruh   mat-dang yi daiya.**
    buru   madaŋ   di daya.
    bamboo   dawn   east
    嫩竹   黎明   東
    軟竹黎明在東。
    嫩竹和黎明在東方。
    (There was another) bamboo sp. and dawn in the east.

14. **burruh   mat-dang yi daiya, aunusasipudah   rakihan   tinnating.**
    buru   madaŋ   di daya,   aunu saa-si-puda   rakihan   t<in>atiŋ.
    bamboo   dawn   east,   for   used-cut-navel   baby   Prf-little
    嫩竹   黎明   東   為了 用來切臍帶   嬰   小
    軟竹黎明在東可以割臍帶，小孩赤子。
    嫩竹和黎明在東方，此嫩竹可用來切斷（新生）嬰孩的臍帶。
    The bamboo sp. and dawn in the east, and the bamboo was used to cut off the navel cord of a (new-born) baby.

15. hauliak   kakatduhu   ni apu-tia.
    hauriak   ka-kaduxu   ni apu   tia.
    very good Red-chant incantation   old lady name
    很好   施咒   阿婆   女名
    好哉法術，祖知仔之賜。
    幸好有阿婆 Tia 施咒。
    It was fortunate that the old lady Tia chanted incantations.

16. nahhah-dah datduwa, di rubbuh rubbuh a kauwas.
    nahada   dadua   di ruburubu   a kawas.
    have   all   below   sky
    有   全部   下   天空
    俱各有□在地下。
    萬物在天空之下生存。
    All (things) existed (on earth) under the sky.

17. uka   kakka hukahui,   uka   sasumusumul.
    uka   kaa-kahu-kahuy,   uka   saa-səmə-səmər.
    other Red-Red-tree   other Red-Red-grass
    其他   樹   其他   草
    眾樹木類及眾草類
    有各種樹和草。
    There were all sorts of trees and grass.

18. aiya nu aiyan, saisaih   ya wilan.
    ayan nu ayan,   saysay   yawira.
                    everything end
    根源   根源   全部   結束
    論至此可以也。
    根源歌到此全部結束。
    This is the end of the song ayan.

全體意譯（黃秀敏譯）：

　　雖然講述往昔的面貌，但那是久遠以前的太空，我們的祖先名叫 Tia，是位俊傑。以手遮目遠遠的俯視大地，則是如何的遼闊，無邊無際地空虛，空無一物；這樣到底有誰去地面治理呢？仰著頭說：「Magiauwas。」今天一旦有遊天之樂，竟在白雲之上，任憑好好遨遊，才下到大地，身上確負所賜與的美好權能。且說光明之起源在東方，正因如此□Adamadaŋ，也讓 Dahamadaŋ 和 Silabaŋ（是蚋望）往東；且說讓另一個 Silabang 治理西方，如此國家平定了，其次讓事物開始。東方有的確很美好的嫩竹，節竹茂密，拿此割斷臍帶則吾子變為小孩，小孩變成成人，永遠繁榮興盛如竹，種植高而直的民草……。

Appendix 2. The Lord's Prayer

The following material about Sek-hoan [Pazih] appears in Campbell (1896:102). It appears that Campbell was unaware of the great linguistic difference between Favorlang and Pazih, so that he inserted this Pazih material in Favorlang materials.

"The foregoing sheets had just been printed when a communication was received from Rev. D. Ferguson, M.A., of the English Presbyterian Mission in Formosa, which may be inserted here. It is dated Tainanfu, 31st March 1896, and was sent in reply to a request that he would have the Lord's Prayer written out in the language now spoken by the Toa-sia aborigines; Toa-sia being the name of a Township about fourteen miles north of the city of Chiang-hoa. Hundreds of families of this same tribe are also found among the villages of the Pawsia Plain, some two days' journey to the east of Chiang-hoa. The version he sends in is as follows:----

The Lord's Prayer in the Present-day Sekhoan Dialect of Formosa[1]"

1. **Niam a   A-bah kai-dih ba bau ka-wuss.**
   niam a   aba   kaidi   babaw   kawas.
   our   Lig   Dad   stay   above   sky
   我們   的   父   在   上   天
   我們在天上的父啊。
   Our God is above in the heaven.

2. **Ni-suh a   la-ngat tsah, ma sü-zau-u hau riak.**
   nisu   a   laŋat   ka,   ma-səzaw   hau-riak.
   your   Lig   name   Top   Sta-clean   very-good
   你的   名   乾淨   很好
   你的名字乾淨良好。
   Your name is clean and very good.

3. **Pa-pang-a-sai   ni-suh-ah ki-n ü la-an.**
   pa-paŋasa-i   nisu   a   k<in>ulaʔ-an
   Cau-bring-Imp   your   Lig Prf-lead-Loc
   帶   你的   引領的地方
   請引領我們到正確的地方（天國）。
   Please lead us to the right place (your kingdom).

---

[1] The following ten Pazih sentences were interpreted by Pan Jin-yu (female, 88) on March 27, 2002, edited and translated by Paul Li. In each sentence the first line in boldface is the original transcription given perhaps by Rev. D. Ferguson.

4. **Pa-pa i ta-du-i ki-ni-siu-a**   **li-ni xa-dan, di-ni da-xüh, hai-ki, ba bau**

pa-paitadu?-i   ki   nisiw   a   l<in>ixad-an,   dini   daxə   haiki   babaw

Cau-arrange-Imp   Nom   your   Lig   here   earth   like   above

安排   主   你的   這裡   地   好像   上

ka-wuss.

kawas.

sky

天

安排得井然有序，在地上這裡就像在天上一般。

Put your ... in order, then this world is like the heaven.

5. **Ba-xei au-no da-li-o nu-sau-a.**

baxa-i   aunu   dali   nu   nu   saw.

give-Imp   for   day   Gen   Gen   man

給   為   日   屬   人

請賞賜我們人們日常所需的（飲食）。

Please give us our daily needs (food and drinks).

6. **ki-na-sa-de-lan yam-i-kah, i-la a na pi-ter-üt-o**

k<in>a-sadial-an   yami   ka,   ini   pitərət   u

Nmz-Prf-bad-Loc   we   Top   not   remember   Obl

壞的地方   我們   不   記

niam-a-ki-na sa-de-lan.

niam   a   k<in>a-sadial-an.

our   Lig   Nmz-Prf-bad-Loc

我們   壞的地方

請赦免我們的罪惡，我們也將對有負於我們的人不計仇。

And forgive our sin, just as we will not remember those who have sinned against us.

7. **A-na pa-pa xi-ta-lam-i yam-mi-a ai-za sei-sei.**

ana   papa-xitalam-i   yami   a   aidisaysay.

don't   Cau-try-Imp   we   Lig   all sorts of things

別   試   我們   的   各式各樣的事

不要讓牠試探我們各種東西。

Don't let him try on us all sorts of things.

250

8. **Tu-tul-i   niam-mih   pa-ter-ia-di   de-sa-del.**
   tutul-i   niam   patər   lia   di   sadial.
   save?-Imp   our   hooked Asp Loc evil
   救?   我們   了   兇惡
   把我們從兇惡中解救出來。
   Save us from the evil.

9. **Hhamoh   ki-nü la-an,   wa-rüt   xi-na ria-ria-kan,   ka   kai-i-swoan   da-duah,**
   ?   k<in>ula?-an   warət   x<in>a-ria-riak-an[2]   ka,   kai-isuan   dadua,
                Prf-lead-Loc   capable XA-Prf-Red-good-Loc   Conj   stay-you/Loc all
                帶領   好   在   全

   mau sei-o   ma-si-lo   ba-zu ba-zoach.
   mausay u   ma-siriw   bazu-bazuah.
   will go   AF-wear   Red-peer group
   去   穿   同輩
   你做的好事都會跟著你，你的同輩也將會分享。
   For the good things you have done, they will all stay with you, and (your) peer group will go and get awarded.

10. **Lai-ki   niam-a   hi-niss-a   xi-na la-tü-dan.**
    laiki   niam   a   hinis   a   x<in>alatəd-an.
    in this way our   Lig mind   Lig Prf-origin-Loc
    如此   我們   的   心   根源
    我們內心所想的就是如此。
    Deep in our mind is like this.

   "Mr. Ferguson remarks on the above; …'A good many of the brethren helped in making this translation, especially A-sin, Hau-hi [xauxi][3], A-iam, Ta-muli [damuri], Aw-hoan and Bau-keh [bauki]. Every petition is kept separate, and begins with a capital. The letter "ü" is pronounced as in German, "x" as in Greek, and "Hh" as a somewhat aspirated form of the single letter. Several words had to be translated in a roundabout way, as they have no such expressions as "kingdom," "hallowed," "glory," "will," and one or two others.'"

---

[2] In Ogawa's unpublished field notes, he suggested the possibility of deriving this form from *hauriak* 'very good'.

[3] The forms in square brackets [   ] are given by Paul Li.

中文版如下：

在天我等父者　我等願爾名見聖
爾國臨格　　　爾旨成行於地如於天焉
我等望爾　　　今日與我　我日用糧
而免我債　　　如我亦（也）免負我債者
又不我許陷於誘惑乃救我於兇惡

Appendix 3. Pazih Sentences Recorded by Steere in 1873

The following sentences were recorded by Joseph Beal Steere in 1873.[4] In each sentence the first line in boldface is the original transcription by Steere, while the second line is the edited version by Li. Where there is a discrepancy in our understanding of the Pazih sentence, the English gloss is given on the right of each sentence.

1. **ríák kālisú**
   riak ka mulasu
   Rice is good.

2. **haimā ālá̄o paisú**
   haima alaw pai siw?
   How many fish do you have?

3. **nāhádzá sūpātá ālá̄ō yākó**
   nahaza supad-a alaw yaku
   I have four fish.

4. **íní̄mārá ālá̄o yākó** 'I have no fish.'
   ini mara alaw yaku. 'I didn't catch (any) fish.'

5. **sarawan mausai mālúp yākó**
   sarawan mausay malup yaku.
   Tomorrow I will go hunting.

6. **ōkaijíhá íní̄mālúp yākó** 'Yesterday I went hunting.'[5]
   ukazixa malup yaku. 'Yesterday I went hunting.'
   ukazixa ini malup yaku. 'Yesterday I did not go hunting.'

7. **sārāwá̄n kāōsá mālúp íssú**
   sarawan mausay malup isiw.
   Tomorrow you will go hunting.

---

4 See Steere (1874:332-333), in which Pazih is called "Sek-whan", but mistyped as "Lek-whan". Steere's original field notes are kept at the Bentley Historical Library, University of Michigan, Ann Arbor.

5 Actually the sentence means 'yesterday-not-hunt-I = I did not go hunting yesterday.'

8. **yākó̍ mausai mālúp**
   yaku mausay malup.
   I am going hunting.

9. **mausaí mārāó̍ ālāō yākó̍**
   mausay mara u alaw yaku.
   I am going fishing.

10. **māké̍ yākānúń yākó̍**
    makiakanən yaku.
    I am hungry.

11. **mausaí paisú̍**   'Where are you going?'
    mausay pai siw?   'Will you go?'
    mausay asay siw?   'Where are you going?'

12. **mausaí Po̍lisíá yākó̍**   'I am going to Posia.'
    mausay purisia.   'I'm going to Puli.'

13. **si Po̍lisíá yākó̍**   'I have been in Posia.'
    di posia yaku.   'I'm in Puli.'

14. **mūlízáh húhúl.**
    murizax xəxəl.
    'The sun is very hot.'

15. **kāsaián paiká̍ dūlaí**   'When will you start?'
    kasayan pai kadul-ay?   'When will you set out?'

16. **sāsai ín̍ílá**
    sasayən la?
    How must I do?

17. **ōkāzā kowá̍s pōré̍hāt nākí̍ ābá̍ ín̍á**
    ukazixa kawas purihat naki a aba ina.
    Last year my father and mother died.

18. **ōkāzā ko̍wá̍s pōrē̍hāt nākí̍ ābá̍**
    ukazixa kawas purihat naki a aba.
    Last year my father died.

19. **pōzáhā ōzáng kǒwás pǒwríházai nākí ābá**
puzah adang a kawas purihaday naki a aba.
My father will die next year.

20. **ōkǎjíhá kāmōkoun āláo yākó**
ukazixa ka məkən alaw yaku.
Yesterday I ate fish.

21. **kākán āláō yākó**
kaakən alaw yaku.
I am eating fish.

22. **sārāwán kākānaí āláō yākó**
sarawan kaakanay alaw yaku.
Tomorrow I will eat fish.

23. **ōkǎjíhá mōdouh o dālúm yākó** 'Yesterday I drank tea.'
ukazixa mudaux u dalum yaku. 'Yesterday I drank water.'

24. **dādouho dālúm yākó**
daadaux dalum yaku.
I am drinking water.

25. **sārāwān ka dādouhaí dālúm yākó**
sarawan ka dadauxay dalum yaku.
Tomorrow I will drink water.

26. **mōpūzá haimú**
mupuzah haimu.
You(pl) have come.

27. **mousai yāmí** 'You are going.'
mausay yami. 'We(exc) are going.'

28. **mousaí lā** 'You wish to go.'
mausay la. '(I'm) leaving.'

Appendix 4. Sample of Previous Scholars' Notes on Pazih

(1) A Sample of Steere's (1873) Notes of Pazih Sentences

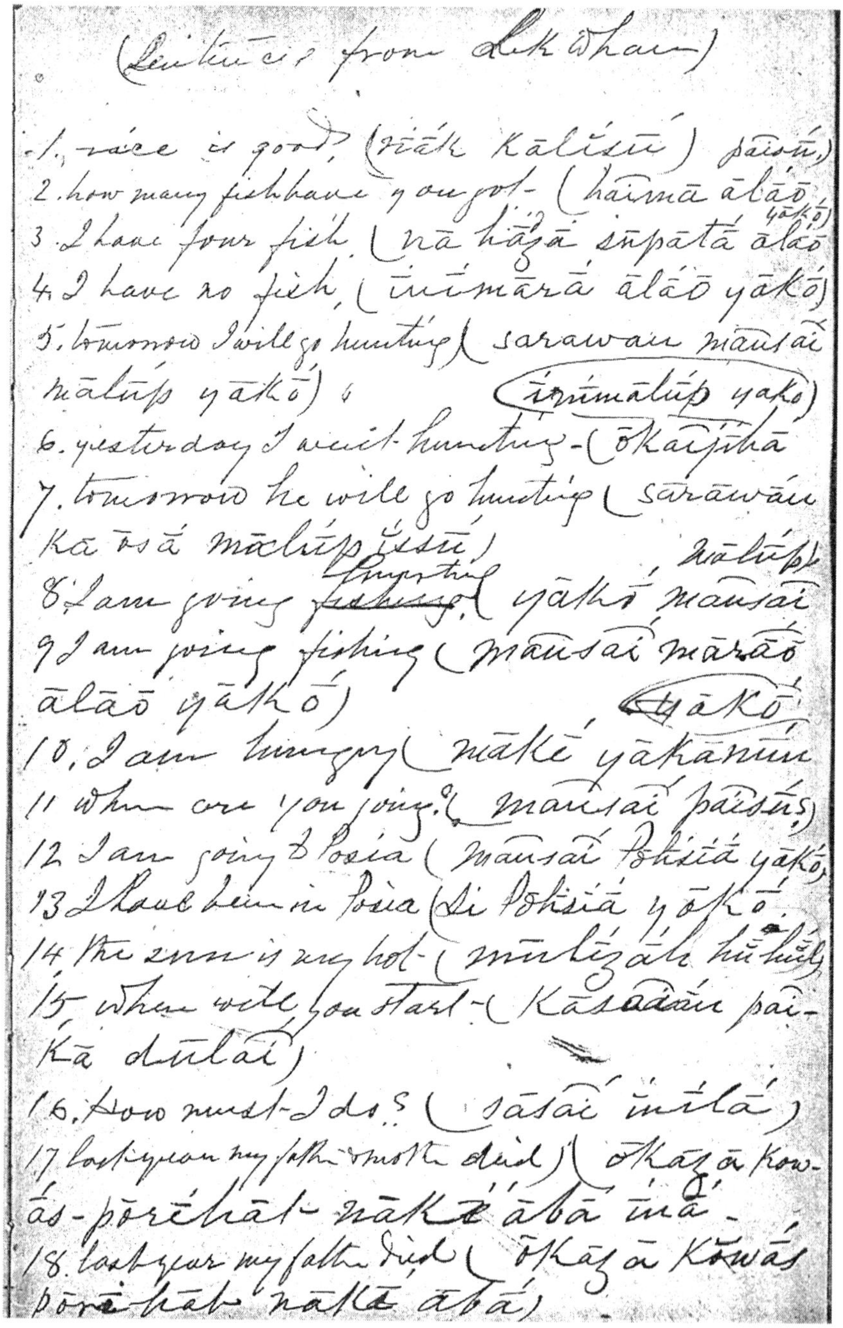
(Sentences from Lik Ohau)

1. rice is good? (siāk kālisu) paisu)
2. how many fish have you got- (haimā ālāō,
3. I have four fish. (nā hāzā supātā ālāō yākō)
4. I have no fish. (inimārā ālāō yākō)
5. tomorrow I will go hunting (sarawau mausai mālup yākō) ; (inimalup yako)
6. yesterday I went hunting - (ōkaijihā
7. tomorrow he will go hunting (sarawāu kā ōsā mālup issu) mālup
8. I am going ~~fishing~~ hunting (yākō mausai
9. I am going fishing (mausai mārāō ālāō yākō) yākō
10. I am hungry (māke yākanun
11. where are you going? (mausai paisus)
12. I am going to Posia (mausai pohsiā yākō)
13. I have been in Posia (si pohsiā yōkō
14. the sun is very hot- (mulizali hu huli)
15. when will you start- (kāsāaau pai- kā dulai)
16. How must I do? (sāsai inilā)
17. last year my father & mother died (ōkazā kowās-pōrēhāt- nākā ābā inā.
18. last year my father died (ōkazā kowās pōrēhāt nākā ābā)

(2) A Sample of Ino's (1897) Notes of Pazih Text

小児は犬をつれて山に遊んで居る

Rubo-rubo binayu ka nahara

Rahong, De barubarud rahong

iria ka, daho a umama ka karid,

山の下に川があり其の川の両側りに多く
の田と畑とがある

kaiZiZaka bābaha sao a maruĭguhu,

かしこにあまたの人が土をすきかへし
て居る　　第七節

Ahowan a dare inapa a hahehahe-
-mai a Paranaha ka Paizahio u
Rahong,

夕暮に荷を積んで舟が川を下り行く

Uka de myadoa binayu a daran
ka tātarao noang a Rahehal,

又あちらの山路を小児が牛を逐ふて行く

Noang liza ka mamuruk u susumai
Panate a muhalid u paripari,

257

(3) A Sample of Ogawa or Ino's Handwriting of *Ai-yan*

maha masik-kulaih Tap-ban na mataro
mahah pabaruddai, rahab-lu hauliak
mausai haiyamu, maha dahoh, dahoh saraumoh
ada mahah roaro, Tap-ban na mat-taro
inilau issia, mahah pau sug-ngut-dai
sug-ngut du ma bit-da-bit, i Tat-tu maumauwan
Taumaumauwan, pis-su lik-khit di sug-ngut
alu lai siah, Tattu maumauwan
Us-sa laisu, mausaih-yakuh
mahah luk-khut, luk-khut-tu noang
Tatu maumauwang, mahah mausai
— mahah dakho
aiyan iu aiyan, saisaiya wilan.

國家圖書館出版品預行編目資料

巴宰族傳說歌謠集 = Pazih texts and songs /
李壬癸, 土田滋著.-- 初版.-- 臺北市：
中研院語言所籌備處, 民 91
　　面；　　公分.--（語言暨語言學專刊. 甲種；2-2）
參考書目：面

ISBN　957-671-888-0 (精裝附光碟片)

1. 民謠歌曲 － 臺灣

539.1232　　　　　　　　　　　91017069

《語言暨語言學》專刊甲種二之二

巴宰族傳說歌謠集

著　　者：李壬癸・土田滋
出版者：中央研究院語言學研究所籌備處
發行者：中央研究院語言學研究所籌備處
　　　　台北市南港區研究院路二段 128 號
　　　　電話：(02) 2786-3300
　　　　網址：http://www.ling.sinica.edu.tw
印　　刷：久盛彩色印刷股份有限公司
初　　版：中華民國九十一年十一月
定　　價：新台幣 600 元／US$20
　　　　國外郵寄及手續費每本另加美金 10 元
　　　　Please add US$10 handling charge for each volume.

ISBN　957-671-888-0 (精裝附光碟片)
GPN　1009102911